RESEARCH
@
LIBRARY AND INFORMATION SCIENCE
Prof (Dr) G Devarajan Festschrift

Research @ Library and Information Science

Prof (Dr) G Devarajan Festschrift

Edited by

Dr. A.Gopikuttan

Dr. K. P. Vijayakumar

Ess Ess Publications

New Delhi

Research @ Library and Information Science

ISBN: 978-81-7000-638-1

Rs.995/-

First Published 2011

Published by:
Ess Ess Publications
4837/24, Ansari Road,
Darya Ganj,
New Delhi-110 002.
INDIA
Phones: 23260807, 41563444
Fax: 41563334
E-mail: info@essessreference.com
www.essessreference.com

Cover Design by *Patch Creative Unit*

Printed and bound in India at Salasar Imaging Systems.

Prof. Dr. G. Devarajan

Contents

Preface (xi)

Dr. G. Devarajan- A biographical sketch (xvii)
Dr. Gopikuttan, A

1. Works of Dr. G. Devarajan: A Bibliometric Study ... 1
Fathima beevi
Dr.Gopikuttan A
Dr.Rekha Rani Varghese

2. Children's literature in Malayalam: A Survey and Bibliometric Study ... 15
Dr. Ajikumary T

3. Research trends in physics: An Analysis of Doctoral Theses ... 49
Dr. Sudhier K G

4. Social Science Books in Malayalam: A Survey and Bibliometric Study ... 73
Dr. Beena S

5. Manpower Utilization in the University Libraries : An Investigation ... 100
Dr. Vijayakumar K P

6. The Impact of Factors on Professional Library Manpower Development in the College Libraries ... 125
Dr.T Mohana Kumar

7. Total Quality Management in University Library : A Case Study ... 141
Dr. Bindu P Nair

8. Knowledge Management in Digital Age: Librarian's Perspective ... 172
Dr. Adarsh N Gokul
Dr.Ambili K S

9. Development of Knowledge Management Based Organizations: New Role of LIS Professionals ... 183
Suresh Kumar N

10. British Council Libraries in India- Policy & performance : An Analysis with Special Reference to Higher Education ... 194
Dr. Lalitha M

11. Role of Library Associations for the Professional Development of Librarians ... 233
Dr. Gopikuttan A
Hima P R

12. Information Needs and Information Seeking behaviour of Ayurveda Information Users ... 253
Dr. Joshi George P

13. Learning Object Repositories in Higher Education: A Survey ... 265
Jayaraj J R

14. E-book Aggregators ... 277
K Ravindran Assari

15. Impact of 'Theory Y' Assumption on Superior Subordinate Relation in Academic and Public Libraries in Germany ... 289
Dr. Mini Devi B

16. Preservation and Conservation of Library Materials ... 298

Vasudevan TV

Jineesha V

Index ... 312

Preface

Much of the research work in Library and Information Science in India, as in many other disciplines, is carried out through academic research programmes leading to M. Phil., Ph.D. degrees. This is not to suggest that practical research carried out as part of the effort to find out solutions to real life problems by practitioners are altogether absent. But the fact remains that they are few and far between. This is quite natural in the absence of prominent funding agencies apart from UGC and ICSSR to finance project proposals in Library and Information Science. The result is that there is a shortage of research studies aimed at finding solutions to the various professional issues and practical problems and developing benchmarks and best practices. This is the impression we got while attempting to make a survey of research studies in the LIS field.

The contents, as is customary of a Festschrift, start with a bibliographical sketch of Dr. G. Devarajan. It is followed by a bibliometric study of the publications of Dr Devarajan who has earned a reputation as a prolific writer, in addition to being an ardent researcher and illustrious teacher. This paper by Mrs. Fathima Beevi, Dr. A. Gopikuttan and Dr. Rekha Rani Varghese serves as a real tribute to Dr. Devarajan.

In the paper Children's literature in Malayalam: a survey and bibliometric study, Dr Ajikumary has attempted the subject-wise distribution of books, areas of publication in various subject groups, authorship pattern, publishers and publishing patterns, chronological distribution, translations, language wise distribution, distribution of illustrations, page and size analysis, price-page analysis and a number of correlative studies of the different variables of the children's literature.

Through an analysis of doctoral theses of the University of Kerala, Dr K. G Sudhier attempts to find out the research trends in Physics. He tries to do this by analyzing the subject wise distribution of research in Physics, the different bibliographic forms of citations used by the physicists and by identifying the core journals and books and the most cited Indian journals.

Dr. Beena focuses her attention on Social Science books in Malayalam published from the very beginning. The study concentrates on subject wise distribution of books, concentration of publications using Herfendahl Index, share of books in various subjects, types of books in Social Sciences, types of authorship, author productivity, prolific authors, gender distribution of authors, books with geographical appellations, various aspects of publishers, translations, cost analysis and correlative studies of the determinants of publication output of Malayalam books in Social Sciences like population, total literacy, SDP and real per capita.

Dr. S.R. Ranganathan had evolved a job standard suitable for university libraries half a century ago, but it is doubtful whether the universities follow this in the planning of human resources. Dr. Vijayakumar, K. P. tries to investigate the problem at a deeper level to see the rhyme or reason, if any, which is followed in manpower planning in the university libraries of Kerala. The study also examines the qualifications and skills possessed by the professionals and how far they are suitable to the changing information scenario. The output analysis of the employees reveals the adequacy or inadequacy of staff in the libraries based on which ways and means of redeployment of staff are suggested. The most significant contribution of the study is the development of an Activity Time Schedule Manpower (ATSM) Model that can be used to estimate the professional and non-professional manpower in libraries in the manual and computerized environments. The paper also offers a number of suggestions for the better utilization of staff in libraries.

The impact of factors on professional development of college library manpower in Kerala is the area of concern of Dr. T. Mohanakumar. He identifies motivation, encouragement, recognition, environment, opportunity, facilities, difficulties, responsibility, will and vision as the factors which have a bearing on professional development. In addition, he also tries to measure the present level of influence of these factors on manpower development.

Dr. Bindu P. Nair explores the bases of quality measures adopted by Kerala University Library, Trivandrum based on the opinion of the users and staff and the awareness of TQM and other quality efforts within the Library. She offers a number of suggestions for improving the quality of services of the library.

A theoretical projection of the application of knowledge management (KM) from the point of view of LIS professionals forms the crux of the paper of Dr Adarsh N. Gokul and Dr. K. S. Ambily. They subscribe to the view that Knowledge Management in libraries is to promote relationship in and between libraries, between library and user, to strengthen knowledge internetworking and to quicken knowledge flow.

Mr. Sureshkumar, anchoring on his rich experience in an industrial information system argues that in the coming days, all the staff functions would be outsourced. In such a scenario, the job of LIS centre would to manage / provide the necessary knowledge/information services to not only the parent organization but to market the LIS services to the potential user companies. These services include identification of agency, making standard terms of reference, provide MIS services to monitoring the work and providing information about legal problems arising out of such activities.

Dr. M. Lalitha, with her background in the British Libraries, makes a survey of the changes in the game plan of the British Council Libraries right from their inception to the present. Then she attempts to analyze whether the aims of the libraries are framed to meet the development needs of India and the regions and whether the changes are really reflective of the aspirations of the users. She establishes that British Libraries have contributed much to India's development in the field of education.

The library associations in India, in general, cannot boast of a glorious history in terms of the impact made on the profession in comparison with developed countries. Several reasons can be attributed to this. However, an area where they have done some service is in the organization of continuing education programmes. In this background, Dr. A. Gopikuttan and P. R. Hima try to investigate the role of library associations in the professional development of librarians. The study reveals that the overall attitude of the professionals to the associations is positive despite criticism of the way they function.

The 1970s and 80s were characterized by a plethora of user studies, more so in the western world. When the trend started waning there, it gained momentum in India.

But of late, here also the emphasis has shifted to bibliometrics and related areas. Still there are studies in the area. The contribution of Dr. Joshi George assumes significance in this context because of the uniqueness of the user category - researchers, teachers, employed doctors, practitioners and students of Ayurveda. The study vividly brings out the differences in the information seeking behaviour of the teachers and students on the one hand and practitioners on the other.

In India also, interest in Learning Object Repositories (LOR), though not as popular as institutional repositories, is catching up with the advent of e-learning. In this backdrop, the attempt by Mr. Jayaraj serves as a curtain raiser. He introduces a dozen widely used LOR initiatives at the global level. The fact that there is at least one such Indian initiative - e-Gyan kosh of IGNOU - makes us proud.

Purchase of e-books has become a really difficult affair mainly due to the variety of publishers, different licensing agreements, platforms and different pricing policies. A solution to this is the use of e-book aggregators. They provide a single platform or interface to host countless titles with international coverage thus proving to be a tremendous boon to LIS professionals. In his paper Sri. K Ravindran deals with a grouping of e-book providers, the main factors to be considered while selecting an e-book aggregator, the characteristics of aggregators, the market trends, developments in platforms, bibliographic issues and induction of new technologies in the field.

Dr. Mini Devi in her paper tries to examine the applicability of the principles of Douglas McGregor, especially the Theory Y principles, among the LIS professionals in Germany. She presents the results of an e-mail survey to find out the relation between librarian's assumptions about human beings in general, particularly subordinates in two libraries. She observes that librarians who believe in pure 'Theory Y' are less and the opposite category is dominant at all levels. She advocates the periodical appraisal of the superior by the subordinate to reduce the problems caused by 'low Y' librarians.

In the paper entitled Preservation and conservation of library materials ,Vasudevan TV and Jineesha V try to examine various aspects of preservation and conservation of various types of materials.

Almost all the contributors and papers in this volume are connected to Dr Devarajan in one way or other. Their variety bears ample testimony of his research interests. He has always been a source of inspiration for the youngsters in the profession. We have immense pleasure to place this volume before the professional fraternity.

Editors

Dr. G. Devarajan – A Biographical Sketch

Dr.A.Gopikuttan

Dr.G.Devarajan was born on 18th November 1947 in a middle class family named Pavoor at Manappally, Thazhava Village, Karunagapally Taluk, Kollam District ,Kerala as the third son of Mr.Pavoor.S Janardhanan and Mrs. Lakshmi. Dr. Devarajan had his primary education at Manapally Govt. LPS and secondary education at Thazhava Government High School. He studied pre-degree and B.Sc Botany with first class from D.B. College, Sasthamcottah in 1970. While in the college he was very active in student politics.

Dr.Devarajan did his Bachelor's degree in Library Science from the University of Kerala during 1971-72 and M.L.I.S from the University of Madras in 1980 with distinction and first rank. He did his M.A in Russian Language and Literature from University of Kerala in 1978. He received Ph D in Library and Information Science under the guidance of Prof.K.A Isaac from the University of Kerala in 1992. He married in 1977, to S. Sugatha Kumari, who worked as Senior Superintendent in Civil Supplies. The couple has two children, a son , Vishnu D Pavoor working as a

Software Engineer at IBM, USA and a daughter, Bhagya who is a research scholar in the University of Kerala.

Dr. Devarajan started his career in 1973 as Library Assistant in the Kerala University Library. He worked in the Centre for Development Studies library as Assistant Librarian from 1974 to 1983 May. He joined as Lecturer in the Department of Library and Information Science, University of Kerala, on 13th June 1983. He was elevated to the positions such as Senior Lecture in charge in 1993, Reader and Head in 1996 and Professor and Head in 2002.He was in-Charge of the Director, College Development Council while he was Professor & Head .He retired from service on superannuation in March 2007.

Dr. Devarajan has served in a number of bodies both in academic and professional at the State and national level, in responsible capacities. He was the Dean, Faculty of Arts, Chairman, Board of Studies in Library and Information Science, Member of Senate, Member, Academic Council, Member, Faculty of Arts and Member ,Research Monitoring Committee in the University of Kerala. . He was also Member of Board of Studies of several other Universities in India. He served as an advisory board member in Kerala University Library, State Central Library and SCERT Library, Trivandrum. He was an expert member (Library Computerization) in State Central Library and Secretariat Central Library Committee, Trivandrum. He served as Member or Chairman in a number of , Boards of Examiners in Library Science in various Universities in India. He served as subject expert in Committees and Commissions appointed by the State Government and Central Government. He is associated as a Technical Consultant of M/S Enter Technology, Techno Park, Trivandrum. . Presently he is the Member of the Senate and Syndicate in the University of Kerala nominated by the Government of Kerala .

Dr.Devarajan has been very closely associated with the activities of national and state level professional associations. He served as a secretary, Centre for Information and Technology Studies (CITS), Trivandrum, General Secretary, Kerala Library Association (Three terms) and president, KLA (Two terms). He is also a life member of KLA, KUTA, ILA, IASLIC and IATLIS. He organized a number of state ,regional and national level seminars in Trivandrum. He served as organizing Secretary and Convener of IATLIS and IASLIC National seminars. Dr. Devarajan has widely travelled all over India and has maintained a high degree of intimacy with library professionals working in almost all important libraries in the country. He has prepared a number of expert committee reports for the reorganization and development of libraries in the State, like State Central Library, Trivandrum. Institute of Engineers Library (Trivandrum), High court Library Ernakulam), Industrial Documentation Centre (Trivandrum), and Secretariat Central Library, Govt. of Kerala.

As a researcher Dr.Devarajan has made significant contribution in the field of Library and Information Science. He is a research guide in Library and Information Science in the University of Kerala, Annamalai university, Alagappa University and Bharatidasan University. He has guided more than 65 MPhil studies in Library & Information Science. He has also produced so far 14 Ph.Ds and a number of students are being guided by him for Ph.D. Presently he is UGC-Emeritus Fellow engaged in a UGC research project entitled 'Digital archiving of indigenous knowledge in agriculture'

Dr. Devarajan is a significant name in the field of library and Information Science literature. He has published a large number of publications. There are 27 books brought out to his credit Among them ,the significant titles include: ' Users' approach to information in libraries, Information

Technology in Libraries, Library Information user and use studies, Library Science Education and Manpower, Resource Allocation in University Libraries, Reading: pain or pleasure?, Information Science Oru Amukhom(Malayalam) and Social Reform Movements in Kerala'. He considered Journal as the major vehicle for reporting the significant research findings and for publishing papers on the theory and practice of knowledge. Journals play a key role in research work because it contains the latest information about current developments in the field of knowledge. Considering this aspect in mind Dr.Devarajan has published 41 papers on various aspects of library and information science in the National and International journals. He has presented 24 papers in various national conferences/ seminars etc. There are 7 research reports and 9 radio / TV scripts telecast in the media.

Dr. Devarajan is associated with the editing of journals. He is the editor of Kerala University Communicator which is a refereed, half yearly journal published by the University of Kerala. He is the associate editor of Southern Sociologist. He is also a reviewer of Annals of Library Science and Review Prospect (India)

Dr.Devarajan's infinite capacity of taking pains in the pursuit of knowledge makes him a genius in the subject. His contribution to Library Science is so significant and valuable. He was the recipient of Rastriya Gowrava Award instituted by India International Friendship Society, New Delhi. He has got certificate of honour from the IASLIC for the development of Modernization of Library and Information Science in India. Considering the significant contributions in the field of Library and Information Science the UGC has awarded to him the Emeritus Fellowship in Library & Information Science in 2009.

Dr.Devarajan has distinguished himself by selfless

service, amazing academic scholarship and commendable administrative sharpness during the past three decades. His quality along with dedications has brought success in his every endeavour. His contributions towards the development of Library Science education, research , publication and professionalism in library services at the State level and the national level are gratefully valued and widely acknowledged.

1

Works of Dr. G. Devarajan: A Bibliometric Study

Fathima Beevi
Dr. A Gopikuttan
Dr. Rekha Rani Varghese

Library and Information science means the study and practice of professional method, use and exploitation of information whether from an institution based or not, for the benefit of users. An umbrella term abbreviated as LIS used to cover terms such as Library science, Librarianship, information Science, information work etc. It is an interdisciplinary science incorporating the humanities, law and applied science to study topics related to libraries, the collection, organization, preservation and dissemination of information resources. There is no generally agreed distinction between library science, library and information science, and librarianship. To a certain extent they can be considered equivalent terms, perhaps adopted to increase the "science" aspect.

Library and Information Science as a discipline owes

very much to the contributions made by Melvil Dewey. Dewey system of Classification for the organization of knowledge in libraries, his founding of the first professional periodical 'Library Journal' and then setting up the first Library education school, all these happened in the year 1876 which is a golden year in the annals of Librarianship. The contribution by Melvil Dewey helped in promoting the publications of Library science literature all over the world.

The term Library and Information Science (LIS) is sometimes used by most librarians as only a terminological variation, intended to emphasize the scientific and technical foundations of the subject, and its relationship with information science. LIS should not be confused with information theory, the mathematical study of the concept of information, or information science, a field related to Computer Science and Cognitive Science.

Library and Information Science Education in India started as early as in 1911. It was only after the World War II that it was gradually recognized as a full fledged discipline and separate departments were setup in universities offering courses leading to bachelor and master degrees.

With the constant effort of Dr.S.R.Ranganathan, the discipline of librarianship took the form of Library Science as it adhered to all the norms and principle of scientific research in the second half of 20th Century. When S.R.Ranganathan (1892-1972) came in to Library Science field in 1924, as an impeccable law of history such a situation gave birth to charismatic leader and a trendsetter. Thus the stage for the advent of a revolutionary in the person of Ranganathan had already been set by the milieu of the times. In 1924 Ranganathan joined as Librarian of the Madras University.

A systematic training programme was started in India at Madras University in 1931 under the leadership of

Dr.S.R.Ranganathan. In India, Ranganathan can rightly be called a genius and innovator par excellence. He has made much seminal contribution to almost all branches of Library Information Science. Some of his books became classics in the field.

Foundation of any systematic, scientific or other enquiry depends upon studies conducted in the past. In the area of productivity studies, we have numerous articles mainly based on bibliometric techniques. These studies are based on productivity of individual scientist, institutional productivity, productivity of country/region, specific discipline's productivity etc. Sangam and Kiran Savarnur conducted a study about communication and collaborative research pattern of professor Ramachandran. He is considered to be one of the founders of the rapidly developing field of molecular biology. His contributions are mainly to the theory of molecular structure of biopolymers in relation to their biological activities. In his 49 years of productive life, he has collaborated with 81 colleagues and students and has published 304 papers during 1942-1990.

Kedamani et al provided the scientometric portrait of Nobel Laureate Harold W. Kroto. Scientometric analysis of 190 publications by Harold.W. Kroto the Nobel laureate in Chemistry (1996) published during 1985-2000 in various fields. His productivity co-efficient was 0.68 which clearly indicate that his productivity increased after 50 percentage of his 16 years of research publication career. His highest collaboration co-efficient (1.00) was found in 1985, 1993,1995, 1996 and 1998-2000.

BIBLIOMETRICS

Bibliometrics is a type of research method used in Library and Information Science. It utilizes quantitative analysis and statistics to describe pattern of publications within a given field or body of literature. Researchers may use Bibliometric methods of evaluation to determine the influence of a single writer or the relationship between two or more writers and their works.

The term Bibliometrics was first coined by Pritchard in 1969, in his article 'Statistical Bibliography or Bibliometrics' published in Aslib's publication, Journal of Documentation. Bibliometrics is a new branch of Information Science. It is a quantitative evaluation of publication pattern of all macro and micro communication along with their authorship by mathematical and statistical calculus. Bibliometrics can be applied to any subject area and to most of the problems concerned with written communication. It is the quantitative analysis of the bibliographic features of a body of literature. Hawkin's interpreted it as quantitative analysis of the bibliographic features of body of literature. Potter defined it as the study and measurement of the publication pattern of all forms of written communication and their authors.

Bibliometric technique has extensive applications in identifying the research trends in a subject, trend in authorship and collaboration research and to get factual and accurate data for information handling and transfer. It provides the background or basis for a move to particular task. It provides information about the structure of knowledge and how it is communicated. Studies of the size and growth of literature can show developing and declining areas over a time.

DR.G.DEVARAJAN

The present study is a Bibliometric analysis of the works of Dr.G.Devarajan. Dr. Devarajan is one among the professional and an eminent teacher in the field of Library and Information Science. Dr. Devarajan has completed his

BLISc, MA and PhD from the University of Kerala and MLIS from the University of Madras. He did his Ph.D in Library and Information Science in 1992. He worked as a Librarian and gained very good professional experience even before joining as lecturer in the Department of library and Information Science, University of Kerala. He is a person who is associated with many academic and professional activities.

1. Statement of the problem

As a researcher, Dr.Devarajan has made significant contribution in the field of Library and Information Science. He is research guide in Library and Information Science in the University of Kerala, Annamalai university, Alagappa University and Bharatidasan University. He has guided more than 65 MPhil studies in Library & Information Science. He also produced so far 14 PhDs and a number of students are being guided by him for Ph.D.

He has published a large number of publications. There are 27 books brought out to his credit and has published 41 papers on various aspects of library and information science in the National and International journals. He also has presented 24 papers in various national conferences/ seminars etc. In this context it is appropriate to examine the total publications of Dr.G Devarajan using bibliometric techniques, a new discipline which employs quantitative methods to the problems of scientific communication process by measuring and analysis of various aspects of written documents.

2. Need and significance of the study

A large number of Library and Information Science literature produced by Dr.G.Devarajan is scattered in various sources. The present study is mainly focused in two areas. One is to compile a comprehensive database of Dr

G Devarajan's contributions and the second one is to make a bibliometric analysis of his works which will in turn reveal the publication productivity of Dr.G.Devarajan.

3. Objectives of the study

The main objectives of the study are given below:

1. To findout the bibliographic forms of document published by Dr. Devarajan and to findout the peak period of productivity
2. To findout the language-wise distribution of publicatios produced by Dr. Devarajan.
3. To asses the year-wise and subject-wise distribution of books and journal articles contributed by Dr. Devarajan
4. To measure the scattering of articles in various journals.
5. To investigate the year wise distribution of research projects and Radio/T.V programmes handled by Dr.G.Devarajan.
6. To findout the year- wise and subject-wise distribution of seminar/conference papers presented by Dr. Devarajan
7. To determine the year- wie distribution of research work(PhD, MPhil, MLISc) conducted under the guidance of Dr.G.Devarajan

4. Hypotheses

For the purpose of the present investigation, the following hypotheses have been formulated.

1. Dr. Devarajan contributed the maximum number of publications in the area of Library and society

2. Dr. Devarajan produced the maximum number of publications during 1990s.

5. Methodology and Data Collection methods

For the present study, the main methods employed in data collection were: review of related literature along with an informal discussion with Dr. Devarajan. For review of literature the relevant primary journals were consulted. In addition the C D ROM version of the database- LISAPLUS and Indian Library science abstract (ILSA) were also searched for relevant results. The list of publications of Dr. Devarajan was compiled as comprehensively as possible from his personal collection as well as from journals, conference proceedings, books and so on. The list of MLISc dissertations was collected from the library of Department of Library and Information Science, University of Kerala where he has been working as professor and Head of the Department. The list of publications and the details regarding the research guidance was noted down and a database created. The collected data were analysed using bibliometric technique.

The database based on the publications and other works of Dr. Devarajan from 1979-2007 (29 years) constitute the baseline data for analysis and interpretation.

Table 1. Works of Dr.G. Devarajan

Works	Number	Percentage
Publication	115	57.5
Research guidance	85	42.5
Total	200	100

Dr.G.Devarajan published 200 items out of which 115 (57.55) are publications and 85 (42.5%) are works relating to research guidance. The details of bibliographic forms are also given in table number 2.

Table 2. Bibliographic forms

Forms of Documents	Number	Percentage
Journal article	41	36.65
Conference/seminar papers	24	20.86
Books	27	23.47
Radio/TV programmes	10	8.69
Research project	9	7.82
Bibliographies	4	3.47
Total	115	100

Table 3. Course-wise distribution of research guidance

Guided Research	Number	Percentage
PhD	9	10.58
MPhil	33	38.82
MLISc	43	50.58
Total	85	100

6. Data Analysis Techniques

Data collected from various sources are subjected to bibliometric analysis using different variables such as bibliographic forms, year, subject and languages etc.

7. Limitations

The first article of Dr.G.Devarajan was published in 1979. The present study is confined to a period of 29 years (1979-2007). Research productivity after 2007 is not considered for this study.

8. Major Findings

The major findings of the study are given below:

1. Out of the 115 publications produced by Dr. Devarajan, the journal articles constituted the maximum number

(35.65 percent). The second place goes to books with 27 (23.47 percent) of the total documents. Bibliographies are the least in number (3.47 percent).

2. Age and productivity

Many studies are available where age as a factor for productivity, but with conflicting results. Bland and Berquist(1997) reports that ' the average productivity seems to drop with age. How ever, many senior faculty members remain quite active in research activities and their products are comparable to those of younger faculty members. Einstein was twenty six when he worked out his special theory of relativity, and Darwin was twenty nine when he developed his theory of natural selection. The amount of important scientific research done by young scientists leads many scientists to believe that age is negatively correlated with scientific creativity and research productivity. Dr. Devarajan gave more contributions during 1994-1998 with 33 (28.69 percent) of the total publications. This is the peak period of productivity. Productively went down to 8 (6.95 percent) during the last four years from 2004-2007. It shows that the most productive age is in between 46-50.

Table 4. Year- wise distribution of Publication

Year	Number	Percentage
1979-1983	11	9.56
1984-1988	22	19.13
1989-1993	28	24.34
1994-1998	33	28.69
1999-2003	13	11.30
2004-2007	8	6.95
Total	115	1.00

3. Dr. Devarajan produced the maximum number of publications in English (78.26 percent). About 21.73 percent of his publications are in Malayalam.

4. Out of 27 books, the maximum number of books (37.03 percent) was published during 1989-1993. During the periods 1999-2003 and 2004-2007 he contributed the same number of books i.e. 18.5 percent.

5. About 37.03 percent of the books are dealing with Library and Society. The Information Technology occupies the next position with 22.22 percent of the total literature output.

6. Granthalokam has been identified as the top ranking journal in terms of literature productivity which accounts for 21.95 percent of the total journal articles. Second and third place go to ALIS Bulletin (12.95 percent) and Yojana (9.75 percent) respectively.

7. During the period 1984-1988, Dr.G.Devarajan published the maximum number of journal articles (31.70 percent). Articles were relatively less during 1999-2003.

8. Dr. Devarajan contributed the maximum number of articles in the area of Library and Society which accounts for 46.34 percent of total journal articles. Second position goes to Information Technology with 8 (19.54 percent) of the total. The least number of articles is contributed in Research Methodology and Bibliometrics.

9. Dr. Devarajan presented the majority (62.5 percent) of the conference papers during 1986-1990, whereas the growth of conference papers in the field was relatively less during the rest of the years.

10. A good number (45.83 percent) of the conference papers deal with Library and Society. The papers contributed on Information Science are relatively less with 12.5 percent of the total output.

11. Dr. Devarajan conducted a large number (90 percent) of the Radio/TV programmes during 1994-1998.The visual media programmes were relatively less during 1989-1993.

12. Dr. Devarajan handled the same number of research projects (33.33 percent) each during the periods 1992-1996, 1997-2001 and 2002-2006.

13. Nine Ph.D theses were produced under the guidance of Dr. Devarajan. He also guided 43 (50.58 percent) M.L.I.Sc. dissertations and 33 (38.82 percent) M.Phil dissertations.

14. Majority (66.66 percent) of the Ph.D theses were produced during the period 2004-2007.

15. Dr. Devarajan guided a large number (87.87 percent) of M.Phil dissertations during 2004-2007. About 12.12 percent of the dissertations are produced during the period 2001-2003.

16. During 1999-2003, Dr.G.Devarajan guided 27.9 percent of the M.L.I.Sc. Dissertations. This is the highest number compared with the last two years from 2004-2007 which account for 6 (13.95 percent) of the total output.

13. Tenability of Hypotheses

The tenability of the hypotheses framed for the study is tested based on the findings drawn out of the study.

i. Hypothesis 1

Dr. Devarajan contributed the maximum number of

publications in the area of Library and Society.

About 37.03 percent of the books are dealing with Library and Society. Dr. Devarajan contributed the maximum number of journal articles in the area of Library and Society which account for 46.34 percent of total journal articles. A good number (45.83 percent) of the conference papers deal with Library and Society. The findings 5, 8 and 10 substantiated the validity of the hypothesis.

ii. Hypothesis 2

Dr. Devarajan produced the maximum number of publications during 1994-1998.

The findings 2 show that Dr.G.Devarajan gave more contributions during the period 1994-1998 with 33 (28.69 percent) of the total publications. This is the peak period of productivity. Productively went down to 8 (6.95 percent) during the last four years from 2004-2007. Hence the tenability of the 2nd hypothesis is tested.

CONCLUSION

The findings of the study reveal that Dr. Devarajan is one of the most prominent person in the field of Library and Information Science. He has an excellent record of achievements as an academician as well as professional. His contributions in the field of Library and Information Science is significant. No area of Library and Information Science had been left untouched by Dr. Devarajan. Analysis of his works has thrown light to his valuable contribution in the field of Library and Information Science. Dr. Devarajan can be treated as a model, for his contributions and his inspiration to many young Library and Information Science writers and students.

REFERENCES

Bland, C and Berquist W. (1997) The vitality of senior faculty members, Snow on the roof-fire in the furnace (ERIC Document Reproduction No. ED 415733)

Encyclopedic Dictionary of Library and Information Science (1992). (Ed.), by Pammar. Delhi: Anmoli Publications.

England: Gover publishing company, P.375

Glanzel, w. (2003). Bibliometric as a Research field: A course on theory and application of Bibliometric Indications. Retrieved August 23, 2007, from http://norslis.net/2004/bib-Modole-kul.pdf.

Hertzel, D.H. Bibliometrics: History of the Development of ideas. In Encyclopedia of Library and Information Science ed. by Allen Kent, Vol. 42, Suppt. 7, pp. 144-219, Marcel Dekker, Inc. New Yor.

http://www.wikipedia.org/wiki/Library

Kawatra, P.S. (2000). Library and Information System in the 21st Centaury. New Delhi: Crest Publishing House.

Levin, Sharon G and Stephen, Paula E (1991). Research productivity over the life cycle: Evidence for Academic Scientists. The American Economic Review, 81, 114-32.

Pritchard, A. (1969). Statistical Bibliography/Bibliometrics. Journal of Documentations, 25, 328.

Ray, pray Therch. (1995). Harrod's Librarian Glossary (8th ed.)

Satija, M.P. (1998). Who do we serve? Doctoral Research in Library & Information Science in India. DESIDOC Bulletin of Information Technology, 18 (1), 19-24.

Sengupta, I.N (1990). Bibliometrics and its application/Information Science and Libraries, edited by Pushpa Dhyani, New Delhi: Atlantic.

Sengupta, I.N. (1985). Bibliometrics: A Bird's Eye View. IASLIC Bull, 30, 167-174.

Sewa Singh. (1998). Library and Information Science Literature. In M.K.Jain (Ed.), 50 years of Library & Information Services in India (9.309). New Delhi: Shipra Publications.

Varma, A.K (1997). A Bibliometrics study of Ph.D theses in Botany. In R.G.Prasher (Ed). Library & Information Science: Parameters and perspectives (Vol. 2, PP. 326-327). New Delhi Concept Publishing Company.

2

Children's Literature in Malayalam: A Survey and Bibliometric Study

Dr. Ajikumary.T

1. INTRODUCTION

The future of a society depends upon its children, because they herald the future and constitute what is to come. The famous sociologist, James Bossard, articulated this self-evident understanding in succinct way. "if society is to control and direct its development (call the process social planning, social reconstruction or what you will) then the place to begin with is incoming generation. The remaking of the world is essentially a process of trading in social features... and the future is the child".

In the contemporary world children are considered as individuals, different and distinct from adults. Those who are at the age group of five to fourteen are generally grouped as

'Children'. During this span of age, creative talents and cognitive capacities are developed in them. Unless the energies of children are properly parented and guided during this period, there is the possibility of developing behavioral anomalies.

A child has to learn about this world, about himself and his relationship with this world, through his experience and from the experience of others. Experience of others are mainly transmitted through listening and reading.[3] In fact, in one's self learning and self perfecting processes, reading books plays an important role and it can be cultivated and pruned through proper library facilities and providing qualitatively preferred literature. Children are complex individuals growing up in a rapidly transforming world. Even in today's technological age, books and reading them are indispensable for both early development and life long learning. The early access to literature is an essential part of any child's early-reading experience and needs reinforcing as they become more sophisticated readers, learners and thinkers. Listening to orally transmitted narratives is quite often followed by reading books; especially children's literature. It may be apt to briefly reflect on the central terms that moulds this thesis i.e. literature in general and children's literature in particular.

2. LITERATURE FOR CHILDREN

The enjoyment, pleasure, inspiration and cultural development of human mind have been intimately bounded to production and reception of literature and art. The genre of literature for children covers a variety of themes and can be said to cover everything read by children. They are written especially for the enjoyment and pleasure of children. Children's literature exists as a portion of universal literature, which reflects excellence in writing and designing. The essential feature of modern children's literature is that, it can be distinguished from other branches of literature by the artistic representations and illustrations. The uniqueness of children's literature lies in the specifics of its addressees. Every child is curious about life and adult activities, and lives in the midst of tensions, love and hate within the family and the society. The author who can invoke these experiences with imagination, ideation and insight, and communicate them to children is the ideal author of children's literature.

Books are essential to children if they are to enjoy their childhood and satisfy their quest for knowledge. The books help to develop fine feelings and good habit among children. Need to develop habit of reading among children is very vital to the success of education. Children's literature forms an important part of curriculum, because it develops the children's own language, it aids their reading habit and it enriches their activities in any field. Books can foster racial and multi-cultural understanding and offer children replicable role models from the stories where children of different ethnic groups can be seen participating as equals and co-operating together in a realistic way. Reading books inculcates curiosity among children to know about their country, its origin, the culture and language of their parents and grand parents which fosters them to strengthen a sense of belonging. Books can help children to a deeper understanding of themselves and others and lead them to mature as balanced personalities.[10]

In promoting reading habit among children many publishers and institutions have been playing crucial functions. In India, National Book Trust, and Children's Book Trust have brought out quite good number of books for children. National Centre for Education Research and Training (NCERT), Kerala State Institutes of Children's

Literature, National Centre for Children's Literature etc. are other publishers of children's literature. This study pay attention not only to the diversity and growth of children's literature, but also examines how this genre is linked to the processes of publication and institutions involved in enabling reading

3. RELEVANCE OF THE STUDY

Children's literature can play an important role in the educational as well as cultural development of a child. We can provide literature to children as supplement to the curriculum materials in various forms such as informative literature and creative literature. Even though we have considerable stock of children's literature, in Malayalam language, the quality stands far behind international standards. We have lot of books based on various subjects for children, but it is difficult to ferret out good literature from them. There is no standard written criterion for evaluating these works. Even though we have many children's books published by different agencies especially commercial publishers, still we have no dependable and comprehensive bibliography of this literature is available. The relevance of this study lies, partially, in the fact that it attempts to fill this literature gap.

We can assess the growth of knowledge in any discipline by qualitative and quantitative approaches. The qualitative approach demands some structural or descriptive models. As there are no such models for evaluation and the lack of critical studies on children's literature in Malayalam, the qualitative assessment cannot be completely carried out. The quantitative approach is based on the consolidation of statistics and interpretations. Many such studies have been conducted on the growth of literature in various subjects except children's literature. That is why this study becomes all the more relevant.

4. TITLE OF THE STUDY

The title of this study is **"Children's Literature in Malayalam: A Survey and Bibliometric Study".**

5. DEFINITION OF KEYTERMS

Let us now proceed to define select terms that are indispensable for the present study. For this purpose the key terms that appear in the title and methodological description are delineated.

5.1. Children's Literature

According to the New Book of Knowledge Encyclopedia, " children's literature consists of an enormous and exciting array of books written and published especially for young readers and listeners". According to the New Encyclopedia Britanica, children's literature is "... the body of written works and accompanying illustrations produced in order to entertain or instruct young people. The genre encompasses a wide range of works, including acknowledged classics of world literature, picture books and easy-to-read stories written exclusively for children, and fairy tales, lullabies, fables, folk songs and other primarily orally transmitted materials".

5.2. Malayalam

Malayalam is the language spoken predominantly in the State of Kerala, in South India. It is one of the 22 official languages of India, spoken by around 37 million people. A native speaker of Malayalam is called a 'Malayali'.. Malayalam language belongs to the family of Dravidian languages and considered to be one of the four prominent Dravidian languages of South India. Malayalam has a script of its own, covering all the symbols of Sanskrit as well as special Dravidian letters.

5.3. Survey

The Collins Cobuilld English Language Dictionary defines survey as a "... detailed investigation of something". According to the Oxford English Dictionary, survey is "... the examining or inspecting in detail especially for some specific subjects." In the present study, literature for children published in Malayalam language is surveyed.

5.4. Bibliometric Study

The British Standard Glossary of Documentation of Terms explained Bibliometrics as the " study of the use of documents and patterns of publications in which mathematical and statistical methods have been applied". Alan Pritchard defines Bibliometrics "... as the branch of information theory that attempts to analyse quantitatively the properties and behaviour of recorded knowledge".

6. OBJECTIVES OF THE STUDY

The main objectives of the study are:

1. to assess total number of the children's books in Malayalam published up to 2006;
2. to assess the growth rate of children's books in Malayalam from 1824 to 2006;
3. to assess the subject-wise distribution of children's books;
4. to identify the major publishers of children's books in Malayalam;
5. to identify the authorship pattern in each of the subject-group;
6. to decompose the total number of translated books into Malayalam in terms of their original languages;

7. to estimate the rate of increase in the cost of children's books over the period up to 2006;
8. to estimate the price per page of children's books and to find out the price - page correlation;
9. to assess the quantity of illustrations in children's books in Malayalam; and,
10. to find out the determinants of publication output of children's literature in Malayalam.

7. HYPOTHESIS

The following hypotheses are formulated in this study.

1. The growth in the production of children's literature in Malayalam fluctuates between years.
2. There are significant variations in the production of books in various genres and subject-groups within children's literature.
3. The contribution of government and public sector publishers in the field of children's literature is higher than that of publishers in private sector.
4. The translations of children's literature into Malayalam from other languages are relatively less.
5. There are socio-economic factors such as population, total literacy, female literacy, real State Domestic Product and Per Capita Income which determined the growth of publications of children's literature in Malayalam.

8. METHODOLOGY

Methodology applied in the present study involves Survey of Literature and Bibliometric Analysis; they are schematized in the following sub-sections.

8.1. Survey of Literature

A comprehensive survey of children's books in Malayalam including books and primary sources like indices and bibliography, are undertaken. In addition, the CD-ROM database of 'LISA Plus' was searched for relevant studies. There is no bibliometric study conducted on children's literature in Malayalam. However, the literature search provided a lot of background information such as studies on literature, bibliometric studies on other genre, studies about Malayalam language etc.

For the collection of data various sources have been consulted. The most important and dependable among them was the Malayala Grantha Soochi published by Kerala Sahithya Akademy, Trichur. It is an authentic bibliography which provides a comprehensive account of books in Malayalam upto 1995 in Seven Volumes. The seventh volume was published in 1997. The compilation of Grantha Soochi was started under the editorialship of K.M.Govi and A.K. Panikkar. The first volume came out in 1973, and the second volume in 1974. The first volume was exclusively devoted for literary works and the second volume for non-literary works. The other five volumes contain both. Entries were arranged alphabetically with the name of the author under each subject. The Grantha Soochi also provides the name of the author, subject and title index. The CD-Rom version of Malayala Grantha Soochi came out in 2006 which includes books published in Malayalam up to 2000. The investigator had to depend for the details about books published between 2000 and 2006 on publisher's catalogues, various book exhibitions that were conducted all over the State and information provided by the leading publishers.

In addition, the children's section of Trivandrum Public Library, collections of other major children's libraries and Kerala Sahithya Akademy library were examined to fill information gaps and for searching titles of children's literature in Malayalam which are not entered into the sources mentioned above.

8.2. Bibliometric Analysis

In order to carry out the bibliometric analysis, the details of 7497 books were consulted. The variables such as form, author, subject, title, publisher, place of publication, year of publication, price, page number, size of the book, illustration etc. are dealt with for the analysis and interpretation of the base line data using the SPSS programme.

9. SCOPE AND COVERAGE

In children's literature, as in any other literature, there are multiple classificatory schemes. For the purpose of the present study, various genre of literature for children are identified and examined. Therefore, they are classified into poetry, plays, stories including fiction, biographies, science, social science, language, religion, music, folk tales and folk songs, sayings and proverbs, history of literature, fine arts, general books, translations, essays, philosophy, education and so on. They together accounted for 50 subjects.

Since the study is about the literature produced in a regional language, it was considered apt to follow the pattern followed by Ranganathan in Colon Classification (6th Ed.). For the analysis, the 50 subjects are classified into eight subject- groups in a logical sequence. They are Generalia, Science, Linguistics, Social Science, Humanities and Religion, Arts, Malayalam Literature and Biographies.

Subject-group Distribution of Children's Literature in Malayalam Language up to 2006 AD

Sl. No.	Name of subject -group	Total books	Percentage
1	Generalia	277	3.7
2	Science	1015	13.5
3	Linguistics	157	2.1
4	Social Science	432	5.8
5	Humanities and Religion	297	4.0
6	Arts	149	2.0
7	Malayalam Literature	4537	60.5
8	Biography	633	8.4
	Total	7497	100

The data collected for the present study is confined to a period of 184 years. ie, from 1824 to 2006. It was found that the first Malayalam book for children was published in 1824; hence the initial year under focus of this study is that year.

10 LIMITATIONS OF THE STUDY

As the study covers 184 years from 1824 to 2006, right from the appearance of the first printed book for children in Malayalam, physical verification of all the books was impossible. Therefore, published bibliographies had to be employed to a certain extent. Though every effort has been made to compile a comprehensive database of children's literature in Malayalam, there may be some gaps in the list due to the lack of bibliographic control after 2000.

11 MAJOR FINDINGS OF THE STUDY

The major findings of literature survey and bibliometric analysis are summarized and presented below.

11.1. Children's literature in Malayalam

The book entitled "Cherupaithangalkkuu Upakarartham Inkleeshil Ninnu Paribhashappeduthiya

Kadhakal" published in 1824 was the first prose work for children in Malayalam. Thereafter, up to 1860 no exclusive work for children got published, although many of the myths and legends reached children's hands. From the year 1861 onwards, publications for children were on an increasing path and it had gained consistency.

11.2. Subject -wise distribution of books

The main findings of the bibliometric analysis conducted to comprehend the subject-wise composition reveal the following:

i. The subject- group 'Malayalam Literature' constitutes 60.5 percent of the total number of children's books published in Malayalam.

ii. Books on 'Science' constitute 13.5 percent.

iii. Biographies constitute 8.4 percent

iv. 'Social Science' books comes to the next position with a percentage of 5.8

v. Books on Humanities and Religion, Generalia and Social Science together have significant share when compared to books on 'Arts' and 'Linguistics'.

11.3. Areas of Publication in various subject - groups in children's literature

Apart from the discipline based analysis, we have conducted thematic distribution of the published works for children. That is, all the eight subject-groups were decomposed to gain an idea about their scatter and composition.

11.4. Generalia

i. General essays constituted more than half of this subject - group (56.3 %).

ii. General books on children's literature consisted of 39.0 %

iii. Books on Library Science and Journalism were found to be rare. (4.7 %).

11.5. Science

i. General books on Science, especially basic books, constituted 29.1 % of the total number of 'Science' books.

ii. Books on Mathematics constituted 22.3 %.

iii. 10.8 % were Zoology books.

iv. Published books on other branches of Science were comparatively less in number.

11.6. Linguistics

i. Books on proverbs had the highest share in the subject-group 'Linguistics' (29.9%)

ii. General books on linguistics constituted 22.9%.

iii. Grammar books and dictionaries had notable number.

11.7. Social Science

i. Books on Geography and Travelogues had the highest share in terms of the number of publications (32.2%); it was followed by Indian History (19.6%).

ii. Books on Education, Gandhi and World History came close to the first.

iii. Books on Politics, Economics, Kerala History and General Social Science books had only a small share.

11.8. Humanities and Religion

i. About 39.4 % of the books were on Hinduism; while on Christianity, the percentage share of it was 24.9%

ii. Books on Islamism and Budhism are lesser in number when compared to the above religions

iii. Philosophy books accounted for 18.5 %.

11.9. Arts

i. Books on Fine Arts, Music, Sports and Entertainment contributed for about 54.4 % of the total books published in 'Arts'.

ii. Songs and folk songs had a contribution of 39.6 %.

iii. Books on Art forms of Kerala were very few (6%).

11.10. Malayalam Literature

(i) In the classificatory scheme of Malayalam Literature, short story and fiction predominated with 69.5% share.

(ii) Poetry had a share of 14.2 %.

(iii) Plays shared 4.5 %.

(iv) Translations of literary works constituted 6.2%.

(v) 3.7% were Folk tales.

(vi) Thinner areas of publication were history of literature, criticisms, comedy and collection of poems.

11.11. Biographies

(i) Individual biographies constituted the major portion; i.e. 51.82 %

(ii) 43.91 % were collected biographies.

(iii) Autobiographies came in black and white were very few.

11.12. Ready Reference Books

(i) Ready reference books for children numbered 102 inclusive of all subject-groups. (1.36%).

(ii) The share of ready reference books were more in 'Science' (39) followed by 'Linguistics' (32) and 'Generalia' (19)

(iii) Hand books, Yearbooks and Directories, which can be classified as children's literature, did not appear during the period at stake.

11.13. Authorship pattern

Authorship pattern was analyzed by taking into account of the difference in author types, gender, prolificacy and performativity of authors. The schematic presentation provided in the following sub-sections brings out some of the main findings of this exercise.

11.14. Types of Authors

(i)B ooks written by single author constituted 94.9 %. Books written by two authors constituted 0.3%

(ii) Single authorship had been prevalent in 'Malayalam Literature' (59 %), however, it is relatively low in 'Arts' and 'Linguistics' (1.9 %).

(iii) Dual authorship was more in 'Science' (0.8 %) and the lowest in 'Generalia'.

(iv) The share of multiple authorship was found to be very low (0.3 %)

(v) Edited works were also scanty (0.2%).

(vi) Books which do not specify the names of authors (anonymous works) appear in all subject - groups and they constituted 2.6 percent of the total

11.15. Productivity of Authors

We have found that productivity of authors differ dramatically in terms of the number of books authored. Some of the outcomes of bibliometric analysis are presented below.

(i) The analysis shows that there is an inverse relationship between the number of authors and number of books.

(ii) 2523 authors have produced one book each. 511 authors produced two books and 213 authors produced three books.

(iii) There are 61 authors who have produced more than 10 books.

(iv) Lotka's 'Inverse Square Law' on the productivity of authors was found to be applicable here with slight variation in the value of index number 'n'. In this study the value assigned was 2.22.

11.16. Prolific writers in children's literature

Some authors were found to be prolific; while there were others who were not. The analysis on the prolificacy of authors enabled the following observations.

(i) The following are the most prolific writers in children's literature as a whole.

1. Madhavan Nair, V (Mali)
2. Sivadas, S
3. Kunjunni.
4. Narendranath, P.
5. Mathew M. Kuzhiveli

(ii) The following authors have contributed the largest number of books in each subject-group.

I	**Generalia**	-	Kunjunni
Ii	Science	-	Sreedharan Palliyara
Iii	Linguistics	-	Velayudhan Panikkasseri
Iv	Social Science	-	Mathew M. Kuzhiveli
V	Humanities and Religion	-	Madhavan Nair, V. (Mali)
Vi	Arts	-	Rajendran, K
Vii	Malayalam Literature	-	Madhavan Nair, V. (Mali)
Viii	Biographies	-	Prasannan G. Mullasseri.

11.17. Gender - wise Distribution

i. The percentage of women writers (10.4 %) was less than that of male writers. (89.6%).

ii. In the subject- group 'Malayalam Literature', out of 1379 authors 150 were females (10.87 %) while the male counter parts were 1229 (89.12 %).

iii. The share of female writers was less in other subject - groups.

11.18. Publishers of children's literature

As we have already noted, publishers play a critical role not only in the number of books and other reading materials published, but also they determine the quality and distribution of them. Therefore, we have examined the profile of publishers as well using quantitative techniques.

(i)Altogether , 727 publishers could be identified

(ii) The main categories were Private, Government (State and Central), and publishers in Public - sector.

(iii) Out of 727 Publishers, the private-sector constituted maximum 5153, i.e. 68.7%. The Government publishers produced 1186 books (15.8 %) and the number of publishers in the public sector was 1158 (15.5 %).

(iv) Sahithya Pravarthaka Sahakarana Sangham, Kottayam ranked as the topmost publisher, which alone had been responsible for the production of 629 books for children within a span of 61 years.

(v) Among the private publishers, DC Books, Kottayam, stood first with 426 books.

(vi) Among Government Publishers, Kerala State Institute of Children's Literature stood first by producing 585 books within a span of 25 years.

(vii) Among public sector publishers, Sahithya Pravarthaka Sahakarana Sangham (SPCS) led with 629 published books in its credit.

11.19. Geographical Location of Publishers

The books for children are not only published from Kerala but also from outside Kerala and India. Therefore, it was found worthwhile to examine the geographical spread of the publishers and publications.

11.20. Publications from Kerala

(i)9 5.3 percent of children's books were published by various publishers from within Kerala.

(ii) Thiruvananthapuram is the most productive district, which accounted for 30.2% percent of books from Kerala.

(iii) Wynad district did not publish any children's literature.

(iv) Kasaragod and Idukki districts lag behind in the production.

(v) In terms of publication, Thiruvananthapuram always maintained a lead during fifty years between 1906 and 1956; Kottayam had taken on the lead since 1956 to 2006.

11.20. Publications from other States

i. There were 393 Malayalam books published from outside Kerala but within the country.

ii. New Delhi had contributed most of the children's literature in Malayalam as it brought out 285 books.

iii. National Book Trust and Children's Book Trust were the most prominent publishers from NewDelhi

iv. Kolkatha, Mysore, Mahe and Bangalore had only little

role in the production of children's books in Malayalam language.

11.21. Publications from outside India

Progress Publishers located in Moscow was the only publisher which brought out Malayalam books for children.

11.22. Author as publisher

i. Books published by the authors themselves constituted 1.49 percent of the total.

ii. Publishing of books by authors themselves had been more wide spread in the subject - group 'Linguistics' (3.82 %) and lowest in the case of 'Social Science' (0.23 %).

iii. The highest number of self-published books was in the subject-group 'Malayalam Literature'.

11.23. Various editions of children's literature

Certain books are published only once and they do not get print form later due to several reasons. At the same time, some find repeated reprints of editions. Therefore, this aspect was also subjected to bibliometric analysis.

i. The single edition books constituted 88.86 percent of the total.

ii. 7.16 percent of books came in the subject- group 'Malayalam Literature' and 6.50 percent of 'Science' books found their second edition.

iii. In the subject-groups such as Science, Social Science, Humanities and Religion and Biography there had been 3rd edition books.

iv. The subject - group 'Malayalam- Literature' possesses the large number of books with several editions. Some of them had been published up to 22 editions.

11.24. Year - wise Distribution of children's literature in Malayalam

Publication of books in general and children's literature in particular, vary over years. Although no particular pattern can be traced, it is important to analyze year-wise variations in the publications of the books that fall in the latter genre.

i. The publication of children's literature started in 1824. The book entitled "Cherupaithangalkku Upakarartham Inklishil Ninnu Paribhazhappeduthiya Kathakal" is considered as the first prose for children in Malayalam.

ii. There were no publications for children between 1824 and 1861.

iii. The books in the subject-group 'Malayalam Literature' retained its first position throughout the period covered by this study.

iv. The period 1991 - 2000 had been the most productive decade of children's literature in Malayalam.

v. Of the five periods taken while estimating the period-wise growth (25 year intervals), the fifth period (1981-2006) witnessed the highest growth rate of 92.6 per cent when compared to the fourth period.

vi. Books in Malayalam Literature maintained the highest level of production during all the five periods.

vii. Though the number of publications increased, the actual growth rate had declined during all the five periods.

11.25. Translations

Arts and ideas are not localized within a language; they get translated and transmitted to other languages and cultures. It was found, therefore, relevant to analyze the profile of the translated works.

i. Translated works for children constituted only 8.3 percent of the total children's literature.

ii. The highest number of translations was in 'Social Science' (11.34 %).

iii. There were no translations in the subject - group 'Linguistics'.

11.26. Language - wise distribution of translations

i. The majority of works were translated from English language.

ii. Hindi occupied the second position and Russian occupied the third position.

iii. Almost all prominent foreign language literatures were translated to Malalyalam.

iv. Translations from only six Indian languages appeared in Malayalam children's literature.

11.27. Period-wise Distribution of translations in 25 - year interval

i. The most productive period of translations had been 25 years from 1981-2006.

ii. The lowest number of translations took place during the period 1906 - 1931.

iii. From the beginning of 20th centaury there had been stable growth of translations in most of the subject - group.

11.28. Publisher - wise distribution of Translations

i. National Book Trust, New Delhi, Kerala State Institute

of Children's Literature, Thiruvananthapuram, Sahithya Pravarthaka Sahakarana Sangham, Kottayam and D.C. Books, Kottayam were the top four publishers of translated works.

ii. The prominent publishers belonged to all the three sectors; government, public and private.

iii. The share of government publishers had been more than that of private publishers.

11.29. Prominent Authors in Translations

i. The analysis shows that maximum number of translations in terms of single author is of the Russian writer Leo Tolstoy. Next comes that of William Shakespeare.

ii. Other prominent authors whose works were translated into Malayalam are Vishnu Sharma, Grim Brothers, and Yeshpal Jain.

11.30. Prominent Translators

i. The study reveals that smt. Omana stands first among the translators of Malayalam Literature. All her translations were from Russian Language.

ii. K.K.C Nair and Evoor Parameswaran were the other two prominent translators.

11.31. Gender - wise distribution of translations

i. Female translators constituted only 20.2 percent of the total, while the male counterparts accounted for 79.72 %.

ii. The share of female translators in the subject- group 'Social Science' was higher than that of other subject-groups.

11.32. Illustrations

It is well known that illustrations fascinate children and also they persuade them to read books. Therefore, we have included in our analysis decipherment of appearance of illustrations in printed texts. Paradoxically enough, we have found that books with illustrations are not forthcoming as much in number as warranted or desired. The following findings derived from the analysis attest this fact.

i. Out of total number of books produced in children's literature, illustrated books are less than non-illustrated books.

ii. The 'Science' books contained more illustrations than other subject-groups.

iii. 'Linguistics' had the lowest number of illustrated books.

11.33. Distribution of illustrations in modes of publication

i. The government publishers brought out more illustrated books than any others.

ii. The private publishers brought out books with lesser illustrations.

iii. The publishers in the public sector gave more space for illustrations than the private publishers.

11.34. Distribution of illustrated books according to geographical area

i. The publishers in Thiruvananthapuram district published more illustrated books than those of other districts.

ii. Kottayam stood in the second position in the magnitude of the illustrated books.

iii. Outside Kerala, publishers of New Delhi stood first in the production of illustrated books.

11.35. Distribution of pages in children's literature

Number of pages contained in a book matters for a child-reader. Lengthy books are formidable, although it may be of great worth to read them. Therefore, an analysis was conducted about the distribution of pages in children's literature in Malayalam language. Select results are invoked here.

i. Most of the books published had pages ranging between 51 and 100 (43.4%).

ii. The books having more than 500 pages were comparatively less (0.4%).

11.36. Distribution of pages in each subject-group

i. Books in almost all subject-groups restricted page numbers within the range of 51-100.

ii. Books with more than 500 pages were rare in subject-groups except 'Malayalam Literature'. Books published in Malayalam Literature had maximum pages.

iii. The lengthiest book ever produced is 'Puranakathamalika' written by Madhavan Nair, V. (Mali) which runs to 1028 pages.

11.37. Decade-wise Distribution of books by pages

i. The earlier decades of the second half of the 20th century published books below 300 pages.

ii. The latter half of the 20th century published books with more than 500 pages. That is over time the length of the running matter increased in terms of page numbers.

11.38. Size of the books

Appearance of any dimensional matter matters; this is so especially when it is concerned with those things that children handle. Hence, size of the book varies inversely with age; children's books generally come out with larger in size than those of adults. The bigger font size and illustrations may be the factors that make books bigger in size. Whatever may be the reason behind the determination of size, it is important to analyze the physical appearance of books in terms of its width and length.

i. Majority of books came out with the size 21 x 14 cms.

ii. Books of the size 18 x 12 cms came in the second position and it was the run of the mill during 19th century.

iii. Except 'Humanities and Religion' in all other subject-groups, most of them were of the size 21 x 14 cms. size.

iv. In the subject-group 'Malayalam Literature' it varied so much that the average value has no statistical significance.

11.39. Estimation of price per page

Price of books and ability to purchase them are closely related. In other words, logic of market matters when it comes to buying of books. It is true not only for individual buyers but also for institutions like libraries. Taking this into account, we have paid attention to the price of the books in this sub-section and in the subsequent sub-section it is correlated with the number of pages.

i. The average price per page had been 20 paise

ii. There was significant variation in average price per page over the decades.

iii. From the decade 1971-1980 onwards, there was steady increase in the price per page.

iv. In the years from 2001 - 2006, the prices per page had been 55 paise.

v. The price per-page variation was found to be statistically significant

11.40. Estimation of price per page of different subject-groups

i. There was considerable variation of price per page among each subject-group

ii. 'Linguistics' books had the highest price (25 paise per page) and Biography had the lowest price (15 paise per page).

iii. The variation of price per page in each subject - group was statically significant.

11.41. Decade - wise Estimation of price per page in each subject- literature

i. During the period between 1991 and 2008, prices reached their peaks for books of almost all subject-groups with the exception of 'Humanities and Religion'.

ii. Linguistic books are rather more expensive and Biography books are found to be the cheapest.

iii. The price per page had increased from the early decades of twentieth century to the later decades.

11.42. Estimation of price per page according to the mode of publication

i. Books published by government publishers cost 20 paise per page. Books published by private agencies cost 22 paise per page where as publishers in the public sector cost only 19 price per page.

ii. The ANOVA result shows that these variations in price per page among the three types of publishers are statically significant.

11.43. Decade - wise Calculations of price per page according to the mode of publication

i. The average price per page of books published by public sector agencies was found to be below 20 paise and it shows fluctuations across decades. For instance, during 1931-1940 the price per page was 34 paise and during 1941-1950 it dropped to 24 paise per page and during 1951-1960 the price per page declined further to 15 paise.

ii. The price of books published by Government institutions had remained more or less stable. Price per page of these books also showed same tendency.

iii. The average price per page of Government publishers was 20 paise, and the highest price during the decade 1941-1950 was 33 paise per page.

iv. The unit price and price per page of books published by private publishers fluctuated and the highest price per page was during 1921- 1930 (26 paise).

v. The average price per page of private publishers was 22 paise.

vi. The comparison of the relative prices of three publishers shows that private publishers charge more than that of the other two types of publishers.

11.44. Price and page number correlation

In the analytical part of this thesis, the correlations

between prices and number of pages of books in different subject-groups were found out. Both cross section and temporal analyses were carried out and the results are presented here.

i. The correlation between the pages and real price was significant.

ii. The real price increased along with increase in the number of pages.

11.45. Correlation between number of pages and real price among various subject-groups

i. The correlation between the number of pages and the real price was highest in 'Humanities and Religion'.

ii. The lowest value of correlation between the number of pages and real price was in 'Science'

11.46. Determinants of publication output of children's literature in Malayalam

Although supply-demand relation is more or less evident, we considered that it is important to examine the determinants of publication output of children's literature in Malayalam. The most important determinants were literacy rate, population, personal income etc.

(i)P opulation was found to be the most important determinant, which influenced publication output of children's books in Malayalam. One percent change in population would lead to 0.72 percent change in publication output.

(ii) Total literacy is the second important factor, which influenced the publication output.

(iii) SDP and Per Capita Income also had some extent of influence.

(iv) The existing relationship between publication output and explanatory variables is found to be statistically significant.

12. SUGGESTIONS AND RECOMMENDATIONS

Children's Literature as an independent genre in Malayalam has a history of nearly two centuries (184 years). In spite of this fact, a comprehensive and up-to-date bibliography is yet to find print. This might have served as the basic reference source for bibliographic control as well as for the systematic planning and co-ordination of the production of literature for children. This study has identified the above lacuna as a strong reason for the imbalance in the growth of children's literature in Malayalam.

Sahithya Pravarthaka Co-operative Society (SPCS), while serving as the most prominent publisher of Malayalam literature, has contributed its own share to children's literature. Nevertheless, as a co-operative society it gradually confronted several problems which affected its performativity. This has also dampened its heralding role in the promotion of children's literature.

This study has also identified the remarkable promotional role played by the Kerala State Institute of Children's Literature for the betterment of children's cognitive, emotional and personal capabilities through literature. There are also many isolated endeavors in the public and private sectors that supported the production and distribution of children's literature in Malayalam. However, lack of co-ordination of these disparate efforts has been a serious lacuna that hindered desired results and realization of the potential of children's literature. Even though the Kerala State Institute of Children's Literature has played an impressive function in the production and promotion of children's literature, it has to go a long way in the contemporary world to meet the needs of children.

Let us now proceed to propose specific recommendations for the betterment of Children's Literature in Malayalam:

i. The State government may designate the Kerala State Institute of Children's Literature as the nodal agency to act as the 'State Resource Centre' for children's literature in Malayalam. It should acquire as well as produce quality literature in all the branches of knowledge. Such an agency is expected to take-up specific responsibilities for preserving and promoting children's literature besides coordinating every endeavor for bettering children through literature.

ii. The Institute should establish a 'Depository Library' for children's literature which can collect, organize and stock all the materials published for children; especially those in Malayalam including translations. It should be designated as the 'State Depository for Children's Publications in Malayalam'.

iii. The Institute should also organize and maintain a 'Model Reference Library' for children. It should have choicest works for children in various subjects and languages which attracts and persuade children. It must be up-to-date and contemporaneous with new media materials, and storage and retrieval facilities.

iv. The Institute should execute a time-bound project for preparing a comprehensive bibliography of children's books. Most modern technologies should be made use of for this end.

v. The Institute should prepare a time-bound 'Development Plan' for the enhancing the quality of literature for children. The plan should focus on a reasonably balanced growth of children's literature with the specific intention to effectively address the current interest of children. It should also pay sufficient attention to the production of quality reference books in all relevant subject areas in all its variety.

vi. It should conduct regular workshops, seminars and orientation classes to the publishers, authors, illustrators and readers of children's literature.

vii. Another agency role of it could be the regular conduct of book exhibitions for general public and in schools for bringing books and children closer.

viii. It could also encourage the production of children's films, children's theatre and documentaries.

ix. There is a need for good translations of famous children's books from other languages. This may require an efficient and effective panel of translators.

x. The Institute should form a high level committee consisting of the representatives from the State Library Council, State Central Library, Kerala Sahithya Akademy, Kerala Sangeetha Nataka Akademy, Kerala State Institute of Languages, and also the prominent publishers and authors in the field of children's literature to ensure proper co-ordination for the effective implementation of the Development Plan and other activities.

xi. It is also important to create websites for important children's writers in Malayalam.

12.1. Other recommendations

I. The Kerala Public Libraries Act has not given due importance to the children's Library Services. It has a definite responsibility to provide the best literature and service to children through the large number of public libraries within the state. It requires proper amendments to the existing provision for bettering children's library services. When a revision of the Act has to take place, due importance should be given to children's libraries.

II. The State Library Council is the agency to develop and implement fruitful library services for children through public libraries. The existing children's corners in the large number of public libraries affiliated to the Council should be developed following proper guidelines to provide better service for children.

III. Each District Library Council should establish a children's library in every district. A delivery station for children's books in each revenue district is required. The District Children's Library, in addition to its normal functions, should serve as a link between the State Resource Centre and Delivery Stations.

IV. Children's Libraries should be established at Taluk, Village and Panchayath levels. These libraries should be made to work in close co-operation with the school libraries in the region. The establishment and functioning of these libraries should be planned with foresight and due recognition for children's growth and development.

13. THE TENABILITY OF HYPOTHESES

The hypotheses formulated at the beginning of the study were:

i. The growth in the production of children's literature

in Malayalam is fluctuates between years.

ii. There are significant variations in the production of books in various genres and subject-groups within children's literature.

iii. The contribution of government and public sector publishers in the field of children's literature is higher than that of publishers in the private sector.

iv. The translations of children's literature into Malayalam from other languages are relatively less.

v. There are certain socio-economic factors such as population, total literacy, female literacy, real State Domestic Product and Per Capita Income which determined the growth of publications of children's literature in Malayalam.

The findings of the analysis explicate that the proposed hypotheses stood the test of verification and they hold good.

14. CONCLUSION

Fiction, short story, play and poem predominate in the genre of children's literature. Authors and publishers prefer them as if children cherish those forms of articulations. Perhaps, this liking of children could be an outcome of the market driven responses of the publishers. When we dream of children's literature, it is desirable and expected that they are written by children. But this is not usual, as we have found in the histories of this genre circulating all over the world including Kerala, the elders write for the young. Children's literature has been found to be the creation of adults. Adults imagine a child and address her/him through that imaginative image. In this context, realism is an out of the way. In fact, within the genre that is studied in this thesis, we have found that even the narratives from the ancient past, i.e. before the compartmentalization of verbal expressions and formalization of the category 'Children's Literature', continued to the present. They continued through orally transmitted narratives and printed books. The distinction between an adult and a child are blurred within the gamut of literary world to which children are introduced or they enter into by themselves. At the same time, it is possible to formulate the following proposition. Mothers tell tales and fathers write works; they together create Children's Literature.

REFERENCES

Agarwal, S P. Ed.(1989) Libraries for Children. Development of Documentation in

Baskara Rao, U.(1989)Bringing Children and Books Together. Indian Book Industry. XLI.(3), 7.

Better Books For Children. Editorial.(1988) Indian Book Industry XLI.(3), p.4.

Bossard, James.(1960) Sociology of Child Development. New York: Harper, p.17.

British Standards Glossary of Documentation of Terms.(1976). London: British Standards Institution.. p.7.

Collins Cobuild English Language Dictionary.(1987) London : William Collins Sons & Co. Ltd. p. 1474.

Elkin, Judith and Lonsdale, Ray. Ed. (1996) Focus on the Child: Libraries, Literacy and Learning. London: Library Association Publishing. p. 16.

Ibid.P.4

Funk and Wangnell's (1971) New Encyclopedia. Vol.5 New York: Funk and

Govi, KM. (1988) Balasahithya Granthasoochi. Vinjana Kairali. 19(6), 31-32.

Gupta, V.P.(1990) Children's Literature for Today and Tomorrow. The Indian Book Industry. XLIII (2),11-13.

India: Social Science Information. New Delhi: Concept Publishers.

Kurup, CRG. (1990) Publishing of Children's Books: Development of the Reading Habit. Indian Book Industry. XLIII (2), 5-10.

Pritchard, Alan. (1989) Statistical Bibliography or Bibliometrics. Journal of Documentation, 25 (4),348.

The New Book of Knowledge Encyclopedia. (2003). Vol.3 Danburry: Scholastic Library Publication Inco. p. 228.

The New Encyclopedia Britanica.(1993). Vol.23. Chicago: Encyclopedia Britanica Inco. p.229.

The Oxford English Dictionary. Ed. 2 (1989).Vol.XVII. Oxford: Clarendone Press. p.309.

Wikipedia Online Encyclopedia.[available at http://en.wickipedia.org/wiki/ Malayalam_ language]

3

Research Trends In Physics: An Analysis of Doctoral Theses

Dr. K.G. Sudhier

1. INTRODUCTION

Research is an indispensable component for any discipline for the generation of new knowledge, which, coupled with skill leads to effective action. According to Varalakshmi[1] 'research is a means of continuously developing a discipline; it endows a discipline with the capability to utilize the knowledge generated in other discipline; it makes use of scientific method and it is helpful; it admits of being learnt and admits of organization'.

Cito analytical studies of doctoral dissertations, which are the products of research activity, form an important source of information. A number of such studies based on dissertations have been conducted in India and abroad, in order to understand the pattern of materials used by the scientists for their research purposes in different branches of science.

Dissertations are current, impartial reviews with extensive reference list. They are also actually inaccessible, because many institutions still insists on time based theses that are assembled in the least number possible. Usually a copy is provided each for the candidate, supervisor and examiner and one is kept in the candidate's university library.

Research Programmes at the Ph.D level in Library and Information Science carried out in India during the seven years (1997-2003) have been analyzed by Mahapatra and Sahoo[2] to find out the trends and areas of research. In a case study of citation analysis of Ph D thesis by NEERI scientists in the field of Environmental science and Engineering during 1977-1991 has been carried out by Madkay and Rajyalekshmi[3]. Raza and Zarrin[4] analysed 16 doctoral theses submitted to the Department of Chemistry, Aligarh Muslim University in 1997 and 1998. The study revealed that researchers in the field of Chemistry mainly use journals, 80.69% and minimum citation for reports was 0.08%. Most productive country of journals was USA with 32.03% followed by UK 27.1%. Bandyopathyay and Nandi[5] reported results of a citations analysis study of 9 doctoral dissertations in Political Science submitted to the Burdwan University (West Bengal) from 1991-1995. The study conducted that the most favoured form of literature was books (56.2%) followed by journals. Doraswamy and Reddy[6] assessed the citations in Ph.D. theses in Geography submitted to Sri. Venkateswara University, Tirupati (India) during 1983-1995. There were 2471 citations in the theses and books contributed the highest member of citations accounting for 41.89% and journals were the second highest group accounting for 37.96% of total citations. Varma[7] assessed the Ph. D theses awarded by Pt. Ravishankar Shukla University, Raipur during the period from 1964 to 1990. Analysis of the citations of 30 theses revealed that in Botanical Research the trend is towards Ecological studies as 40.54% of theses belong to Ecology class. This has been followed by two other branches of Botany; Physiology and Plant Pathology. Adiyodi[8] made a comparison of information generation of different faculties of University of Calicut, in his book titled New Frontiers of Knowledge. In his publication he attempted to compile all the relevant details regarding the research activities, includes all theses (474) and over 6,000 titles of books, research papers, creative writings, chapters in books, reviews, conference proceedings and reports that have appeared form the University of Calicut during 1968-1993 Other similar studies include Krishna and Kumar, Biradar and Thippeswamy[10], Srivastava and Lahiri.

The purpose of this article is to identify the trend of doctoral research programmes of Physics in University of Kerala during 1999-2003.

2. OBJECTIVES

The main objectives of the study are :

- To study the trend of Physics research
- To know the subject wise distribution of research in Physics
- To study the different bibliographic forms of citations used by the physicists
- Identify the core journals and books
- Most cited Indian journals

3. THE UNIVERSITY OF KERALA

The University of Kerala, which occupies the position of the mother university in the State, has been at the centre of all higher education activity in Kerala since its very inception. The University of Travancore which eventually became the University of Kerala was established in 1937 by a promulgation of the Maharaja of Travancore, Shri. Chithira Thirunal Balarama Varma who was also the first Chancellor of the University. Sir C.P. Ramaswamy Ayyar, the then Diwan of the State, was the first Vice-Chancellor[13].

Formation of the first university in Kerala - University of Travancore, the predecessor of the present university of Kerala was an important landmark in the cultural history of Malayalam speaking people. The University of Travancore was the third University to be started in any princely state in India and one of the 16 Universities to be started in pre-independent India, and one of the oldest universities in the commonwealth.[14]

At present, the university has 16 faculties and 41 departments of teaching and research. There are 121 affiliated colleges, of these, 46 are aided Arts and Science colleges, and 13 are unaided Arts and Science colleges.[15]

During 1997, the university celebrated its diamond jubilee. The National Assessment and Accreditation Committee (NAAC) have placed the University at the B^{++} grade[16].

4. PH. D PROGRAMME

The university has been trying to organise its Ph.D programme in various disciplines with great care and devotion. Despite its financial difficulties, the university has been making liberal allotment in the Annual budget for the provision of fellowship to scholars. The fellowship amount has been revised periodically while the number of scholars on the rolls has steadily increased. This has naturally given rise to a steady enhancement in the number of Ph.D awardees every year. In 1960 only one Ph.D was awarded in the University where as the number of rose to 94 in 1990. On the whole 2,566 Ph.D awards have been made till the end of 2003 out of which 1,214 were in Science.

Ph. D programme is part of the regular work of the teaching and research departments of the university. Many teachers have, at the same time, research projects financed by external funding agencies, which add substantially to the general research output of the departments. The university has also taken important measure for the qualitative improvement of research like, for instance, the linking of university research with Industry, the formation of the Research Development Council, identification of thrust areas of research etc.

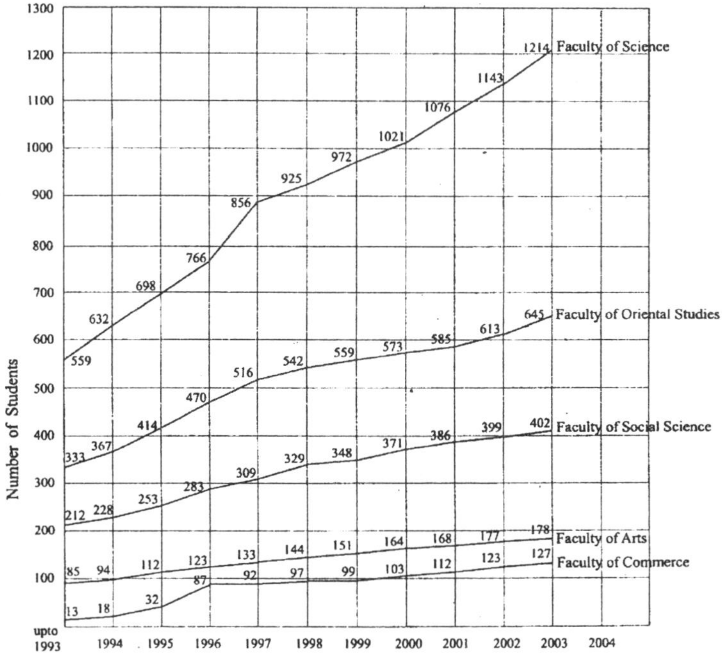

Fig. 4.6. Ph.Ds awarded up to 2003 from University of Kerala

5. DEPARTMENT OF PHYSICS

The Department of Physics was formally established in August 1970. Prof. K.S. Viswanathan has been the head of the department since its inception. Earlier the department was at Cochin and Prof. Venketeswara Lu was the head of the department. When Cochin University of Science and Technology was formed in 1970, a new department started at the Kariavattom Campus of the University of Kerala

The postgraduate teaching in the department was started from 1971 onwards. The post M. Sc Diploma course in Space Physics started during the period 1974-77 and was later replaced by the M. Sc Course with specialisation in i. Applied Electronics, ii. Space Physics and Electronics with an intake of 18 students every year.

Ph. D programme has been in operation since the inception of the department. 91 students of the department have been awarded Ph. D since 1971. Over 600 research papers and monographs have been produced from the department. Ratio of students to teachers was 46:6 and the Research scholars to teachers (guides) ratio were 30:5. The ratio of research papers published to number of teachers is two papers/year/teacher.

The Table 1 shows the detailed statement related to the number of Ph. Ds awarded from the Department of Physics and the total number of the University as a whole during 1999 to 2003.

From the Table1, it is seen that 12 out 32 total numbers of Physics doctoral degrees awarded from the University are from the Department of Physics. There were 84 Ph. Ds awarded from the department up to 2003 and the first Ph. D was awarded to Smt. K. Revathy, in the year 1974. Prof. K. S. Viswanathan was the supervising guide and the topic of research was 'the magnetosphere and the collision less Plasma'.

Table 1. Research output of the Department of Physics, 1999-2003

Year	Total Ph.Ds from University	Total Phyiscs Ph.Ds	Department of Physics				
			No. of Ph.Ds.	Research Publi-cations	Students enrolled		
					M.Sc.	M.Phil	Ph.D.
1999	113	7	Nil	15	34	10	13
2000	106	6	3	21	33	10	27
2001	66	Nil	Nil	20	33	16	27
2002	207	7	4	08	33	10	23
2003	136	12	5	11	35	10	23
Total	**628**	**32**	**12**	**75**	**168**	**56**	**113**

(*Source:* Annual Reports, University of Kerala and from the sources of Dept. of Physics)

Department of Science & Technology, New Delhi identified the department as a FIST-assisted department and sanctioned Rs.25 lakhs as level-I assistance to upgrade the M.Sc. Programme. DST also approved a major research project programme, 'Nano materials Science & Technology Initiative - Phase II'. The major thrust areas within the subject in which research activities are being actively pursued are:Space Physics, Materials Science, Spectroscopy, Geophysics, Non linear Optical science

The other areas in which research are being carried out includes Electronics, studies on Crystal and Vibration Spectroscopy, oxidation studies of metals on transparent conducting media, preparation and characterization, magnetosphere and Physics, Ionospheric and Thermospheric Physics etc.

6. ANALYSIS

6.1. Year-wise distribution of theses

The Table 2 represents the year-wise distribution of

Ph Ds awarded from the University of Kerala during 1999-2003. It can be seen that there were only 12 Ph Ds are awarded from the department during the period of the study.

Table 2: Year-wise distribution of theses

Year	Count	%	Cum %
1999	Nil	0	
2000	3	25.00	25.00
2001	Nil	0	25.00
2002	4	33.33	58.33
2003	5	41.67	100.00
Total	**12**	**100.00**	

It is interesting to note that not even a single Ph. D is awarded in the year 1999 and 2001. The Table also shows that the highest number of 5 theses are awarded in the year 2003, and 3 theses were awarded in the year 2000.

6.2. Subject-wise Distribution of Theses

In order to determine the direction of Physics research in broad subject categories, the analysis has been made in the Table 3. Taking consideration of research works in Physics, the subject categorization has been made according to the Classification Scheme followed in Physics Abstracts. In Physics Abstracts the entries are arranged by subjects in accordance with special classification scheme. The classification scheme is the result of co-operation between INSPEC, the American Institute of Physics, the European Physical Society and the Physics working group of the ICSU-AB.

It is seen that 'Optical properties and condensed matter Spectroscopy' and "Solid Earth Physics' both having the highest number of 3 theses each are awarded. The research topics in the areas of 'Super conductivity', 'Crystallography and stellar systems', etc. has not the thrust areas in the university.

Table 3: Subject categories of theses

Sl. No.	Subject	Count	%	Cum %
1	Solid Earth Physics3		25.00	
2	Optical Properties and Condensed matter Spectroscopy	3	25.00	50.00
3	Fundamental Astronomy and Astrophysics	2	16.67	66.67
4	Materials Science	2	16.67	83.34
5	Magnetic properties and Materials	1	8.33	91.67
6	Surface interfaces: Thin films and whiskers	1	8.33	100.00
Total		**12**	**100.00**	

The classification scheme employed for grouping the Physics literature consists of 69 subject headings. While classifying the 12 theses using the subject headings, all theses fall under 6 headings. This shows that many areas of Physics are untouched by the researchers. In University of Kerala the major thrust areas within the subject in which research activities are being actively pursued are Space Physics, Materials Science and Spectroscopy.

6.3. Page-wise distribution of theses

Page number wise analysis of theses are shown in the Table 4.

Table 4. Page-wise distribution of theses

Pages	Count	%	Cum %
Up to 100	1	8.33	-
101-200	9	75.00	83.33
Above 200	2	16.67	100.00
Total	**12**	**100.00**	

The Table 4 shows that majority of theses having the page numbers of 101-200 range. The theses having number of pages 101-200 are found to be 9 (75%) and theses having number of pages below 100 is 1 (8.3%). The average number of pages per theses is found to be 167.5.

6.4. Guide-ship Pattern

The analysis shows that majority of 11 (91.67%) scholars are guided by single guides and only one (8.3%) scholar has chosen two guides for the research work. It indicates that joint guide-ship is not common in the University of Kerala.

Inter-institutional and institution-industrial collaboration are rare in the University of Kerala. The researchers in the department could get the opportunity of Regional Research Laboratory (CSIR) and Vikram Sarabhai Space Centre (ISRO) scientists for their collaborative research. This may be the reason for the less joint guide-ship.

6.5. Productivity of Guides

The Table 5 shows the contributions of most productive guides towards the creation of Ph. D theses in Physics during the period of study.

Table 5. Most productive Guides

Sl. No.	Name	Rank	Count	%
1	Nayar, S.R.P.	1	3	25.00
2	Renuka, G.	1	3	25.00
3	Devanarayanan, S.	2	2	16.67
4	Nair, V.U.	2	2	16.67
5	Khader, Abdul	3	1	8.33
6	Vaidyan, V.K.	3	1	8.33
	Total		**12**	**100.00**

It can be seen from the Table that, Dr. G. Renuka and Prof. S.R. Prabhakaran Nayar are the two supervisors who have guided 03 research scholars each followed by Prof. S. Devanarayanan and Prof. V. Unnikrishnan Nair, two each.

The gender- wise analysis of research guides shows that three out of seven research guides in the department are females. But there is only one female research guide is included in the list of top ranked guides.

6.6. Gender-wise Analysis of Research Productivity

In order to ascertain the productivity of doctoral theses of male and female scholars of the University of Kerala, an analysis has been made and the results are shown in the Table 6.

Table 6. Gender-wise analysis of Research scholars

Year	Male		Female	
	Count	%	Count	%
1999	0	0	0	0
2000	2	40.0	1	14.29
2001	0	0	0	0
2002	0	0	4	57.14
2003	3	60.0	2	28.57
Total	5	100.00	7	100.00

As far as the University of Kerala is concerned, out of 12 Physics doctoral theses awarded during the 5 year period, 7 are produced by female scholars and 5 goes to male scholars. A maximum of 4 theses are awarded to female scholars in 2002 and one in 2000. The Table 6 shows that, in 2002 all the four Ph. Ds awarded from the University Physics department are by female scholars. In the case of male scholars, three Ph. Ds are awarded in 2003 and two in 2000. The analysis revealed that female scholars are awarded more doctoral degrees (58.33%) than male scholars.

6.7. Distribution of Citations in Theses

The number of citations in the theses are analysed to determine the trend of citations and the data is presented in the Table 7.

Table 7. Number of citations in theses

Number of Citations	Count	%	Cum %
Up to 100	0	0	
101-200	2	16.67	16.67
201-300	7	58.33	75.00
Above 300	3	25.00	100.00
Total	**12**	**100.00**	

It is interesting to note that, there is not a single thesis having citations of below 100 numbers and majority of theses (58.33%) are having citations in the range of 201-300. The remaining 25% theses having 300 and above citations are included. The average number of citations per thesis is calculated to be 265 during the period of study.

6.8. Gender-wise Analysis of Average Number of Citations

The Table 8 highlights the distribution of average number of citations of male and female research scholars.

Table 8. Gender-wise analysis of average number of citations

Sex	Mean	Std. Deviation	t	p
Male	295.8	138.7	0.82	p>0.05
Female	243.0	43.5		

The average number of citations for the male scholars is calculated as 295.8 (SD 138.7) and for females it is 243.0 (SD 43.5). The t statistics is 0.82 with a p value greater than 0.05. It means that the average number citations per theses of male and female scholars are statistically not significant.

There is not much variation between the number of citations of male and female research scholars.

The result also indicates that the average number of citations of male scholars is more than that of female scholars, even though the number of theses produced by the female scholars are more than the male scholars.

6.9. Year- wise Analysis of Average Number of Citations

The Year- wise analysis of average number of citations per theses is shown in Table 9.

Table 9. Year-wise average number of citations

Year	Mean	SD	F	p
2000	235.0	142.1	0.4	p>0.05
2002	249.5	57.0		
2003	295.4	97.6		

The maximum value of the average number of citations per thesis is calculated in the year 2003 is 295.4 (SD 97.6) and the minimum in the year 2000. Here the F value is 0.4 with a p value greater than 0.05. It shows that the average number of citations per thesis over the years is statistically not significant. It means that the period of time or the year in which the citations are made has no impact on the average number of citations.

6.10. Bibliographic Form-wise Distribution of Citations

The entire 3186 citations made in the 12 doctoral theses included in the study are classified under 10 broad bibliographical forms and placed in their order of ranking in Table 10.

The study provides an interesting result in regard to bibliographical forms and the extent to which, the Physics scholars have opted. It is observed that, journals and books are the first (83.65%) and second (12.99%) most preferred form of documents respectively cited by the research scholars. Theses, patents and seminar proceedings occupy the third position with 23 citations each.

Table 10. Form-wise distribution of citations

Sl No	Forms	Count	%	Cum %
1	Journals	2665	83.65	-
2	Books	414	12.99	96.64
3	Theses	23	0.72	97.36
4	Seminar Proceedings	23	0.72	98.08
5	Patents	23	0.72	98.80
6	Technical Reports	16	0.50	99.30
7	Others	13	0.41	99.71
8	Standards	4	0.14	99.85
9	Lecture notes	3	0.09	99.94
10	Private Communication	2	0.06	100.00
Total	**3,186**	**100.00**		

(Others includes chemicals, software, monographs and unidentified citations)

The bibliographical forms that drew the least attention by the scholars are, private communication (0.06%), lecture notes (0.09%) and standards (0.13%). None of the scholars of University of Kerala have made any citations of websites (URLs), e-prints, communicated and unpublished documents in their doctoral theses.

From the Table10 it is clear that the journals are the most preferred sources of citations used by the researchers followed by books. Journal is the most favoured medium of reporting and publishing scientific contribution the world over so is the trend in the university. Patents, theses and seminar proceedings (0.72% each) are the other forms of citations preferred by the scholars of University of Kerala.

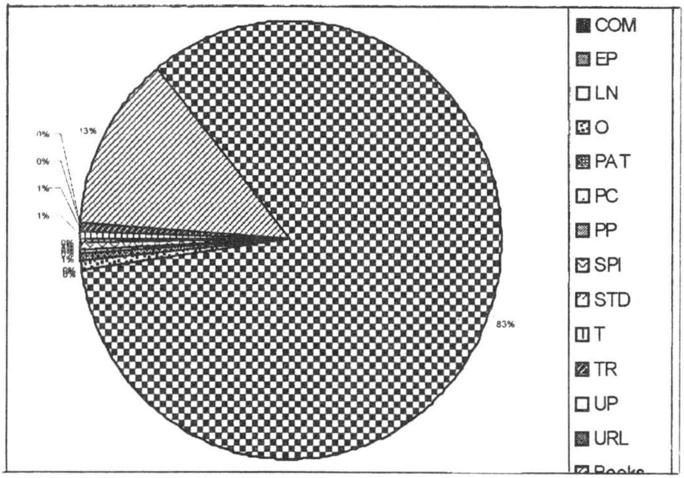

Fig. 1. Bibliographic forms of citations

6.11. Institution-wise distribution of cited theses

On further analysis of the institutional affiliation of theses, it is found that most of the theses cited by the researchers are from the university itself, i.e., 86.4% (19). 9.1% (2) are from Katholieke University and only one thesis is from University of Ljubljana.

Table 11: Institutional affiliation of cited theses

Sl. No.	Institutions	Rank	Count	%	Cum. %
1	University of Kerala	1	19	86.4	86.4
2	Katholieke University	2	2	9.1	95.5
3	University of Ljubljana	3	1	4.5	100.0

This trend may because of the availability of theses in the same institutions and since the theses are the unpublished documents and restricted for in house use only.

Author- wise analysis of the cited theses shows that the most cited authors are of Isaac, M (17.4%), Joe, I.H. and Suresh, G. (13% each)

6.12. Seminar Proceedings

Of the seminar proceedings cited by the Physics scholars, 80% of them are international seminars and the remaining 20% are national seminars. Out of the ten places of seminars indicated, Tokyo with three seminars and New Delhi with two are in the top positions.

6.13. Ranking of Journals

Frequency of citations or use of a journal is governed by many factors such as availability, language and country of publication, size and frequency of publication, coverage in secondary journals, reprint dissemination, reputation of the authors and so on. The use of citation frequency as a measure of journal significance is based on two assumptions (a) citation is a valid index of use and (b) use is a positively related to value.

The journals are arranged in their respective descending order of frequency and in alphabetical order among the same rank number. The journal contributing the largest number of articles is ranked as number one, next is ranked two and so on. The criterion for ranking is purely quantitative not qualitative.

Table 12: Ranked list of Journals

Sl. No.	Journals	Year	Country	Publisher	Rank	Count	%
1	J.Geophys. Res.	1896	USA	AGU	1	345	12.97
2	Spectrochim. Acta A	1978	UK	Pergamon	2	116	4.36
3	J. Atmos.Solar. Terr. Phys	1950	UK	Pergamon	3	95	3.57
4	Geophys.Res. Lett.	1974	USA	AGU	4	90	3.38
5	J.Raman Spectrosc.	1973	Netherlands	John Wiley	5	78	2.93
6	Phys.Fluids	1958	USA	AIP	6	67	2.52

7	Thin Solid films	1968	Nether-lands	Elsevier	7	64	2.41
8	Phys.Plasmas	1958	USA	AIP	8	50	1.88
9	Indian J. Radio & Space Phys.	1972	India	CSIR	9	49	1.84
10	J.Solid State Chem.	1699	USA	Academic	9	49	1.84
11	J. Appl. Phys.	1931	USA	AIP	10	48	1.80
12	J.Mater.Sci.	1966	Nether-lands	Springer	11	46	1.73
13	J.Chem.Phys.	1931	USA	AIP	12	45	1.69
14	Phys. Rev. Lett.	1958	USA	APS	12	45	1.69
15	Solar Phys.	1967	Nether-lands	Springer	12	45	1.69
16	J.Mol.Struct.	1985	Nether-lands	Elsevier	13	44	1.65
17	Phys.Rev.B	1893	USA	APS	14	40	1.50
18	Ann.Geophysicae	1983	Germany	EGU	15	37	1.39
19	J.Phys.Chem. Solids	1956	USA	Pergamon	15	37	1.39
20	Am.Ceram. Soc.Bull.	1922	USA	ACS	16	36	1.35
21	J.Am.Ceram.Soc	1918	USA	ACS	17	35	1.32
22	Planet Space Sci.	1959	USA	Pergamon	18	33	1.24
23	Plasma Phys. Contr.Fusion	1959	UK	IOP	18	33	1.24
24	Nature	1969	UK	Nature Pub.	19	32	1.20
25	Phys. Rev.	1983	USA	APS	19	32	1.20
26	J. Am. Chem. Soc	1879	USA	ACS	20	31	1.17
27	Nanostruct. mater.	1967	UK	Acta Mattal	21	29	1.09
28	Acta Cryst.A	1948	Denmark	Blackwell	22	28	1.05
29	Astrophysical Journal	1895	USA	UCP	23	27	1.02
30	Space Sci.Rev.	1962	Nether-lands	Springer	23	27	1.02

The analysis shows that the Physics literature are scattered in 303 journals accounting 2665 citations.

Of the 303 journals cited in the doctoral theses 54 are cited at least 10 times or more. In the rank list, the Jl.Geophys. Res. published by American Geophysical Union top the list with the highest contribution of 345 (12.97%) citations followed by Spectrochim Acta A, with a share of 116 citations (4.36%). J.Atmos.Solar-Terr.Phys occupies the third place with 95 citations (3.57%).

6.14. Indian Journals

Table 13: Ranked Indian journals

Sl. No.	Journal	Year	Publisher	Rank	Count	%
1	Indian J. Radio & Space Phys.	1972	CSIR	1	49	39.84
2	Bull.Mater.Sci.	1979	IAS	2	15	12.20
3	Ind.J.Phys.	1926	IACS	2	15	12.20
4	Pramana-Jl. of Physics	1973	IAS	3	10	8.13
5	Ind. J. Pure & Appl. Phys.	1963	INSA	4	8	6.50
6	Proc. Indian Acad. Sci.	1988	IAS	5	7	5.69
7	Current Science	1932	CSA&IAS	6	6	4.88
8	Ind. Ceram.	-	BHU	7	3	2.44
9	Bull.Mat.Res.	-	-	8	2	1.63
10	Trans. Ind. Ceram. Soc.	-	ICS	8	2	1.63
11	Ind. Min. Aug.	-	-	9	1	0.81
12	Indian J. Pure and Appl. Maths	1970	INSA	9	1	0.81
13	Indian J.Meteorol. Geophys.	-	IMG	9	1	0.81
14	J.Astrophys.Aston	1980	IAS	9	1	0.81
15	Proc. Ind. Ceram. Soc.	-	ICS	9	1	0.81
16	Ultra Science	-	-	9	1	0.81
	Total	123	100.00			

An analysis has been made to identify the list of Indian journals preferred by the researchers and the results indicate that 16 (5.28%) out of the 303 journals are Indian.

Indian Jl. Radio & Space Phys with 49 citations (39.84%) is the top ranked Indian journal preferred by the researchers. Bull. Mater.Sci and Indi Jl. Phys. with 15 citations each (12.20%) are in the second rank and 'Pramana' occupies the third place with 10 (8.13%) citations.

Out of 303 journals cited by the researchers of University of Kerala, only 16 are Indian journals and it amounts 123 (4.62%) of the total 2665 citations.

6.15. Ranking of Books

In every subject, like journals, there are also few books which are frequently cited by the Physicists because of the close association between the subject of books and area of works of the researchers.

The core books in Physics have been derived on the basis of frequency of occurrence of a book in the form of citation. The rank of a particular book is derived on the basis of number of times it was referred during 1999 to 2003.

The Table 14 represents a total of 414 books cited in the theses. The titles of the books with their authors and year of publication, the number of citations up to a minimum of 6 are shown in the Table.

Infrared and Raman Spectra of Inorganic and coordination compounds ranked first with 23 citations (5.6%) and infrared and Raman selection rules for molecules and lattice vibrations occupies the second position in the ranking order with 21 citations (5.1%). The third position jointly shared by three titles with 10 citations each (2.4%). This may because of the different research areas, approaches, interest and availability of books in their respective libraries.

Table14: Top ranked Books

Sl. No.	Title	Rank	Count	%	Cum %
1	Infrared and Raman Spectra of Inorganic and Coordinaion compounds/ Nakamoto, 1997	1	23	5.6	5.6
2	Infrared and Raman Selection Rules for Molecules and Lattice Vibrations: The Correlation Method/ W.G. Fately; F.R. Dollish and N.T. Mc Devitt, 1972	2	21	5.1	10.6
3	Hydrogen Bonding/ S.N. Vinogradov and R.H. Linnel, 1971	3	10	2.4	13.0
4	Introduction to Space Physics/ W.J. Hughes, 1995	3	10	2.4	15.5
5	Source Book on Raman Effect/ R.S. Krishnan, 1989	3	10	2.4	17.9
6	Semimetals and Narro-band gap Semiconductors/ D.R. Lovett, 1977	4	8	1.9	19.8
7	Vibrational Spectroscopy of Solids/ P.M.A. Sherwood, 1972	5	7	1.7	21.5
8	Chemical Applications of Infrared Spectroscopy/ C.N.R. Rao, 1963	6	6	1.4	22.9
9	Statistical Physics/ L. Landau and E.M. Lifshitz, 1980	6	6	1.4	24.4
10	The Infrared Spectra of Complex Molecules: Advances in Infrared Group Frequencies/ L.J. Bellany, 1975	6	6	1.4	25.8

7. CONCLUSION

The study revealed that 12 theses were awarded from the Department of Physics of the University of Kerala during 1999-2003. There were no Ph Ds awarded in 1999 and 2001 and the highest number of 5 theses are awarded in the year 2003. The highest number of theses are awarded in Optical properties and condensed matter spectroscopy and in Solid earth physics fields. The average number of pages per theses is found to be 167.5. Majority of 11 scholars (91.7%) are guided by single guide and only one scholar has chosen two guides for his research. Theses productivity of guides shows that, Renuka and S.R. Prabhakaran Nayar share the highest number of 3 theses each.

Seven out of 12 theses are produced by female scholars and male scholar's share is 5. The average number of citations per theses is found to be 265 and the average number of citations of male scholars is more than that of the female scholars.

The study shows that journals are the most preferred form of citations used by the researchers followed by books. None of the scholars have made any citations of websites (URL's), e-prints, communicated and unpublished items in their theses. The researchers cite a total of 303 journals amounting to 2655 citations. Journal of Geophysical Research is the top ranked journal, followed by Spectorchimika Acta A and Journal of Atmospheric Solar Terro.- Physics.

Out of the 303 journals cited by the researchers, only 16 (5.28%) are Indian journals with 125 citations. Indian Jl. Radio & Space Phys. is the top ranked Indian journal preferred by the researchers. Seven out of the 16 Indian journals cited by the researchers are covered in JCR and five of them are Physics journals. The books titled 'Infrared and Raman spectra of inorganic and coordination compounds' is the top ranked book.

Scientific research and scientific communication are bound together so closely that the two always go hand in hand. There exists a cyclic relation between the scientific research and literature production in a region. The higher the research output, the higher the publication of literature. The growth of scientific literature of a country or a region can, therefore, be used as a significant indicator to measure the progress of science and technology.

The scientific and technological productivity of the universities in Kerala are at low level, in spite of acquiring different systems and components of modern technologies especially with the assistance from the University Grants Commission and the State and Central governments.

As far as Kerala is concerned, though the state was in the forefront of education, the same thing could not be claimed in scientific investigations. Serious research activities in science and technology started only after the establishment of the University of Travancore in 1937. It is generally accepted both by the educational administrators and general public that though the achievements of Kerala in the field of general education are incomparable, the State has miserably failed in the diversification of courses at the higher level. In the field of academic research also the state has fallen short of expectations.

REFERENCES

1. Varalakshmi, R S R (1994). Library and Information Science research in India: Subject perspectives. Library Science with a slant to Documentation & Information Studies. 31(2); 91-109.
2. Mahapatra, R K and Sahoo, Jyotshna (2004). Doctoral dissertations in Library and Information Sciencein India 1997-2003: a study. Annals of Library and Information Studies. 51(1); 58-63.
3. Madkey, V D and Rajyalakshmi, D (1994). Citation analysis of Ph D thesis in Environmental Science and Engineering used by NEERI scientists during 1977-1991. Annals of Library Science and Documentation. 41(2); 63-78.
4. Raza, M Massom and Zarrin, Zeba (2004). Citation analysis of Doctoral Dissertations submitted in the Department of Chemistry, AMU, Aligarh: A utility assessment approach. In

Responding to user's need in changing information landscapes: sojourn of libraries from palm-leaf to palm-top. Seminar papers: 49th All India Library Conference. Bundelkhend University, Jhansi 29 December 2003- 1 January 2004. N. Laxman Rao, Ed. Delhi: ILA; 256-264.

5. Bandyopadhyay, A. K. and Nandi, A. (2001). Citation analysis of references used in doctoral dissertations of Political Science. Herald of Library Science. 40 (3-4); 192-200.

6. Doraswamy, M. and Pulla Reddy, V. (2000). Citations in Ph.D. thesis in Geography: an analysis. In Books to Bytes: Library and Information technology in the new millennium. N.S.Jagga Rao and M. Ramachander, Eds. New Delhi: Ess Ess publication; 188-196.

7. Varma, A. K. (1997). A bibliometric study of Ph. D theses in Botany. In Library and information science: Parameters and perspectives. Vol. II. R.G. Prasher, Ed. New Delhi: Concept Pub; 326-334.

8. Adiyodi, K. G. (1993). New Frontiers of knowledge. Kozhikode: Publication Division. University of Calicut.365p.

9. Krishna, K. M. and Kumar, S. (2004). Authorship trends in Agriculture research: A bibliometric analysis. SRELS Journal of Information Managemen., 41(2); 229-234.

10. Biradar, B. S. and Thippeswamy, K. (2004). Information use pattern by pediatricians: A bibliometric study. SRELS Journal of Information Management, 41(1); 107-120.

11. Srivastava, Ranjana (2002). Information use pattern of research in Chemistry: A citation study. IASLIC Bulletin. 47(4); 185-192.

12. Lahiri, Ramansu (1996). Research in Library Science in India (1950-95): an account of the Ph. D programme. Annals of Library Science and Documentation. 43(2); 56-68.

13. Sreedhara Menon, A. (2003). History of the University of Kerala. Vol. I. Thiruvananthapuram: University of Kerala, Dept. of Publication. p.1

14. Sukumaran Nair, A (1998). Making of the first university in Kerala: a retrospective of early events and people. In Diamond jubilee Souvenir 1997-98, University of Kerala. p.29.

15. Annual Report-2005. University of Kerala. Thiruvananthapuram.

16. http/ /:www.keralauniversity.edu/

4

Social Science Books in Malayalam: A Survey and Bibliometric Study

Dr. Beena, S.

1. INTRODUCTION

Social sciences play a vital and significant role in improving the quality of life because more than any branch of study, they are about every day life of people. They bring together those who wish to know more about people and the social forces which shape and determine their lives. Social sciences open up a whole host of alternative perspectives about society in social arrangements that exist today and have done so in the past. There can surely be no great or more worthwhile endeavour for human beings than to understand their fellow beings better.

Social science information is a vital national resource which is essential to a nation's well being, socio-economic development and security, as any other natural resource. It provides an important basis for international relations, peace, prosperity and overall global development. A substantial part of human culture has been handed down to generations in the form of recorded knowledge. This resource consists of documents such as clay tablets, books, journals, other categories of text, audio-visual material and other units of information or data.

As far as social sciences are concerned a very interesting and useful area of knowledge covers the organized human behavior. The creation of social institutions - political, economic, legal, administrative and educational - and the relationship of these bodies to individuals is a major field of study. The activities of all these institutions influence human behaviour. Since social sciences are very comprehensive there exist a very large number of books, including several of the valuable classical titles which are in use even today. Many new books are emerging in this field, which are very valuable to people especially to students and researchers. This is more so in the case of books in a regional language, especially Malayalam.

2. RELEVANCE OF THE STUDY

Even though there are a lot of books available in social science in English language, the number is comparatively low in Malayalam. This is mainly because of the wide spread use of English as the medium for study and teaching, especially at the higher levels of education. But today the shift in emphasis to Malayalam could be evinced. The government's initiative to switch over to Malayalam as the official language gave a fillip to the production of more books in the language. Therefore, it is worthwhile to study the rate of production of social science books and other related aspects of book production in Malayalam.

For effective communication, the language of communication should be in the language most familiar to the users. In spite of the importance attached to books in social sciences, very few studies are available about their production and growth. This is more so in the case of Malayalam. The scarcity of previous studies regarding Malayalam books in social sciences and the personal interest of the investigator in the literature of social sciences prompted the present study.

3. SCOPE AND COVERAGE

The social science have a very wide connotation and the demarcation between different disciplines is not clear cut as in science. For the purpose of the study, the definitions of notable social scientists like Jean Piaget, Thomas M.Little, Maurice B.Line, Professor Seligman and D.J.Foskett have been examined to identify the subjects to be incorporated into the social sciences. The Indian Council of Social Science Research (ICSSR), the principal objective of which is to promote social science research in India, identifies certain disciplines to be incorporated into the social sciences. Thus it was observed that Anthropology, Commerce, Demography, Economics, Education, Geography, History, Law, Linguistics, Management, Psychology, Public Administration and Sociology could be incorporated.

The treatment of social sciences in various classification schemes like Dewey Decimal Classification (DC) Universal Decimal Classification (UDC), Library of Congress Classification (LC) and Colon Classification (CC) was also examined. While examining the clusters of definitions, it was found that there is no unanimity of opinion regarding the subjects to be incorporated into the social sciences. So the subjects commonly appeared in all these definitions, which are suitable for the study have been chosen. Since the study was about books in a regional language where considerable number of books are not available in all the peripheral areas of social sciences, it was considered better to adopt the pattern followed by Ranganathan in Colon Classification (6th Ed) since it covers all the disciplines mentioned above within seven disciplines in a logical sequence. Under Social Sciences the following disciplines are listed. T - education, U - Geography, V - History, W - Political Science, X - Economics, Y - Sociology and Z - Law.

The present study is confined to a period of 166 years i.e. from 1835-2000. The study started from the year 1835 because it was found that the first social science book in Malayalam was published in 1835 and hence the study started from that year.

4. OBJECTIVES OF THE STUDY

The main objectives of the study are

1. To assess the share of Malayalam books in each social science discipline;
2. To assess the share of each type of books like biographies, children's literature, ready reference books, text books and multivolumed books in individual disciplines.;
3. To assess the growth rate of social science books over decades;
4. To identify the authorship pattern in each discipline;
5. To identify the major publishers of social science books in Malayalam;
6. To assess the translations and the source language from which they are translated;
7. To estimate the price per page of social science books and to find out the price- page correction and
8. To find out the determinants of publication output of Malayalam books in social sciences.

5. HYPOTHESES

(i)T hough there is a rich collection of social science books in Malayalam, there is an imbalance in the growth of books in different subjects with the result that while some are well developed, others are lagging behind.

(ii) The government is not keen on providing translation services in the field of social sciences so that many good works on various social science disciplines available in other Indian languages are not translated into Malayalam

(iii) There are certain socio-economic factors which determine the growth of publication in any subject or language like population, total literacy, female literacy, Real State Domestic Product and Real Per Capita Income and this is true of social science books in Malayalam.

6. Methodology

Methodology applied in the present study involves the following

i Literature survey

ii Bibliometric analysis

6.1. Literature survey

An extensive survey of literature on social sciences including books and primary periodicals was done. In addition, the CD - ROM databases, LISA plus, ERIC and other electronic databases were also searched for relevant studies. But a bibliometric study as envisaged here could not be located. However, the literature search provided a lot of back ground information.

For the collection of data, various sources have been consulted. The most important among them was the 'Malayala Granthasoochi' published by the Kerala Sahitya Academy, Trissur. It is an important bibliography which provides a comprehensive account of books in Malayalam in seven volumes. The compilation of bibliography was started under the editorialship of K.M Govi. and AK Panikkar. The first volume came out in 1973, the second volume in 1974. The 7th volume was published in 1997. A notable feature of the Granthasoochi is that the first volume is exclusively devoted for literary works and the second volume for non- literary works. The other five volumes contain both literary and non-literary works. Entries are arranged alphabetically in the name of the author under each subject. The Granthasoochi also provides indexes of author, title and subject. The CD - ROM version of the Malayalam Granthasoochi came out in 2006. It includes books published in Malayalam up to 2000.

Another source used was the Malayalam edition of the Indian National Bibliography. It started publication in 1958 and was published by the Central Reference Library, Kolkata. As per the Delivery of Books Act of 1954 a copy of each book published in India would be deposited in the National Library, Kolkata. Based on these books they prepare the bibliography of Malayalam books in all subjects and publish it in every 10 years. It is classified according to the Dewey Decimal Classification and is provided with an index consisting of authors, translators, publishers, titles and subjects.

'The catalogue of Malayalam Books in the British Museum' edited by Albertine Gaur, catalogues of major publishers in Malayalam and catalogues of the Kerala University Library; State Central Library, Thiruvananthapuram; the Legislative Library, Thiruvananthapuram; the Kerala Sahitya Academy Library, Trissur were some other sources consulted.

In addition, the entire Malayalam books in the social science subjects available in the Kerala University Library and Departmental Libraries, the State Central Library, Thiruvananthapuram and the Sahitya Academy Library, Trissur were examined to identify gaps and for missing information in the data bases of social science books.

6.2. Bibliometric analysis

In order to carry out the bibliometric analysis the details of 5920 books were recorded in the computer. They were recorded on the basis of individual subjects in social sciences. Using the SPSS program the following analyses were made.

1) Subject - wise distribution of social science books in Malayalam
2) The Concentration of publication of social science books in Malayalam
3) Areas of publication in various subjects in social sciences
4) Types of books including Biographies, Children's Literature, Ready Reference Books, Text Books and Multi- volumed books.
5) Decade-wise production of social science books
6) Authorship pattern which includes type of authorship, productivity of authors, prolific authors, application of Lotka's Law gender-wise distribution of authorship etc.
7) Countries covered by social science books in Malayalam
8) Social Science titles with geographical appellations
9) Distribution of books in different subjects dealing with Kerala
10) Publishers of social science books
11) Government publications
12) Author as publisher
13) Geographical location of publishers
14) Various editions of Social Science books
15) Share of translations
16) Estimation of price per page in Social Sciences

17) Price and page number correlation
18) Determinants of publication output of Malayalam books in Social Sciences

7. LIMITATIONS OF THE STUDY

Since the study covers 166 years from 1835-2000, right from the appearance of social science books in Malayalam, physical verification of all the books is impossible. Therefore, to be comprehensive, published bibliographies were also depended upon to a certain extant. Though every effort has been made to compile a comprehensive database of Malayalam books in social sciences, still there may be omissions in the list due to the rarity of books and the inadequacy of bibliographic control measures especially in the earlier stages.

8. FINDINGS AND CONCLUSION

The major findings of the literature survey and bibliometric analysis are summarized below

8.1. Social Science books in Malayalam

The publication of Malayalam books in social sciences started from 1835 and it has been constantly on the increase.

8.2. Subject - wise distribution of books

i) History books constitute 41.37 percent of the total social science books in Malayalam
ii) Books on Education constitute only 5.27 percent though Kerala claims 100% literacy.
iii) Law books are also limited in number (2.43%)
iv) Books relating to geography topics are less, but travelogues make up the deficiency in the total number.
v) Specialization in each subject resulted in the reduction of General Social Science books.

8.3. Concentration of publication of Social Science books in Malayalam

The application of the Herfindahl Hirshman Index (HHI) for measuring the degree of concentration of publication of social science books in Malayalam reveals that, though there is a concentration of publication among a few subjects, the intensity of concentration remains almost the same. There has not been any perceptible change either upward or downward with respect to the concentration of publication under various subjects.

8.4. Areas of publication in various subjects in Social Sciences

8.4.1. Education

(i) General books on Education, especially basic books constitute nearly half of the total books on Education. In other words, books on specialized fields of Education are less.

(ii) Books on Higher Education especially technical education are very less. Other weaker areas are Physical Education and Education in other countries.

8.4.2. Geography

(i) Travelogues constitute more than half of the geography books

(ii) Books on Meteorology and Economic geography are very few.

8.4.3 History

(i) Excluding biography books on Kerala History, score the highest member (17.11%) followed by Indian History (14.66%)

(ii) Books on Disarmament, French Revolution League of Nations Parliament are rare.

8.4.4. Political Science

(i) Political theory which includes communism, Marxism, Socialism etc constitute 56.31 of political science books.

(ii) Weaker areas are State, Monarchy, Contemporary Politics etc

8.4.5. Economics

(i) Representation of books in almost all topics is evident in Economics

(ii) One fifth of the Economics books are on general topics

(iii) Weaker areas are 'Budget', 'Finance' and 'Poverty'.

8.4.6. Sociology

(i) The highest number of books is on Caste which account for 15.15 per cent of the total. Topics relating to women constitute 7.27 percent.

(ii) Books on Anthropology, Child Welfare, Social Services etc. are comparatively less.

8.4.7. Law

(i) General books on Law have the major share.

(ii) Publications are more in Civil Law, Law of Inheritance, Service Rules, Muslim Law, Criminal Law etc.

(iii) Books dealing with specific laws like IPR laws and acts are very few.

8.5.1. Types of books

8.5.1.1. Biographies

(i) Biographies form 16.25 percent of the social science books.

(ii) Out of the 962 biographies, 767 are in History

(iii) Biographies are few in Education, Geography and Law

8.5.1.2. Children's Literature

(i) Only 5.69 percent of books fall under children's literature

(ii) The highest number of books on children's literature is in History (7.55%) and the lowest number is in Social Science General (1.25%) and in Law (1.39%)

8.5.1.3. Ready Reference Books

(i) Ready reference works constitute only 0.63% of the total social science books

(ii) Year books and atlases are conspicuous by their absence

8.5.1.4. Text books

(i) Text books form only 1.77 percent of the total and their representation is minimal in almost all subjects.

(ii) Text books are absent in political science and law.

8.5.1.5. Multivolumed books

(i) Multi - volumed books costitute 4.86 percent of the total

(ii) There is an inverse relationship between the number of volumes and the number of titles.

(iii) There are only three books which have more than five volumes.

8.6. Decade - wise production of Social Science books

(i) History books retained the number one position in terms of the total number except during 1861-70 and 1871-80.

(ii) The period 1981-90 is the most productive decade of social science books in Malayalam. 19.27 percent of books were produced during this period.

(iii) Of the three periods taken, while estimating the period wise growth, the second period (1901-1950) witnessed an average growth rate of 7.04 percent when compared to the first period (1835-1900).

(iv) During the second period, the highest growth rate is for sociology (15.5%) followed by Economics (13.33%) and History (11.3%).

(v) The growth rate during the third period is only 3.54 percent, showing a decline compared to the previous period.

(vi) During the third period, Political Science Witnessed the highest growth rate (16.31%) followed by General Social Science (8%)

(vii) Though the number of publication increased, the actual growth rate has declined during the third period.

8.7. Authorship pattern

8.7.1. Type of authorship

(i)B ooks written by single author form 86.08 percent; two authors form 3.06 percent and more than two authors constitute 1.08 percent of the total.

(ii) Single authorship is the highest in Geography, but it is relatively low in Law (72.22%).

(iii) Books written by two authors are more in Geography but are the least in History.

(iv) Multiple authorship is visible in all social science disciplines

(v) Compilations constitute 1.01 percent and edited works 1.52 percent.

(vi) Books written by corporate authors constitute 3.26 percent.

(vii) Books which do not specify the names of authors (anonymous works) appear in all subjects and these constitute 3.99 percent of the total.

8.9. Productivity of authors

(i) The study shows that there is inverse relationship between the number of books and the number of authors

(ii) Lotkas' Inverse Square Law' on the productivity of authors was found to be applicable here with slight variation in the value of index number 'n'. In the study the value assigned was 2.71.

8.10. Prolific writers in Social Sciences

(i) The following are the most prolific writers in each social science subject.

Social Science General	-	Sreevaraham Pillai
Education	-	Erumeli Parameswaran Pillai
Geography	-	S.K. Pottekkattu
History	-	M.K.Gandhi
Political Science	-	E.M.S Namboothirippad
Economics	-	K. Damodaran
Sociology	-	E.M.S. Namboothirippad
Law	-	Sreemandiram, K.P

(ii) A good number of prolific writers are politicians and political thinkers

8.11. Gender - wise distribution

(i) Women writers are far less compared to men

(ii) In the single author category the ration between men and women writers is 27: 1

(iii) The ratio of women is the highest in Geography (17.57:1) followed by Sociology (19.61:1)

(iv) The difference in the ratio is more in law (51:1)

(v) Regarding joint authorship only 7 are women while their male counter parts constitute 174.

(vi) An multiple authorship there is only one women writer while there are 63 male authors.

(vii) The male-female collaboration in authorship shows that the number of women is limited to be

8.12. Countries covered by Social Services books in Malayalam

(i)O ut of the total books, (39.09%) focus on a single country or countries

(ii) Among the countries covered, 79.04 percent are on India, 4.36% on Russia and 3.59 America.

(iii) Among the subjects, 52.59 percent of books in history deal with various countries, and among them 87.34 percent deal with Indian History

(iv) Country specific studies are very less in General Social Science and Law.

8.13. Social Science titles with geographical appellations

(i)O nly 13.24 percent of the books have geographical appellations in the title

(ii) As can be expected it is more in Geography (29.59%) and History (15.11%)

(iii) It is the least in General Social Science books (3.75%).

8.14. Distribution of books dealing with Kerala.

(i)T he study reveals that only 15,88 percent of books deals particularly with Kerala.

(ii) In Sociology and Law a quarter of the books deal with Kerala

(iii) Books dealing specifically with Kerala are comparatively less in Social Science-General and Geography.

8.15. Publishers of Social Science Books

(i)Altogether 929 publishers could be identified.

(ii) The main categories of publishers are Private, State and Central Government, Universities, scholarly

Institutions etc. Books published by the authors themselves are also visible.

(iii) Prabhat Book House ranks as the topmost publisher which alone is responsible for 15.95 percent of the total Publications. Kerala Bhasha Institute, TVM Chinta Publishers, TVM, DC Books Kottayam and Sahitya Prvarthaka Co-operative Society (SPCS) Kottayam occupy the second, third, fourth and fifth positions.

8.16. Government Publications

(i)G overnment/government sponsored institutions constitute only 4.95percent of the total

(ii) The Kerala Bhasha Institute is the top most government publisher of social science books in Malayalam, followed by the Govt Press, TVM and Publication Division of the Govt. of India

(iii) Though there are only 46 government publishers, the number of books produced them are very less.

8.17. Author as publisher

(i)Books published by the authors themselves constitute 5.39 percent.

(ii) Publishing of books by the authors themselves is more evident in Geography (11.12%) and the least in political science (3.73%)

(iii) The highest number of books published by a single author is ten.

8.18. Geographical location of publishers

Social Science books are published not only from Kerala, but also from various other Indian States and even from foreign countries.

8.19. Publications from Kerala

(i)Nearly 93 percent of books are being published from Kerala,

(ii) Thiruvananthapuram is the most productive district which accounts 35.15 percent of the books from Kerala.

(iii) Wynad, Kasargod and Idukki are the districts which lag behind in the production.

(iv) The publishing trends at 50 years intervals show that Thiruvananthapuram has maintained the lead throughout the period.

8.20. Publication from outside Kerala

(i)42 0 books are published outside Kerala of which 393 are published from the various Indian States and 27from outside India

(ii) New Delhi is the largest contribution of social science books in Malayalam from outside Kerala.

(iii) The Indian Atheist Publishers, Publication. Division of the Government of India, the National Book Trust and the Ministry of Information and Broadcasting, Government of India are the major publishers from Delhi

8.21. Publications from outside India

Russian Federation (the erst while Soviet Union) Singapore and Sri Lanka are the foreign countries which publish Malayalam books in social sciences.

8.22. Various editions of Social Science books

(i)The first edition constitute 93.53 percent

(ii) 15 percent of the General Social Science books have run into more than one edition and the corresponding figures for Education, Geography, History, Political Science, Economics, Sociology and Law are 16.03%; 4.47%, 6.49%, 5.46%, 6.15%,4.39% and 9.03%.

(iii) The highest number of editions comes out in History.

(iv) The ratio of social science books, running into first,

second, third and fourth editions is 221.5: 10.2:3:1

8.23. Translations

(i) Translations constitute 22.57 percent of the total social science books in Malayalam.

(ii) The highest number of translation is in Political Science (40.18%). In History; Economics and Law, about 25% of the books are translations.

8.24. Language-wise distribution of translations

(i) The majority of the works are translated from English.

(ii) The next position is occupied by Russian.

(iii) Representation of almost all prominent language could be seen in translation.

(iv) Translations from only seven Indian languages appear in Malayalam.

8.25. Decade-wise production of transactions

(i) Post-independent period witnessed a sudden increase in the production of translations.

(ii) The period 1981-70 is found to be the most productive decade of translations

8.26. Prominent authors of translated works

(i) The study shows that Mahatma Gandhi's works stands first in terms of number of translations.

(ii) Other prominent writers whose works are translated most are Lenin and Karl Marx.

8.27. Gender-wise distribution of translations

(i) Women translators constitute only 5.86 percent.

(ii) The ratio between male and female translators is 16.06:1

8.28. Publisher-wise distribution of translated works

(i) Prabhat Book House and Chinta the propagators of

communist literature occupy the top position among the publishers of translated works.

(ii) Among the major ten prominent publishers of translations only three are government.

8.29. Translations of biographies

(i) Translation of biographies constitute only 9.58 percent of the total translations of social science books in Malayalam.

(ii) Most of these translations are in History

(iii) The biographies of Gandhiji constitute a major share in History.

(iv) Translation of biographies are totally absent in Social Science General, Education, Economics and Law.

8.30. Estimation of price per page in Social Sciences

(i) The average price per page of a social science book in Malayalam is 17 paise

(ii) There has been a variation in the average price over the decades.

(iii) From 1951-60 onwards, there is a steady increase in price per page.

(iv) The ANOVA reveals that the price variation is statically significant.

8.31. Estimation of price per page between various Social Science subject.

(i) There is variation in price per page in each social science discipline

(ii) Among the subjects Sociology has the highest price and Political Science has the least.

(iii) The variation in price per page among subjects is statistically significant.

8.32. Decade-wise estimation of price per page in social science disciplines.

(i) During the period 1991-2000 the price reached its

highest in almost all subjects except Sociology and Law.

(ii) Regarding the lowest price, there is no such visible period. It varies from discipline to discipline.

8.33. Estimation of price per page of text books and other categories of books

(i)T he average price per page of text book is 14 Paise where as it is 17 paise for other categories of books.

(ii) The variation in price per page between text books and non-text books is statistically significant.

8.34. Estimation of price-page variation in text books and other categories of books in various social science disciplines.

(i)The price per page variation between texts and other categories of books is more is sociology

(ii) In General Social Science books, Geography, History and Sociology the price, of text books are low when compared to non-text books.

(iii) In Education and Economics there is no price variation between text books and non-text books.

8.35. Decade-wise analysis of price per page variation between text books and non-text books

(i)D uring 1971-80 both text books and non-text books have the same price while there are some differences in price between the two in other decades.

(ii) The price per page of text books and non-text books is maximum during 1991-2000.

(iii) For the text books, the price is at the lowest during 1941-50 and for the non-text books during the period 1951-60

8.36. Comparison of price per page in Children's Literature and other categories of books

(i)The average price of Children's Literature is 21 Paise

per page whereas that of Other books is only 17 Paise.

(ii) Though there is some difference in price per page between Children's Literature and other books, the variation in price is not statistically significant.

8.37. Estimation of price per page between Private and Government publishers.

(i)Books published by government agencies lost only 16 paise per page whereas books private publishers cost 18 paise per page.

(ii) The variation in price per page between government and private publishers is statistically significant.

8.38. Decade-wise calculation of price per page between government and private publishers

(i)T he price of books brought out by government publishers is found to fluctuate. During 1951-60 the price is 16 paise per page. But during 1961-70 it comes down to 13 paise. The price of private publishers on the other hand steadily increases from 19521-60 onwards.

(ii) For both the publishers the price reached its maximum during 1991-2000

8.39. Price and page number correlation

There is high number correlation between the number of page and real price. The real price charged increases along with the increase in the number of page

8.40. Correlation between the number of pages and real price in various Social Science subjects

(i)C orrelation between the number of pages and real price is the highest in Law followed by Education and Political Science

(ii) The lowest value correlation between the number of pages and real price is in Social Science General.

8.41. Correlation between pages and real price is Social Science subjects among decades.

(i) The correlation between the number of pages and real price is the highest during the period 1961-1970.

(ii) The lowest value correlation is during the period 1981-90.

8.42. Determinants of publication output of Malayalam books in Social Sciences

(i) Population is the greatest determinant affecting publication output of social science books in Malayalam. One percent change in population would lead to 0.83 percent change in publication output.

(ii) Total literacy is the second important factor which influences the publication output.

(iii) SDP and real percapita have the least impact.

(iv) The existing relationship between publication output and explanatory variables are very significant.

9. SUGGESTIONS AND RECOMMENDATIONS

Based on the findings of the study, certain suggestions and recommendations are given below.

i. The existing bibliographical tools do not contain all the necessary information sought by the users. It lacks comprehensive coverage of books. Many voluntary institutions publish social science books in Malayalam which are not covered by any of the existing bibliographies. So the Delivery of Books Act, 1954 should be reviewed and amended suitably so as to ensure effective supply of publications to the National Library, Kolkata, and the other three public libraries of Chennai, Mumbai, and Delhi. The Central government should conduct awareness programmes to individual publishers as well as Publisher's Associations of every state to highlight the importance of preserving all the publications at one place in the country and bringing out a comprehensive bibliography for reference. The National Library should make arrangements to put the details of all the books received under the Delivery of Books Act in their website which may prompt publishers to send their books without fail. Moreover, the Raja Rammohan Roy Library Foundation should be entrusted to give directions to all the state governments not to consider the books of publishers who do not comply with the Delivery of Books Act and also force them to take legal action to those who purposely violate the Act.

ii. A Regional Deposit Library in every state should be established and entrusted with the task of collecting, organizing, and holding relevant literature in a regional language and thus supplement and complement the efforts of the Indian National Library. This regional library in cooperation with the publishers and other bibliographical agencies should prepare current as well as retrospective bibliographies. As far as Kerala is concerned the State Central Library should be charged with the responsibility of enforcing the Delivery of Books Act by modifying the Press and Registration Act, 1867 to ensure that a copy of the book published be vested with the State Central Library.

iii. A High Level Committee consisting of the representatives of the State Central Library, Kerala; the Kerala Sahitya Academy; and prominent publishers and authors has to be constituted to ensure the comprehensive collection and proper bibliographic control of books in Malayalam.

iv. Lack of adequate translation facility hinder the growth of social science books in Malayalam. In many parts of the world, multi-lingualism is a fact of life and highly creative works produced can be intelligibly transmitted to other linguistic communities in the same country or in other countries only through the medium of translation. Translations in the present day world have therefore assumed a unique significance. The National Book Trust, New Delhi; Kerala Sahitya Academy, Trissur; the Kerala Bhasha Institute (State Institute of Languages), Thiruvananthapuram and a few enterprising publishers like Prabhat Book House, Chinta, DC Books, etc., have taken some good efforts in this regard. But the social science books are by and large translated by individuals themselves. The Kerala Sahitya Academy has to take an active role in identifying the works worthy of translation to Malayalam and getting them translated. For this, a panel of translators who are proficient in social sciences have to be identified. Similarly, an index of translations in the model of **Index Translationnum** by UNESCO should be published.

v. The universities should offer courses in translation as part of post graduate degree course in Language Departments of the Universities of Kerala. Similarly, there should also be facilities to translate works from other languages to Malayalam.

vi. The shortage of women writers in the nonliterary field could be made good to some extent by giving training in technical writing by conducting seminars, workshops, and camps. They can also be persuaded to come forward by offering incentives like awards of various sorts.

vii. The International Conference on Science Information, 1948, held in UK and similar conference held in USA in 1958 paved the way for far reaching changes in the information scenario in the science and technology fields. Similarly, the world Malayalam conference which is occasionally held in different parts of the world should seriously consider sessions devoted to SWOT analysis of the Malayalam publications in different subject fields and point out creative methods to overcome the weaknesses and enhance the existing strength.

viii. In the model of the Tamil University, a Malayalam university should be established to foster studies relating to Malayalam. It should offer courses and conduct researches that would help augment the growth of publication of Malayalam books in individual subject fields. Naturally, the university would be able to identify gaps in Malayalam publications and take steps to overcome the lacunae.

ix. Formation of research centers for resource development in language and culture in the pattern of 'Mozhi' in Tamil Nadu can also be thought of. Mozhi is a charitable trust formed in 1990 for the development of resources in Tamil language and culture. It was founded by a group of individuals belonging to disciplines such as Linguistics, language teaching, publishing, Information Sciences, etc., pooling their long experience in respective areas to develop conceptual and technical facilities in language teaching and learning and understanding culture. It is now engaged in creating a library for Tamil studies in collaboration with the University of Chicago. The collection contains about 1,00,000 items consisting of books and a variety of non-book materials. This collection is a rare one covering all major subjects will prove to be a boon to scholars in Tamil studies.

10. THE TENABILITY OF HYPOTHESES

The hypotheses formulated at the beginning of the study are that:

i There is a rich collection of social science books in Malayalam but there is imbalance in growth in different subjects with the result that while some are well developed, others are lagging behind.

ii The government is not keen on providing translation services in the field of social sciences with the result that many good works in various social science disciplines available in other Indian languages are not translated into Malayalam.

iii There are certain socio-economic factors which determine the growth of publication in any subject or language like population, total literacy, female literacy, Real State Domestic Product, and Real Per Capita Income.

The findings show that these hypotheses are proved to a very great extent.

11. CONCLUSION

Kerala is on the threshold of transforming itself into an information society with its upper hand in literacy, education, health, transportation and communication sectors. But as elsewhere there is an over emphasis on study and research in science and technology subjects, sometimes to the exclusion of social science and humanities subjects. This is very much evident from the fact while there is a mad rush of students to engineering and medical fields, social sciences get only a lukewarm attention. Social scientists have already warned of a society which lacks sympathy, empathy, sensibility, and sensitivity to the weaker sections of the society mainly due to the absence of imbibing human values. The human values can be imparted to the generations only through a study of the subjects concerned with human beings and society in general i.e. Social Sciences.

This calls for a concerted policy on the part of the

government of Kerala regarding the production and distribution of books in Malayalam. It is imperative that the government should have an Information Policy and the policy on books can form part of it. The study has shown that the share of social science books in Malayalam, though not deplorable, is not that much high. There are a number of areas where books are not available. These factors have to be taken care of while formulating a book policy as part of the total information policy. Such a policy is indispensable for the proper growth and development of the information society and the transformation into a knowledge society. It is relevant to note here that a proposal of the National Knowledge Commission (NKC) to set up a National Translation Mission (NTM) to promote and disseminate good quality translations to broadbase education that has perennially suffered from limited access to well translated material in various domains of study. Some of the activities proposed as part of the NTM are creation of a National Register for Translators, translation education, translating pedagogic materials at all levels - including primary to tertiary education - particularly in natural and social sciences, a national web portal on translations as a one - stop shop for related information and promoting machine translation.

REFERENCES

1. Samantharay, Sudhir K(.2001) Restructuring of social sciences in the twenty first centur. University News, 39 (25), 14
2. Sangam, S.L. and Kesava. (2003) Growth pattern of literature in the field of social science. SRELS Journal of Information Management, 40 (1), 77
3. Piaget, Jean (1970) The place of science of man in the system of sciences. Main Trends of Research in the Social and Human Sciences: Part 1. Social sciences. Paris: Unesco. P.2
4. Little, Thomas M. et. al. (1964). Sources of information in

the social sciences. New Jersey. P.3

5. Line, Maurice B.(1962) Information requirements in the social sciences. Journal of Librarianship 1(1),. 2
6. Seligman (1968) International Encyclopedia of the Social Sciences. Ed. By David L. Sills. New York: Macmillan. P.xxi
7. Foskett, D.J. (1990) Structure and development os social sciences., Social science information: Problems and prospects. New Delhi: Vikas Piblishing House, P.3
8. ICSSR Annual Report 1 (1968). New Delhi: ICSSR, P.15

5

Manpower Utilization In The University Libraries : An Investigation

Dr. Vijayakumar, K. P.

1. INTRODUCTION

The University of Travancore came into being in 1937 by a promulgation of the Maharaja of Travancore, Sri Chitira Tirunal Balarama Varma as the sixteenth university to be set up in India. Soon after the formation of the University, the ten colleges, hitherto affiliated to the University of Madras, were shifted to the new University. After the formation of the Kerala State in 1956, the University of Travancore was renamed as University of Kerala by the Kerala University Act, 1957 (Act 14 of 1957). The University with the entire state under its jurisdiction at that time had three campuses located in three different parts of the State at Trivandrum, Ernakulam and Calicut. In 1968, the university centre at Kozhikode became a full-fledged university covering the colleges and departments located in Kannur, Kozhikode, Palakkad and Thrissur districts of Kerala. Another university meant for Science and Technology namely, Cochin University of Science and Technology and a fourth one for Agriculture and related disciplines located at Kochi and Thrissur respectively also came up in 1971. Again in 1983, the Mahatma Gandhi University was established at Kottayam. Two more universities - the Sree Sankaracharya University of Sanskrit, Kaladi, the place of birth of Sree Sankara and the Kannur University, Kannur were established in 1993 and 1995 respectively. Thus, the number of universities, all of them of affiliating type, increased to seven in about quarter century. The universities in Kerala are the following:

i. University of Kerala, Thiruvananthapuram (1937)

ii. University of Calicut, Tenhipalam, Malappuram (1968)

iii. Cochin University of Science and Technology, Kochi (1971)

iv. Kerala Agricultural University, Vellanikkara, Thrissur (1971)

v. Mahatma Gandhi University, Kottayam (1983)

vi. Sree Sankaracharya University of Sanskrit, Kalady (1993)

vii. Kannur University, Kannur (1995)

Apart from the full-fledged state universities, two institutions of national importance, viz. National Institute of Technology, Kozhikode and Sree Chitira Tirunal Institute of Medical Sciences and Technology, Thiruvananthapuram also came up in the state. In the meanwhile, the number of colleges, both Arts and Science and Professional, were also increasing year by year.

3. UNIVERSITY LIBRARY MANPOWER

The Indian Universities Act, 1904 made it obligatory on

the part of universities to establish well-equipped libraries as essential ingredients and since then started the practice of attaching libraries to universities in India. In conformity with this practice, the universities in Kerala also started their libraries. Thus, the University of Travancore set up its library in 1942 and others, except the Kerala Agricultural University, opened their libraries within a few years after their establishment.

People are the most important assets of an organization. They, in fact, determine the success or failure of the organization. At the same time, managing human resources is one of the toughest challenges faced by the management. The management of staff and their optimum utilization do not take place in a vacuum. It requires a clear idea of what has to be done which calls for an understanding of the cyclical nature of effective management. The starting point is the objectives of the library which, in turn, depend on the objectives of the parent body and the needs of the community it serves. The objectives of the universities and university libraries have been elaborately discussed by Radhakrishnan Commission and Kothari Commission. But the fact is that the external environment of the universities have changed drastically mainly due to the changes in education at all levels, in technology, in the political environment and in the economic environment with the resultant impacts on the internal environment. Naturally, this demands a role redefinition and restructuring of the university libraries, especially the library staff, to cope up with the times. This calls for changes in all aspects related to libraries including staff.

4. STATEMENT OF THE RESEARCH PROBLEM

The number and utilization of university library manpower will be affected by such factors as the number of students, faculties and other clientele, the character and condition of library collections, the number of departmental libraries, the teaching method of the faculty, the number of working hours of the library etc. There are two fundamental problems relating to the staffing of the libraries. Firstly, how best to relate the library to the work of the academic and the research staff and departments it serves. Secondly, there is the need to make the most efficient use of the staff which may not always be compatible with ensuring maximum job satisfaction for individuals.

The seven state universities in Kerala and their libraries present a heterogeneous picture. They differ from one another not only in age but in size of collection, services and number of staff. All the seven universities have central libraries. In spite of these differences, there are common problems. Though there may not be any clear cut division, generally speaking, there are only two tiers in the hierarchy of professional library staff in the university libraries. At the top are the academic-related grades which include the University Librarian, Deputy Librarians and Assistant Librarians. The lower grades are occupied by professional juniors like Junior Librarians/Reference Assistants, Professional Assistants/Library Assistants. Since the vacancies up to the position of Deputy Librarian is filled up based on seniority, the entry qualification still remains as degree in any subject with a bachelor's degree in Library and Information Science. In the absence of a third category of semi-professionals, as seen in libraries elsewhere where a three tier structure is followed, many of the routine duties are left to the professionally qualified junior staff.

An aspect which needs investigation is the question of numerical balance between professional staff and non-professional staff. The current thinking in UK and anywhere else is that three-fourths of all jobs in libraries require something less than graduation from a library school. The professional bodies in developed countries are constantly endeavouring to formulate staffing standards to suit the changing needs and bring out concrete formula for estimating manpower mainly based on the users and collection. They also pinpoint the need for employing para-professionals and the ratio to be maintained. It is worthwhile to examine the structure and position of manpower in our university libraries and how far it conforms to the standards available. In this context, a study about the staffing pattern and staff utilization becomes relevant. In addition to the excellent staff formula put forward by Dr. S. R. Ranganathan, which is widely accepted, some professional associations, conferences and even individuals have put forward performance standards.[6] It is a moot point whether any of these norms are followed in the planning of manpower in our university libraries.

Besides the traditional print media, several non-book materials like audio-visuals, audio and video discs, CD-ROMs, DVDs have also emerged as major information carriers. The new media in their wake facilitated the introduction of new services in libraries. Today computers are used for almost all library house keeping operations. Savings in library staff and time through automation have already been established in many places. One of the greatest benefits which the new communication technology brings to libraries is the ability to interconnect them functionally. As a result, the trend towards the establishment of nationwide networks of libraries is becoming stronger. All these factors are sure to affect the staff pattern and staff utilization in university libraries. In this context, a futuristic approximation becomes all the more necessary. Once the minimum staff required for each service is determined, it is possible to find out whether there is shortage of staff or excess staff that can be deployed for newer services.

The quality of the service rendered by the libraries has a direct bearing on the motivation of the employees. In order to be motivated, the employees should be satisfied with the nature of the job assigned to them and their proper utilization in rendering the services. Therefore, as a corollary of the utilization study it is appropriate to examine the job satisfaction level also of the professional staff.

5. SIGNIFICANCE OF THE STUDY

A sound manpower management policy envisages the use of job analysis, job description, job evaluation, job classification, personnel specification, appropriate recruitment and selection policies, induction and training and employee appraisal. These steps also need refinement to suit the changing environment - both internal and external.

Several factors make the study of manpower utilization an essential component of library management. Declining budgets, increasing allocation for staff, decreasing outlay for materials and services, constant changes in the external and internal environment, competition from other agencies concerned with information storage and dissemination, the need for continuous innovation and a more client-focused approach to library services are a few of them. In addition, organizational restructuring, application of information and communication technology, job reassignments and resultant training and staff development needs also necessitate such utilization studies.

Dr. S.R. Ranganathan had evolved a job standard suitable for university libraries half a century ago, but it is doubtful whether the universities follow this in the planning of human resources. The present study tries to investigate the problem at a deeper level to see the rhyme or reason, if any, which is followed in manpower planning in the university libraries of Kerala. The study would also examine the qualifications and skills possessed by the professionals and how far they are suitable to the changing information scenario.

As a result of the application of IT gadgets, many jobs previously attended to by the professionals could be carried out by non-professional skilled staff. A demarcation of such jobs would go a long way in the effective utilization of professional staff for a variety of novel services that are possible.

The output analysis of the employees would reveal the adequacy or inadequacy of staff in the libraries, as a result of which ways and means of redeployment of staff could be suggested.

Apart from a few studies about the assessment of work of staff members in individual libraries, so far no similar study has been conducted in India covering all the university libraries in a state. The suggestions formulated on the basis of the study would point towards better utilization of staff. This can serve as a guideline for other university libraries in the country.

6. OBJECTIVES

The major objectives of the study are:

i. To determine the size and structure/ pattern of library manpower in each of the university libraries in Kerala.

ii. To ascertain the qualification and skills of the library staff in the university libraries.

iii. To assess the quantum of work involved in the different sections of the chosen libraries for the study.

iv. To compare the extent of utilization of the existing manpower in the university libraries in terms of the quantum of output and by analysis against staff formula of the U G C Committee.

v. To suggest measures towards better utilization of manpower in the libraries.

7. SCOPE AND COVERAGE

As stated earlier, there are seven universities in the state. Of these seven, the first five have got full-fledged university libraries, whereas the libraries of the last two universities are at the fledgling stage with skeletal staff. The first five university libraries have very strong central libraries and separate departmental libraries/constituent college libraries. Therefore, in order to study the utilization of manpower, only these five universities are taken.

The Kerala University Library system comprises the Central Library at Palayam, the Campus Library at Kariavattom, the departmental libraries attached to the teaching and research departments located at the city and Kariavattom campuses, the University Engineering College Library again at Kariavattom and the study centre libraries functioning at three locations within the area of jurisdiction of the university. University of Calicut and Mahatma Gandhi University also have central libraries, departmental libraries and study centre libraries and engineering college libraries. Cochin University of Science and Technology has got a central library, departmental libraries and Engineering College Library. Kerala Agricultural University has a central library and separate libraries for all the ten constituent colleges located at different parts of Kerala.

The scope of the study is confined to library manpower. The manpower utilization part of the study covers only the central libraries of the five universities. The department libraries are left out since most of them have only one professional staff member.

Hypotheses

The study proceeds with the following hypotheses.

i. The existing staff size and structure in the university libraries in Kerala do not conform to any approved manpower standards.

ii. The library professionals in university libraries are under-utilized.

9. METHODOLOGY

The study covers the central libraries of the five universities. The university libraries covered are:

i. Kerala University Library, Palayam
ii. C H M K Library of University of Calicut, Tenhipalam
iii. CUSAT Central Library, Thrikkakara
iv. M G University Library, Kottayam
v. Kerala Agricultural University Central Library, Vellanikkara

The major tools used for this part are the following.

i. Data sheet

The main tool used is a comprehensive datasheet meant for collecting details like documentary resources, membership, equipment, budget allocation, services offered, annual output of work in each and every section and manpower (both professional and non-professional). The datasheet is intended mainly to collect details of manpower and the output of staff members. It was administered to the librarians of the central libraries.

ii. Interview

Of the five university libraries, only two are having university librarians. All others are headed by senior-most Deputy Librarian or Assistant Librarian. All the heads of libraries and Deputy Librarians and heads of sections were interviewed with the help of an interview schedule. The idea was to collect information about the mission of the library, policies on collection building, functioning of the library committees, new services introduced, human resource management policy, in-house training programmes, continuing education programmes, and to obtain suggestions for the improvement of human resource management including proper utilization of staff members. Altogether 22 professionals were interviewed for the purpose and information thus obtained was incorporated at appropriate sections of the thesis.

iii. Observation

With a view to get first hand information about the quantum of work in each section and thereby to get an idea about the utilization of manpower, the investigator spent a few days in each central library of the universities. In order to develop a standard for manpower estimation based on the time involved in each routine in the manual method and in the automated environment, the routines/activities in each section of the Kerala University Library were keenly observed as a case study. Discussions with professionals at the service points also formed part of this method. This university provided an opportunity to study the time required in both manual and computerized modes since both methods are resorted to - simultaneously in some services like circulation – since the library is still in the process of computerizing the services.

iv. Verification of records

Various records in the central libraries, departmental libraries/college libraries of the universities like gate register, accession register(s), budget allocation register, accessions list, binding register, serials control register etc. either in the register form or electronic format were examined for factual data and to clarify doubts.

Analysis

The data collected through the data sheet were subjected to various types of analysis and inferences were drawn.

The data collected through the verification of records and information gathered through interviews are included at the appropriate places. Through participant observation and discussion with professionals at service points the average time required for each routine in the sections was estimated. Based on this, an Average Time Schedule Manpower (ATSM) Model was developed as an alternate method for estimating manpower in university libraries.

10. LIMITATIONS

The study, though tried to be comprehensive, has certain limitations.

They are:

i. Though there are seven universities and two institutions of national importance with deemed university status, five universities which have well-equipped university library systems alone have been selected for the study.

ii. The manpower utilization study is mainly confined to the central libraries of the five universities excluding the departmental libraries most of which are managed by a single staff member.

iii. Since the quality aspect of the services has not been dealt with, the customer satisfaction survey has been left out from the study.

11. MAJOR FINDINGS

11.1. Manpower in the University Libraries

i. In the university libraries of Kerala, there are four grades of professional staff such as University Librarian, Deputy Librarian, Assistant Librarian and the Professional Assistants. The category of semi-professionals or para-professionals is conspicuous by its absence. In addition to the administrative staff, there is the class IV category. The five universities follow the same pattern as far as staff grades are concerned, though there is slight difference in the designations at the junior level. Even for those who belong to the UGC category, UGC stipulations are applicable only for placements and state/university rules are followed for other service conditions like retirement age, pension etc.

ii. Though there is considerable difference in the volume of procurement of documents, the number of professionals in the Acquisition Section is the same in both KUL and CUL. While KUL, CUL, CUSATL and MGUL have only permanent staff among professionals, KAUCL has one apprentice also in the Section. One noteworthy feature is that the professional staff in the KAUCL in the Acquisition has to attend to the work of the Technical Section also. Only CUL has a permanent non-professional staff.

iii. As far as Technical Section is concerned, KUL has the biggest contingent of professional staff, followed by CUL. Only CUSATL has non-professional staff. Even though physical processing, a routine job, is done in the Technical Section KUL, CUL and MGUL do not have non-professionals.

iv. In the Maintenance Section, KUL has 8 professionals and 2 non-professionals, followed by CUL with 4 professionals and 2 non-professionals. MGUL has 5 professionals alone both for Maintenance Section and reference work in the absence of a separate Reference Section.

v. The Circulation Section of all the libraries, except KAUL, work in two shifts and therefore the working time of the charging counter is more, compared to other sections. KUL leads with a total professional staff of 7 and 3 non-professionals. CUL manages the Section without a single non-professional though there is considerable non-professional work.

vi. In all the libraries, except KAUL, the Periodicals Section works in two shifts. KUL with the largest periodicals collection has 5 professional staff and 1 non-professional. MGUL with the second biggest collection has 3 professionals and CUL with less than half the number of periodicals of MGUL also has 3 professionals. The number of periodicals subscribed to in the library does not have any relation with the size of the staff in the university libraries.

vii. KUL with the biggest reference and text book collection has fewer professionals in the Reference Section compared to the volume of work. There is no direct relationship with the volume of work in the Reference Section and the staff members.

viii. CUL, MGUL and KAUCL have no separate Documentation Section. While CUL and KAUCL do not attempt any documentation work, MGUL builds up a reprint collection which is quite unique among university libraries.

ix. The IT Sections in libraries have gained importance in terms of the number of staff in them. KUL and CUL have 6 professionals each in the Section. Only CUSATL has two i.e. the Information Scientist and a temporary staff. There are 7 professionals in the MGUL mainly because it combines in itself the activities of the Documentation Section also. KAUCL has no separate staff for the purpose.

x. In the KUL an Assistant Registrar is charge of the Administrative Section, whereas all other libraries have Section Officers. While KUL has 3 Assistants, all others have 2 each. There is no uniformity in the number of typists. In the case of Class IV staff, Kerala

University takes the lead with 5 including library cleaners and sweepers. Other categories include Security Officer and Guards, Artist and Photostat Operator.

xi. Kerala Studies, one of the prestigious Sections of KUL has 3 professionals, of which one is in the grade of the Assistant Librarian who serves as the Head of the Section. Research Section of KUL has one Head of the Section in the grade of Assistant Librarian and one Professional Assistant. UN & World Bank Section, another unique feature of KUL, is manned by one Assistant Librarian and a temporary professional. Union Catalogue Section of MGUL, concerned with the development of a machine-readable catalogue of documents, has one Assistant Librarian as Section Head and one Library Assistant.

xii. As far as Supervisory staff is concerned, only two libraries, CUL and CUSATL, are having university librarians and the other three are headed by the Senior-most Deputy Librarian/Assistant Librarian at the time of study. Kerala University is functioning without a university librarian right from 1990 and is looked after by the Deputy Librarian-in-charge. KAUL also is controlled by the Senior-most Assistant Librarian.

xiii. The analysis of the total professional staff in the libraries shows that KUL, naturally, has the largest contingent of professionals because of its sheer size followed by CUL. If professionals in the grade of Assistant Librarians and above are treated as professional seniors, the percentage of professional juniors is slightly bigger than that of professional seniors in all libraries except CUSATL. This general trend is visible when the total number of professional staff in all libraries is taken together.

Both KUL and CUSATL have more than one third of the posts lying vacant. While KAUL has one fourth of the posts vacant, the corresponding figure for MGUL is one fifth. In total, more than one fourth of the total positions (26.8%) are lying vacant.

The absence of non-professionals is more glaring in the KUL where more than 70 percent of the posts are lying vacant. While there is gap in the CUSATL (35.71%) and MGUL (38.46%), there is no non-professional at all in the KAUL. CUL is the only library with all the posts filled up.

xiv. While KUL and KAUL have not made any fresh posting of professionals during the period 2000 - 05, CUL, CUSATL and MGUL have made appointments in the range of 10 -12 persons. But fresh posting or allocation of non-professionals has not been made except by CUSATL.

11.2. Output analysis using Staff formula of the UGC Committee

i. The estimate of professionals based on Staff formula indicated that only 1 professional staff is required in the Acquisition Section of KUL in the place of the present 3. CUL, CUSATL, MGUL, and KAUL also need one each instead of the 3, 2, 2 and 0.5 incumbents. Only KAUL is found to have less staff than required.

ii. Based on the study, the technical sections of the university libraries have 6, 4, 2, 2, 0.5 persons in the place of 2,1,1,1 and 1 respectively. The gap is wider in CUL with a percentage difference of 300. KUL comes next in terms of the gap with 200 % more staff. Only KAUCL has less staff than required.

iii. All libraries seem to have excess professional staff in the Maintenance Section, the percentage difference ranging from 33.33 in the KUL to 250 in the CUL. The number of professionals seems to be more because of the present practice of employing professionals full time in the two shifts, though the most of the work in the section is of non-professional nature.

iv. KUL has 7 staff members - largest number among the libraries – including the Section head. While the Section head and other Assistant Librarians work from 10 a.m. to 5 p.m., others work in two shifts. This library has 133.33 percent more staff than the estimate arrived at using the staff formula. Only CUSATL has the optimum number of staff as required according to the formula while KAUCL needs more.

v. As per the estimate, no university library needs more than one staff in the Periodicals Section. KUL with 5 staff members has the highest percentage difference of 400 followed by CUL and MGUL. Only KAUL has the optimum number of staff as required. As far as Kerala and Calicut University libraries are concerned, there is historical reason for more staff. During 1970s, KUL and CUL had more than 1000 and 700 journals respectively. Though the subscriptions have come down drastically owing to the spiralling cost of periodicals, the number of staff remains the same.

vi. The total number of visitors to the Reference Section indicated by the libraries includes all those who come to the Section for making use of the textbook facilities also. From this angle, KUL has less staff than required to the extent of -20 percent. CUL has the optimum number of staff, but CUSATL has double the number. No Section was found to conduct user education program.

vii. Taking into consideration the average annual output, the present staff strength of the Documentation and Information Section of KUL appears to be 50 percent more than the estimation. KUL had brought out many bibliographies which were highly appreciated but has not published any in the last 5 years. Had such bibliographies been brought out, the number of items indexed or abstracted would have justified the present strength of manpower in the Section. CUSATL carries out SDI service to a limited extent and that is the reason why the 1 staff member available at present is justified. MGUL does the indexing of reprint collection and therefore justifies a post of a professional. But since Documentation Section and IT Section are clubbed together, the manpower available is considered as part of the Information Technology Section.

viii. The staff formula is silent on the manpower for the IT since IT applications were not there at the time of its formulation. In the absence of a standard for manpower estimation, it is presumed that at least 1 professional is required to guide users in information search in each shift of the Library. At this rate, KUL and MGUL have 133.33 percent more staff than required. While CUL has 33.33 percent more staff, CUSATL has 33.33 percent less.

ix. As far as other sections are concerned, Kerala Studies of KUL which works for two shifts at present has 3 professionals. This is quite justified because the services of at least one professional are required in each shift, in addition to the Head of the Section who works from 10 am to 5 pm.

The Research Section which works from 10 am to 5 pm has two staff members at present including the Head. Considering the fact that this section involves much administrative work concerned with the research scholars and the services to be provided to the users in the use of theses and back volumes of periodicals, two staff members including the Head of the Section is a must. But one professional with a non-professional can handle the work considering the clerical nature of the work.

The UN & World Bank Section which offers the services for seven hours needs the services of only one full time professional. Since the publications need proper arrangement and physical processing, the services of one skilled staff or an apprentice or a trainee would also be required.

Union Catalogue Section of MGUL needs the services of only two professionals to supervise the activities of the catalogue preparation taking place at different locations of the component libraries since the entire work is outsourced.

x. A generalization that can be drawn from the analysis of manpower is that in the case of all university libraries while there is more manpower in the Sections concerned with behind the screen operations like Acquisition, Technical Processing, Documentation, Periodicals and of late IT Section too, the staff provided in service points, especially Reference Section is less strongly suggesting a redeployment.

xi. The norms followed for the estimation of staff in the Administration Section are those followed in the Administrative Office of the University. It is obvious that there is no standard pattern for deciding the number of staff in the Administration Section. Also there is no policy in the deployment of unskilled staff. Correlation of the number of non-professionals based on the formula of the UGC Committee with the existing staff of the same category shows that there is a shortage of unskilled staff in all the libraries. The gap is more in KUL and less in CUL. Even if all the vacant posts of unskilled staff are filled up, the gap between the estimated number and the total number would persist. In the absence of unskilled staff, libraries have started outsourcing the routine jobs like cleaning. The practice of getting the job done by people on daily wages is also catching up.

11.3. Activity Time Schedule Manpower Model

An Activity Time Schedule Manpower (ATSM) Model was developed as part of the study to estimate the professional and non-professional manpower in the manual and computerized environments. The Staff formula approved by the UGC Committee is applicable to certain Sections alone and is incapable of estimating the manpower in a computerized environment. Since the ASTM Model is based on the average time for each routine, it can be applied in any environment which emerges.

Using this model the study comes to the conclusion that KUL, CUL, CUSATL, MGUL and KAUL require total manpower strength of 56, 23, 23, 31 and 16 respectively. The ratio of professional and non-professional staff is found to be 1:1. The non-professional staff includes both skilled and unskilled staff envisaged by the UGC Committee. The number of non-professionals excludes the supervisory, clerical, Class IV and security staff who form part of the Administration Section, the strength of whom is determined by the norms of the parent university.

In the computerized environment, the number of professional staff arrived at through the ATSM Model is in the order of 45, 22, 22, 27 and 15 in KUL, CUL, CUSATL, MGUL and KAUL respectively. The reduction in staff due to automation is to the tune of 11 in the KUL and 4 in MGUL, but there is a variation of only one each in CUL, CUSATL and KUCL. This finding shows that in an automated environment substantial reduction is experienced in the number of staff, only if the volume of routine work is high. Thus, the premise that IT applications would lead to the reduction of professional manpower is not found to be true. The change takes place mostly in the case of non-professionals. The comparison of the number of professionals obtained through the Staff Formula of the UGC Committee with those arrived at through the ATSM Model shows that the latter is marginally higher in KUL and MGUL but less in CUL, CUSATL and KAUL.

The comparison of the number of non-professionals - semi-professionals and unskilled as envisaged by the UGC Committee - arrived at through the formula and the ATSM Model shows sizeable difference in all libraries. The estimation according to the staff formula is high in all cases. It is observed in the analysis of routines that the unskilled are more needed in the maintenance, circulation and periodicals sections. All other sections need only semi-professionals. In the context of outsourcing the routine and repetitive jobs like cleaning of shelves and overall cleaning of the library, the figures arrived at through the ATSM Model is more realistic.

The application of the UGC Committee Formula and the ATSM Model for the estimation of professional showed that there is more professional staff in all the universities than presently required. At the same time, there is shortage of semi-professionals or para-professionals who are capable of carrying out skilled jobs like ordering documents, accessioning, bill passing, issue and return of documents, ordering periodicals, recording the receipt of periodicals etc. In their absence, even the routine jobs are carried out by the professionals resulting in the underutilization of their skills. The presence of more professionals in the Sections of the five libraries is mainly due to this anomaly. This makes it imperative to employ more skilled manpower as is being practised in western countries so that the valuable time of professionals can be utilized for more creative information services which are in great demand.

12. VERIFICATION OF HYPOTHESES

The study started with four hypotheses. The first one is that the existing staff size and structure in the university libraries in Kerala do not conform to any national and/or global manpower standards.

A category of staff called Semi-professionals is not at all present in any of the libraries. The UGC guideline which acts as a norm is followed in the case of qualification and salary of the senior staff alone who constitute a minority.

The size and structure of the manpower was correlated with the existing staff pattern in each of the sections of the five university libraries. The norm prescribed by the Committee was not found to be followed in any of the sections in any University Library. The interview with the Head of Librarians also revealed that the appointments to the entry posts are made based on the number of sanctioned posts calculated earlier arbitrarily without taking into consideration any norm. Since it was found that no other norm is adopted in the calculation of posts and appointments further correlations were not attempted. Thus, the findings of the study support the first hypothesis.

Correlation of the prevailing staff strength with the desirable strength suggested by the UGC Committee shows that the number of professional staff in most of the sections is more than the recommended level. Only in the Technical and Circulation Sections of KAUL, Reference section of KUL, Documentation Section of MGUL and IT Section of CUSATL, there is less staff than prescribed by the Committee. Circulation Section of CUSATL and MGUL, Reference Section of CUL and KAUL and Documentation of CUSAT have the optimum number of staff. The correlation of the strength of existing professionals with the number arrived at using the manpower model also testifies this.

At the same time there is no non-professional skilled

staff and the number of unskilled non-professionals is very much less than recommended by the Ranganathan Committee and the number obtained by the application of ATSM Model. This indicates that even the non-professional routine jobs in the sections are done by professionals. CUL, CUSATL and MGUL have computerized many of the routines and KUL and KAUL have partially done it and this automation renders even the manpower recommended by the Committee surplus. These findings validate the hypothesis that the library professionals in university libraries are under-utilized.

13. SUGGESTIONS

Based on the study, the following suggestions are offered.

i. Redeployment of Professional Staff
ii. Fixing of MLISc/MLIS as the Minimum Qualification for Professional Posts
iii. Use of Semi-professionals or Para-professionals for routine jobs
iv. Training of Library Staff to suit with the times.
v. Students Assistantship
vi. Strengthening of Library Committees
vii. Centralization of Technical Operations and Decentralization of Services
viii. In-house Training Programmes
ix. Direct Recruitment of Assistant Librarians
x. Establishment of Library Clusters or Specialized Branch Libraries
xi. University Library Staff Web Site
xii. Readiness to Participate in Continuing Education Programmes

xiii. Assessment Mechanism to Evaluate the Success of the Library
xiv. Quality standardization of university libraries
xv. Co-operation with Practising Librarians
xvi. Library - LIS Department Collaboration
xvii. Co-operation with Professional Associations
xviii. Market the Profession to the Society
xix. Conduct Quality of Work and Job Satisfaction Surveys.
xx. Organize Continuing Education Programmes

14. CONCLUSION

If university libraries are not to become obsolete or irrelevant as new technologies and the resultant business models emerge, as pointed by Christensen's Theory of Disruptive Technologies, they have to resort to certain strategies to limit the effect of such technologies and at the same time adopt and adapt them into sustaining technologies.[7] As admitted by Christensen himself later, few technologies are intrinsically disruptive or sustaining in character, but it is the strategy that creates the disruptive impact.[8] The fast changes taking place in the information scenario make it imperative on the part of university libraries to periodically check and update its strategic plans and change priorities continuously. The old hierarchies and divisions are not tenable for long time. There is a strong justification for the traditional hierarchical organization but a flexible and dynamic solution is needed for the areas affected by the rapid changes. This, in turn, changes the workflow forcing library staff to adopt new and additional duties and responsibilities. Unfortunately university libraries in India do not yet have sufficient experience to define and measure the new tasks that are emerging so as to project an alternate model. Even with sufficient experience, it may be difficult to project a lasting model because of the rapid changes taking place in the internal and external environments of the library.

Today's user of the university library ranges from a technologically sophisticated researcher conversant with publications in different formats to a more traditionally focused scholar whose interest is in a relatively narrow yet important part of the library collection. Naturally, the library's role is shifting to provide services and assistance in navigating the vast amount of information available. The organization of electronic databases, subscription of e-journals, the migration to new integrated library systems, the interlinking of print and electronic collections, the proliferation of information resources and the resultant help and guidance additionally needed by the users, the growth of web-based teaching-learning materials, the maintenance and proper use of the emerging new media are some of the challenges faced by the professionals. In this context, libraries should demonstrate that they are positioning themselves to meet the challenges of the new information environment. Instead of the rigid divisions in libraries and information centres, special workgroups and task forces are likely to emerge. This behoves on the part of professionals to sharpen their skills continuously. The parent bodies also have the moral responsibility to ensure that the skills and abilities of their employees get sharpened from time to time. This calls for a new approach in Library Management in which team work, effective leadership, vision and mission should be the catch words.

Restructuring of the manpower, over the long term, would lead the academic libraries to have an expanded workforce concept. In such a scenario those who possess Masters degree or higher qualifications in Library and Information Science would hold key roles as leaders and managers and there would be more diverse and higher number of staff members with more varied qualifications like specializations in Science, Social Sciences, Humanities, Media Studies, Web authoring, Content Development and so on. The nature of jobs, qualifications and skills will have to be rethought continuously to suit the requirements of the clients and the times.

REFERENCES

1. Velu Pillai, T. K. (1940) Travancore State Manual. Vol. III. Trivandrum: The Government of Travancore, 700.
2. Sreedhara Menon, A. (2003) History of the University of Kerala. Vol.1. Thiruvanathapuram: Publications Division, University of Kerala, 3.
3. Ibid.: 16-17
4. Universities Handbook. 30th ed. (2004) New Delhi: Association of Indian Universities, 1282.
5. Likert, Rensis. (1967) The human organization. New York: McGraw-Hill: 12.
6. University and College Libraries. (1965) Report of the Library Committee of the University Grants Commission. New Delhi: UGC.
7. Christensen, Clayton M. (1997) The innovator's dilemma. Harvard: Harvard Business School Press.
8. Christensen, Clayton M. and Raynor, Michael E. (2003) The innovator's solution. Harvard: Harvard Business School Press,

6

The Impact of Factors on Professional Library Manpower Development in The College Libraries

Dr. T. Mohanakumar

1. INTRODUCTION

The challenges facing modern library and information services demand learning, information systems and services, and their speed, responsiveness and capability. The demands can be fulfilled only by persons with good academic background, knowledge, professional skills, expertise, leadership for accomplishment of the library activities and operations. The united efforts of the workforce/ human resource/ manpower can fulfill the objectives of the library and achieve the goals of the organization. The library personnel are heterogeneous consisting of individuals of varying ages, levels of education, areas of expertise, differing motivation, personal characteristics, aspirations, needs and personalities. The library management shall understand how these factors interact in the work environment.

The productive abilities of a nation or a firm are based upon the integration of the abilities of its members with physical resources and technology available to it. The human abilities consist of the capabilities of all the individuals, as modified by environmental factors (Tiwari, 2004).

2. SIGNIFICANCE OF THE STUDY

Manpower is one of the most essential components in any profession. The performance of the personnel plays a vital role in the success and failure of an organization. Libraries are no exception to this phenomenon. The contemporary scenario predominated by information and knowledge provides indicate the pressing needs to educate and train the library and information manpower towards a sustainable professional competence. In the present changing information scenario it is highly relevant to conduct a study on professional library manpower development. The outcome of the study may be useful to authorities and librarians who can plan and execute better manpower development programmes in the college libraries.

3. OBJECTIVES

(i) To study the impact of some of the important factors on professional library manpower development in the college libraries in Kerala.

(ii) To measure the present level of influence of factors on manpower development.

(iii) To make suggestions for developing the professional library manpower.

4. HYPOTHESIS

The influence of factors on manpower development has not reached in a satisfactory level to develop the present professional library manpower in the college libraries in Kerala.

5. METHODOLOGY

The size of the total population of the study is 392 professionally qualified librarians who are working in various college libraries in Kerala. An optimum sample of 68.62 percent of the population (269 Numbers) was selected by stratified sampling technique by representation from all types of colleges. Data required for the study was collected by questionnaire method. The level of factors of manpower development was measured using a scale developed for the purpose. The scale consists of ten items of Likert type on a five point rating scale. Each item, therefore, contained five alternative responses such as Very Good, Good, Average, Poor, Very Poor. It was a self-administering tool. The scoring was based on a five point measurement. The items weighed a score of 5 for Very Good, 4 for Good, 3 for Average, 2 for Poor and 1 for Very Poor. The summated score of all the items provide the total score. Descriptive statistics was applied to analyze data.

6. MANPOWER DEVELOPMENT

The term Manpower Development /Human Resource Development (HRD) has multifaceted meaning. The definition, interpretation and functions of HRD vary depending upon individual author's specialty. Thus, from the economic point of view, HRD is defined as capital, assets, labour, skill and wages. A psychologist perceives it as attitudes, values, perceptions and intelligence. A sociologist visualizes it as the quantum of social relations and value exchange that possible in the development process of society. HRD or MD is a positive concept in human resource management. It aims at overall development of human resources in order to contribute to the well-being of the employees, organization and the society at large. HRD means developing or tapping hidden qualities in people in order to make them accomplish new functions leading to organizational and individual goals.

Nadler (1969) defines HRD as, "an organized learning experience within a given period of time with the objective of producing the possibility of performance change." The term learning experience refers to purposeful or intentional learning and not incidental learning.

Among the Indian authors, T. Venkateswara Rao worked extensively on HRD. He defines HRD in the organizational context as " a process by which the employees of an organization are helped in a continuous, planned way to:

(i)A cquire or sharpen capabilities required to perform various functions associated with their present or expected future roles;

(ii) Develop their general capabilities as individuals and discover and exploit their own inner potentials for their own and /or organizational development process;

(iii) Develop an organizational culture in which superior-subordinate relationship, team work and collaboration among sub-units are strong and contribute to the professional well-being, motivation and pride of employees" (Rao, 1986).

Glossary of Human Resource Planning and Development defines Manpower Development as "the process of persons acquiring skills, knowledge and capabilities over a period of time moving towards levels of higher value. The process also involves the whole amalgam of recruitment, selection, career planning, etc" (Dhar, 1997).

In the strict sense of the study HRD or Manpower Development can be defined as a process in which the employees/professionals of an organization are helped/ motivated to acquire and develop technical, managerial and behavioural knowledge, skills, abilities and mould the values, beliefs, attitudes and interests necessary to perform present and future roles by realizing the highest human potential with a view to contribute positively to the organizational, group, individual and social goals. In simple words Manpower Development can be defined as "the development of the total knowledge, skills, creative abilities, talents and aptitudes of any organization's workforce as well as the value, attitude, belief, involvement and interest of the individuals involved.

7. FACTORS OF MANPOWER DEVELOPMENT

Acquisition and development of professionals are not enough to ensure good performance. There are certain factors, which influence change and encourage developmental needs of professionals. A brief discussion of these factors is given here.

7.1. Motivation

The vital factor in manpower development is motivation of the workforce. Human resources/ manpower is the essential and most important resource in the library. If the library personnel are highly motivated, adequately qualified, sincere in their work, serious to achieve the result-oriented targets and sincerely feel a sense of belonging to the organization, they can be regard as the best resource of the library in comparison to all other physical resources. Only the human resource can overcome the constraints and limitations of other physical resources. Motivation plays a key role in energizing and activating the people to put in their best effort of the accomplishment of goals. As performance is a multiplicative function of ability and motivation (P= AxM), is extremely important to ensure motivation of people in tandem with their development for higher performance and productively. In the words of Mamoria (1980), the "purpose of motivation is to create conditions in which people are willing to work with goal, initiative, interest and enthusiasm, with a high personal and moral satisfaction, with a sense of responsibility, loyalty and discipline and with pride and confidence in a most cohesive manner, so that the goals of an organization are achieved effectively."

Motivation has been variously defined by scholars. As Berelson and Steiner (1964) state: "A motive is an inner state that energizes, activates or moves and directs or channels behaviour towards goals." As commonly understood, motivation means the willingness and eagerness of a person to perform a task. From the standpoint of behavioural science, it is defined as a process of identifying the needs that create drives in the people to engage in work and deciding on the incentives and rewards that would give them the highest satisfaction and fulfilment (Luthans, 1989).

In an organizational context, motivation should be viewed as a continuing process. This is because satisfaction of the existing needs will give rise to fresh needs from the existing employees or from the new employees. Moreover, employees will remain with the organization as long as their personal needs and goals are satisfied on a continuing basis by working in that organization (Simon, 1976). In simple terms motivation can be defined as a willingness to utilize the full energy to achieve a goal and to perform a job successfully. Motivation is thus a process of mental attitude to understand rightly the job and to perform it yielding result in least possible time frame.

7.2. Encouragement

The dictionary meaning of the term encouragement is

the act of encouraging, or the state of being encouraged, incitement, stimulation or to inspire with courage sufficient for any undertaking, to embolden, make confident. For better performance in work the staff should be incited or induced. If there is any weak from the side of the staff they should be advised. Authorities should take keen interest in this respect.

7.3. Recognition

Every employee or library professional expects a word of praise from the users as well as the authority. It gives vigour, energy and confidence to shoulder on a new and little difficult task and deal with it successfully. "Recognition is more important than monetary rewards and can help small men to more mountains" says rightly Dabas (1989). Flener (1975) is of the opinion that in attempting to combine the needs of staff with user demands for library services, many approaches will need to be examined. Recognition will need to be given to staff expectations while, at the same time, considering the possibility of meeting these expectations within the framework of the academic community.

7.4. Environment

As an important factor 'environment' has much influence on manpower development. The professional development of a librarian depends, to a very great extent, on the environment in which he works. He should have a congenial environment that will provide him with the necessary stimulus and encouragement to apply himself to this work creatively. The most important factor in his environment is the clientele making use of the library. In an environment in which there is a demanding clientele, i.e. a clientele who continuously demand different types of service from the library for their academic and research needs, the librarian cannot but respond to the demands. And in the process of organizing and providing the services his professional development takes place. In such an environment, he feels the pressing need for equipping himself adequately in all respects and updating his knowledge that would enable him to provide the services. If, on the other hand, a librarian happens to work in a library where the environment does not put any pressure on him for providing library service, he does not feel the incentive to update his knowledge and, as a consequence, he declines professionally over a period of time. It is observed that librarians working in isolated college libraries, which are not made proper use by their clientele, is declining in their professional competence and librarians working in research libraries and, to some extent, in university libraries developing professionally.

In a situation where a congenial environment does not prevail, the librarians should explore measures of the improvement of the conditions. One step is that they should organize service on their own initiative and do everything possible to demonstrate the effectiveness of such services. The management also should take initiative for creating an environment suitable to carryout all kinds of services including IT oriented services. If the environment is better the services also become better.

7.5. Opportunity

An opportunity is any favourable situation in the organisations' external environment. The opportunities offered to the profession by the instantaneous revolutionary changes in IT are enormous and new services and produced could be introduced to serve the information seekers. The introduction and popularization of internet facilities, e-mail service, on-line searching, are only a few examples. In order to provide efficient IT oriented service, librarians should be provided ample opportunity to update their knowledge and skills.

7.6. Facilities

Facilities are opportunities or favourable conditions, for the easier performance of any action, the physical means for doing something. For performing the duties effectively and efficiently in the changing environment the library staff should be provided facilities for developing their personal and professional competencies by sanctioning leave for study purpose, sponsor them for acquiring higher qualifications, etc. Better infra-structure facilities for library (building, furniture, equipment, etc.) and librarian (convenient seating, toilet facility, etc.) should also be provided. Finance is an important factor in any developmental activities. So, when allocating funds for library, allocate funds for the development of its staff also. Hence, financial facility is also very important.

7.7. Difficulties

Difficulty is an unfavourable condition or state to handle a work. In the practical situation the library professionals feel a lot of difficulties to carryout IT oriented services to the clientele. This is mainly due to the lack of facilities and training.

7.8. Responsibility

Responsibility is the person's obligation to himself to accomplish the assigned jobs. Successful managers or librarians are those who are comfortable with the process of delegation of responsibility and authority (Evans, 1983). The simple dictionary meaning of responsibility is "the obligation to act." However, the meaning of the responsibility in the science of management is the obligation to perform the work activities. Therefore, the obligatory action to be performed to achieve the goal of organization is the responsibility of a person who performs the job. "Responsibility is really a created factor within a person, when an assigned task is accepted by him. Someone who is unwilling to accept the responsibility usually refuges the job to perform and someone who accepts responsibility but feels free that no responsibility, because of he knows that somebody will perform that job" opines by Borse (2000). In short, for the successful performance of the job library professionals should be responsible in the job assigned to them.

7.9. Will

'Will' of a professional has a significant role to play in performing his job especially to carryout the services in the new media and means in the changing information technology environment. The 'Will' which is required in the new library professionals to dedicate themselves to serve the clientele is again an important aspect of manpower development. The dictionary meaning of the term 'will' is power or faculty of choosing or determining. It is the power of the mind to take up a task without bothering about its difficulty. Sridhar (1999) has stressed the importance of will in the following words. "The knowledge and skill are only meeting the necessary conditions of a successful practitioner but the sufficient condition is met only when 'will' of the person motivates him to perform."

7.10. Vision

Vision is an important factor as far as a professional is concerned. Vision has got importance because it will help us to get adjusted with the changing world. The library profession today is changing very fast due to the impact of information technology and the library professionals will need to develop 'vision' or 'visionary skill' to look to the changes that will occur in the profession tomorrow. A library professional must keep one of his eyes at present and another at future. He needs better visualization. Subramaniam (1997) aptly points out that "One must have a vision of what one wants to be. If the vision is clear, the steps that you take to achieve will also be clear."

The factors of manpower development are identified and included in the scale formation are listed as follows.

Factors of Manpower Development

1 Motivation in job

2 Encouragement from the authorities for professional growth

3 Recognition from users

4 Environment to carryout work and provide IT services

5 Opportunity to update your knowledge and use your talents in work including IT service

6 Facilities for developing individual competencies

7 Difficulty/problems/limitations to perform your duties and offering IT services

8 Responsibility in job

9 'Will' to carryout the services in the new media & means

10 Vision and orientation to the future

8. ANALYSIS

The important factors of Manpower Development selected for the study are analyzed and the result is presented in the Table below. Ten items are included in the scale. Out of the ten items Responsibility in job shows the highest score level of 4.29 followed by Recognition from users 4.00. The item which shows lowest score level is Difficulty/problem/limitations to perform their duties and offering IT services (2.90). Motivation in job occupies the third position in a score level of 3.98. The score level of other items in the scale are Vision and orientation to the future (3.93), 'Will' to carry out the services in the new media and means (3.80), Encouragement from the authorities for professional growth (3.49), Opportunity to update their knowledge and use their talents in work including IT services

(3.37), Environment to carryout work and provide IT services (3.33) and Facilities for developing individual competencies (3.22). The average score of the factors of manpower development is 3.63.

Table : Mean score of the Factors of Manpower Development

	Factors	Very good	Good	Average	Poor	Very poor	Mean Score
1	Motivation in job	33.09	38.66	22.68	4.83	0.74	3.98
2	Encouragement from the authorities for professional growth	17.47	35.32	30.86	11.90	4.46	3.49
3	Recognition from users	22.30	57.25	18.59	1.86	0.00	4.00
4	Environment to carryout work and provide IT services.	8.55	36.80	38.66	11.90	4.09	3.33
5	Opportunity to update your knowledge and use your talents in work including IT services.	13.01	30.11	41.64	11.90	3.35	3.37
6	Facilities for developing individual competencies.	8.18	27.51	47.21	13.38	3.72	3.22
7	Difficulty / problems / limitations to perform your duties and offering IT services.	4.46	16.73	57.99	12.64	8.18	2.90
8	Responsibility in job	42.01	45.35	12.27	0.37	0.00	4.29

9	'Will' to carryout the services in the new media & means.	28.25	39.41	24.16	4.46	3.72	3.80
10	Vision and orientation to the future	27.14	46.47	21.56	2.60	2.23	3.93
	Average	20.45	37.36	31.56	7.58	3.81	3.63

The percentage-wise analysis of the items in the scale reveals that 20.45 percent of Librarians is in the Very Good level, 37.06 persent are in the Good status and 31.56 percent are in the Average level. A diagrammatic representation of the Average score of the Factors of Manpower Development is given in Fig. 1.

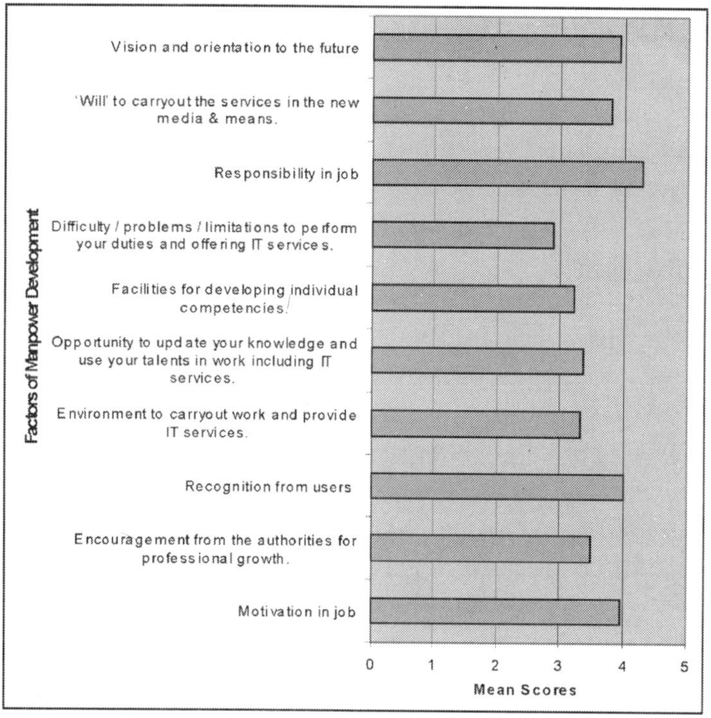

Fig. 1 : Average score of the Factors of Manpower Development

9. FINDINGS AND SUGGESTIONS

The results of the analysis show that only two items (3rd and 8th item in the scale) have got the score level 4 and above. Though the seventh item has the lowest score, it is a positive answer. Librarians feel less difficulty / problems (Just below Average) to perform their duties. It is found that a great majority of librarians are responsible in their job. Librarians are getting a Good (4 point level) recognition from users. As far as the factor Motivation in job is concerned, it shows nearly Good level. 'Will' to carry out the services in the new media and means and Vision and orientation to the future is in an above Average or nearly Good level. But, four important factors such as Encouragement from the authorities for professional growth (3.49), Environment to carry out work and provide IT services (3.33), Opportunity to update their knowledge and use their talents in work including IT services (3.37) and Facilities for developing individual competencies (3.22) are in a low score level i.e., these factors are only in an average level. These four areas should be needed more attention by the authorities.

It is evident from the findings that important factors have not influenced in a higher level to develop the professional library manpower in the college libraries in Kerala. Therefore, the hypothesis is fully substantiated. The following suggestions are made to develop the manpower.

1. The Professional staff should be provided with all possible opportunities to update their knowledge for developing their individual competencies.
2. The authorities should recognize its importance of libraries and follow a policy of providing encouragement for their efficient functioning.
3. The librarian should have a congenial environment that will provide him with the necessary stimulus and encouragement to apply himself to his work creatively.

4. Continuing education programmes in the form of workshops, refresher courses, conferences, seminars, summer institutes, etc. should be organized for this purpose by suitable agencies. Such programmes are particularly necessary for those who work in libraries located at places where they have no access to literature on the subject and no opportunities for interacting with colleagues.
5. All practicing librarians should spend at least two weeks every year updating their knowledge.
6. Facilities for continuing education should be recognized as an essential part of manpower development programme in library and information field.

10. CONCLUSION

From this detailed discussion about the various factors of professional library manpower development, it is evident that Manpower Development or HRD is essential for any growth oriented and dynamic organization, which wants to succeed in the changing and competitive environment. It is the effort and competency of human resource that make the organization dynamic. Personnel policies can keep the morale and motivation of employees in an organization high but, the HRD system/ mechanisms enable the employees to continuously acquire, sharpen and use their capabilities to create an organizational climate, which ultimately stress the organization to success. Therefore, development of human resource is essential for any organization, which wants to grow.

REFERENCES

Berelson, Bernard and Steiner, Gary A. (1964). Human behaviour: An inventory of scientific findings. New York: Harcount Brace & world Inc., 240.

Borse, T. R. (2000). Accountability and responsibility of librarians and libraries. IASLIC Bulletin, 45(4), 161-166.

Dabas, K.C. (1989). Total quality Management (TQM) and its applications in University libraries: Some basic rules. In S.D. Vyas, et al. (Eds). Readings in library and information science. Jaipur: Raj publishing House.

Dhar, Ruby. (1997). Glossary of human resource planning and development. In M. P. Srivastava. Human resource planning: Approaches, needs assessment and priorities in manpower planning. New Delhi: Institute of Applied Manpower Research. 376-377.

Evans, G. E (1983). Management techniques for librarians. New York: Academic Press, 84-85.

Flener, J. C. (1975). New approaches to personnel management. The Journal of Academic Librarianship. 1(1), 17-20.

Luthans, Fred. (1989). Organizational behaviour. Singapore. Mc Graw- Hill, 231-32.

Mamoria, C. B. (1980). Personnel management. Bombay: Himalaya Publishing House, 505.

Nadler, Leonard. (1969). Developing human resources. (Wnd ed). Austin Texas: Concepts, 3.

Rao, T. V. (1986). Recent experiences in human resource development. New Delhi: Oxford and IBH Publishing company, 3-4

Simon, Herbert A. (1976). Administrative behaviour. New York: The free Press, 110-111.

Sridhar, M. S. (1999). Skill requirements of LIS professionals in new E- world. Library Science with a slant to Documentation and Information Studies, 36(3), 141-149.

Subramaniam, C. V. (1997). Human resource management. New Delhi: S. Chand & Co. Ltd, 93.

Tiwari, Ramesh (2004). Human resource management, Jaipur: Avishkar Publishers Distributors, 2.

7

Total Quality Management In University Library : A Case Study

Dr. Bindhu P Nair

1. INTRODUCTION

Libraries can be defined as 'a system which makes right knowledge and information in right time to right person at right place'. Historically libraries used to be turned as the store house of books and the librarian as the custodian of books. The concept of library and librarianship has been totally changed as time passed. Now libraries are treated as gateways to knowledge resources and the librarian as the knowledge manager and interpreter of the content.

The university Grants Commission appointed a library committee under the chairmanship of Dr. S.R. Ranganathan which provided standards and guiding principles for administration and organization of university and college libraries, made recommendations for education for librarianship deals with other relevant matters in a novel and indigenous way.

In view of the objectives of higher education, the university libraries are expected to play at least three roles today.

1. Practical role of information management.
2. Cultural role of preserving human knowledge and culture of the past for posterity.
3. Social and intellectual role by bringing people and ideas together.

Library staff have so far not developed any mechanism to identify the latest potent and dormant needs of the clientele. Libraries have no universal tool and technique to identify and quantify their services and make comparative investigation practices of similar other libraries. Also libraries need to step into the information age and achieve successful development of the library. For the proper growth and development of any institution needs proper planning, same is the case with the library. All these aspects have their influence in each and every field of librarianship.

Library and information scientists can never be silent spectators to this dismal picture of university libraries. In this context the application of Total Quality Management to university libraries is necessary and timely one. The problem under investigation is to study and analyze the existing level of TQM and to prepare developmental plan to achieve quality in Kerala University Library.

2. RELEVANCE OF THE STUDY

The concept of quality in the Library and Information Service context is not a novel phenomenon. Dr. S.R. Ranganathan's five laws of library science imply the quality concepts in library service. Complying with five laws involves a whole range of professional activities including change in the mindset; customer orientation, service strategies, designs and deliveries. For centuries, the purpose of libraries was based on the twin concept of storage and education function. Libraries were thought to have no competition. But this situation is changing due to the rapid advancement in technology and the free availability of information. The internet and increased availability of online services are facilitating self sufficiency of information for students and faculty. Libraries can retain their importance only by providing content based value added services and become electronic learning centers. It is the quality and timelines of information a society gets, determines the quality of that particular society. Gidwani observed that the quality of a university and its library should have a correlation in its structure, organization and objects. He also stated that there is in fact a close co-relation between the nature of the university library and the quality of the university.

Quality management in libraries and information services is built on the solid foundation of past achievements. Because of this, it is often difficult to gauge the extent to which libraries have adopted quality management. Libraries can benefit from TQM in three ways: breaking down interdepartmental barriers; redefining the beneficiaries of library services as internal customers (staff) and external customers (patrons); and reaching a state of continuous improvement. University Libraries should keep abreast with the information needs of the time and this can be achieved by applying TQM principles in library of information services.

3. TITLE OF THE STUDY

The study is entitled

"Total Quality Management in Kerala University Library - a case study."

4. DEFINITION OF KEY TERMS.

i. Total Quality Management

Total Quality Management (TQM) is defined as 'Management philosophy and company practices that aim to harness the human and material resources of an organization in the most effective way to achieve the objectives of the organization'. Atkinson describes TQM as a strategic approach to produce the best products and services possible through constant innovation. John R. Brockman defines TQM as a management philosophy embarking all activities through which the needs of the customer and the community, and the objectives of the organization are satisfied in the most efficient and cost-effective way by maximizing.

Peter Capezio and Debra Morehouse define total quality management as "TQM refers to a management process and a set of disciplines that are coordinated to ensure that the organization consistently meets and exceeds customer requirements. TQM engages all divisions, department and levels of the organization. Job management organizes all of its strategy and operation around customer needs and develops a culture with high employee participation. TQM companies are focused on the systematic management of data in all process and practices to eliminate waste and pursue continuous improvements."

Bently mentions that TQM is a systematic approach to education, management and operations designed to four and co-ordinate the efforts of all employees in an organization to perform certain activities to:

- Know and meet requirements of their jobs;
- Prevent problems which may cause defects;
- Understand the cost of not meeting the requirements; and
- Strive to reduce the cost on a continuous basis.

i. Kerala University Library

Kerala University Library, Thiruvananthapuram is a library which was established in the year 1942, to cater the information needs of the users, researchers, teachers and students of the departments and affiliated colleges and graduate members of the university.

ii. Case Study

Webster's dictionary defines case study as an intensive analysis of an individual unit stressing developmental factors in relation to environment.

5. SCOPE OF THE STUDY

The study is limited to Kerala University Library. The resources and services accessible to the clientele are studied in detail. It is confined to the staff and users of the Kerala University Library, Palayam, Thiruvananthapuram.

6. OBJECTIVES OF THE STUDY

The major objective of the study is to make an in-depth case study of the Kerala University Library, Thiruvananthapuram, based on TQM.

The specific objectives are:

1. To explore the wide range of resources and services available in the Kerala University Library.
2. To conduct an information audit (i.e. the requirements and level of satisfaction of the users).
3. To see whether there is a systematic methodology for measuring customer satisfaction and the level of acceptance of the elements like commitment, teamwork etc.
4. To evaluate the service quality of the Kerala University Library based on a user survey.
5. To evaluate the library quality from the staffs' point of view.

6. To see the management practices prevailed in the library.
7. To see whether there is awareness of TQM or other quality efforts within the library.
8. To explore the barriers within the library to a quality initiative.
9. To see whether there is a systematic methodology for measuring customer satisfaction.
10. To suggest measures for implementing effective services in the library and improving existing services.

7. METHODOLOGY

The research method adopted is case study. Case study is essentially an intensive investigation of the particular unit under consideration. The method enables the qualitative analysis of the library services, after careful and complete observation and efforts can be made to study each and every aspect of the library in minute details and from the case, data generalizations and inferences are drawn.

Data is collected using methods like data sheet, questionnaire, interview, document analysis and observation.

i. Data Sheet

It is meant for collecting information on the library resources, membership, budget allocation, library equipment, output of work and services. It is mainly intended to collect details of the existing services and resources and is administered to the head of each section.

ii. Interview

The Deputy Librarian-in-charge is interviewed with the intention to collect information on the mission, library policies, library committees, services newly introduced, human resource management, continuing education programs, existing services, remedial measures taken, if any, for customer satisfaction and to obtain suggestions and views for maintaining quality in all the aspects of Library and information service.

A questionnaire schedule was prepared for interview.

iii. Document analysis

Various documents like annual reports, accession register, budget allocation register, accessions list, serials control register etc were examined for factual data.

iv. Questionnaire

Structured questionnaires containing closed and open-ended questions were used. The closed ended questions used a five point Likert scale to measure quality management applications.

Questionnaire administered to staff is designed on the basis of LibQUAL dimensions to check the quality of the library. The LibQUAL+ is a useful assessment tool for measuring the quality of libraries. LibQUAL+ helps the library to

(i)I dentify where their services need improvement in the view of their users.

(ii) Compare their service quality with that of others.

(iii) Provide services that are more close to user expectations.

The Questionnaire consists of three sections. Section A deals with personal information. Section B is comprised of 14 questions where the staffs are requested to tick mark appropriate option. Section C consists of 66 questions which the staff has to rate the statements. The rating has to be done in a five point likert scale in which 1 implies 'to 'full extent'; 2 -'to great extent'; 3 - 'to some extent'; 4 - 'to a little extent' and 5 - 'not at all'.

The questionnaire prepared for measuring the service quality from the users' point of view is based on SERVQUAL dimensions. SERVQUAL is a multiple item scale for measuring the service quality and not a tool for improving it. The quality of services provided in a library can be assessed well through questionnaires containing questions on library service quality determinants developed by experts like Thomas Sea, Danuta A.Nitecki etc based on the work of Parasuraman, Zeithaml and Berry[19]. Out of the ten service quality determinants only five are found suitable to Kerala University Library. The Questionnaire consists of three sections. Section A is for user profile, Section B comprises of questions which are grouped into 8 categories and Section C consists of 46 questions which the users are asked to rate. Rating has to be done in the 5 point scale and the questions are based on determinants Reliability, Assurance, Tangibles, Empathy and Responsiveness (RATER).

Questionnaires were given to all the staff and different categories of users - students, teachers, research scholars and Graduate members. Attempts were made to collect as many details as possible through observation and interview. Data collected was analyzed to arrive at the findings and conclusion.

8. SAMPLE

The questionnaire is prepared keeping in view of the SERVQUAL dimensions, and is distributed to 400 users out of which 381 were selected randomly. The sample size is calculated using the following formula.

ss = Z 2 * (p) * (1-p) c 2

where:

Z = Z value (e.g. 1.96 for 95% confidence level)

p = percentage picking a choice, expressed as decimal (.5 used for sample size needed) c = confidence interval, expressed as decimal (e.g.,. 04 = ±4)

9. HYPOTHESES

1. Kerala University doesn't have a strategic plan and policy for giving quality services and for total quality management.
2. Absence of a regular and systematic measure for giving user orientation and for assessing user satisfaction.
3. There are inadequate in-service training programmes for the staff to cope up with the advancements in information technology.

10. FINDINGS AND CONCLUSIONS

The study was designed and executed as an evaluative and descriptive study of the functioning of the Kerala University Library. The sources and services of the Kerala University Library were areas under study. The opinion and suggestions of the clientele on the sources, services and personnel are sought and analyzed. The view and suggestions of the staff and their opinion on the management, work environment etc are sought.

10.1. Preferences of information sources.

Most of the users' prefer current periodicals followed by publications of Institutions/Agencies and conference and seminar papers. Secondly users prefer Index/Abstract/ Reviews next to periodicals. Majority of the users third preference is Conference/Seminar papers. Status-wise analysis also revealed that majority of the users prefer periodicals. This shows the users' interest in primary information sources.

10.2. Adequacy of sources

Periodicals, textbooks and reference sources are only

partially adequate to meet the academic needs of the users; Index/Abstract, Dissertation/Thesis and Online Sources are adequate. Majority of users are unaware of Patents/ Standards/Report and Non book materials collection of the library. Status-wise analysis also reveals that the Post Graduates, M.Phil students, Research scholars and Teachers are of the opinion that the periodicals, textbooks and reference sources collection are not up to date.

10.3. Frequency of use of information sources

The sources which are used frequently are textbooks followed by journals. Reference sources and online sources are also frequently used by the users in their information search. Dissertation/Thesis, Conference papers and Catalogue are used only occasionally. Patents/Standards/ Reports are used rarely. Number of scientific journals required by the majority of the users is three but the journal collection is very poor.

10.4. Routes for seeking information.

Majority of the users are using the contents page of books and journals for locating the required information. Subject index, Author index and Key word index are utilized in the case of reference sources and abstracts. Choosing the right route may enable the user to retrieve right information without loss of time.

10.5. User training/orientation.

The provision of user training is very much helpful to the users in finding out various information sources. But the users of the Kerala University Library are not getting sufficient user training. It should be taken into account that all new members should be given orientation and the current users should be trained while introducing a new service.

10.6. Request and receipt of resources from outside the library

33.1% of the users responded that they have requested resources from outside the library and out of that only 4.7% have received the resources. Majority of the users who have requested materials which are not present in the KUL has not received the resource. This shows that the provision of inter library loan is not effectively practiced in the library.

10.7. Familiarity with the sources and the usage

Familiarity and usage of information sources like E-journal consortium, abstracting indexing journals, subject periodicals, online sources etc was examined. Majority of the users are not familiar with the E-journals consortium and a small number with other sources. Since the users are unaware of the service and the information they could retrieve out of it, the usage is also very low. This indicates the lack of proper training/orientation to users.

10.8. Awareness of services

The effectiveness of the university library is very much dependent to the awareness of the services to the users. The analysis shows that the users are neither aware nor use majority of services and sources offered by the library. All the new members are given guidebook, at the time of enrollment, having instructions and information regarding the rules and regulations, services layout etc. Not all services are listed in the guidebook. Users who don't know what the service is, cannot benefit from the guide book or the board in front of the library. It is evident from the questionnaire that majority of users are unaware of the Inter library loan service, CD ROM search service and Indexing and Abstracting service. Unawareness of the users about the services offered indicates that they don't use those services. In fact this may lead to the failure of the library in achieving the goal of cost effective production of service.

10.9. Level of satisfaction of the services.

Just like user orientation there is no proper system to study the user needs. Also there is no regular mechanism to get the customer feedback and customer perceptions about the services and staff, which is evident from the interview and discussions with the librarians. Majority of the users specifically Teachers, Post graduates students and Research scholars are only moderately satisfied which is an unknown fact to the library staff as there is no proper user study. There should be user studies conducted periodically and the plans, procedures, services etc to be centered on the customer satisfaction.

10.10. Use of online services

Majority of the users utilized Internet for E-mail services followed by online database. Only 25.5% are using the E-journal consortium. From the responses it is evident that 47.5% of the users are unaware of the E-journal consortium and from among those who are using the consortium only 31% are satisfied. Staff should bear in mind that unawareness of the users regarding the services indicates the failure of the library staff in rendering proper guidance.

10.11. User behaviour and use pattern.

Frequency of visit of the users depends largely on the attitude of the staff towards users, the sources and services offered by the library, the working hours etc. Majority of users who are not frequent users opted the reason as shortage of time and unavailability of resources out of which the second reason can be minimized by procuring up to date resources. Most of the users acquired knowledge of using online sources either from their colleagues or by themselves, which shows the lack of help the users are receiving from the staff.

85.3% users utilized the library for 1-5 hours per week

during the UG program and 61.8% used it for 5-10 hours per week for the PG program. 45% of the respondents used it for more than 10 hours per week for the Research purpose. The less percentage of use of library shows the inadequacy of sources, services and facilities.

Out of the 381 respondents 76.6% know how to use the Electronic/Online sources and most of them acquired the knowledge from their colleagues. The rest majority learned it by themselves or by previous experience. Nobody commended that the library staff trained them for using Electronic/Online sources.

10.12. Working hours of the library

Majority of the users (95%) are satisfied with the working hours of the week days. But the satisfaction level of the working hours on Sundays is less and suggested to increase it. Likewise 13.9%suggested reducing the number of holidays. Reducing the number of holidays may facilitate larger use of the library by the general category of the users.

10.13. Library collection

The analysis of the level of satisfaction on library collection gives a variant picture. Majority are satisfied with the collection of Newspapers and general magazines. But when it come to subject periodicals, general books, textbooks and online sources, the level of satisfaction is much less. Regarding newspaper clippings, microfilm, maps, charts diagrams, CD ROM databases etc majority are not in a position to say whether they are not satisfied or not as they are unaware of the services. The users need indexing/ abstracting journals, catalogues, bibliographies, news papers and conference proceedings via computer access.

10.14. Physical facilities

Most of the users are not satisfied with the cleanliness of the library. Around 0% are not satisfied with the lighting and ventilations, reprography, seating arrangements, arrangement of books and refreshments. Some of them even opined that the atmosphere inside stack is suffocating. The racks and books are dusty and congested. Improving the physical facilities may facilitate greater utilization of the library.

10.15. Library staff

More than 50% of the users need the help of staff in their information search. Out of that 82.9% sought assistance in the book search, 56.2% in the periodical search, 73.8% in the catalogue search and 53.5% to understand various reference tools. This shows that the users are in need of aid from the library staff in their search for information.

Only 32% of the respondents opined that the library staff is always ready to help. 41.2% are of the opinion that library staff is helpful but not very often and 16% responded that the staffs are too busy to help. This shows that the attitude of the staff towards users is not very helpful. Also most of the users are of the opinion that the staffs are not approachable. This indicates that the attitudes of the staff need to be changed.

10.16. Reliability

Reliability measures the ability to perform promised services dependably and accurately. Users opined that the library posses reliability only to a little extent which clearly indicates the dissatisfaction of the users in the performance of the library. The statistical analysis also reveals that the users expect good quality services from the library.

Assurance

Opinion on the assurance determinants varies from 'to a little extent' to 'to great extent'. Responses reveal that there is no prompt action on users complaints and it is not at all easy to make a complaint or suggestion about the library services. Users are of the opinion that there should be a Suggestion/complaint box in the library.

Tangibles

Most of the users are satisfied to a great extent in the working condition, the equipments provided but not satisfied with the library web page. The interior of the library is attractive only to some extent. Lighting and ventilation in the building is not adequate. There is no adequate number of computers for online search. The physical facilities and equipments are the areas which need improvement as far as the users' responses regarding this is concerned.

Empathy

Responses reveal that library staffs are courteous and polite to some extent and are not willing to leave the chair all the time. Demonstrations on the use of catalogue and reference sources are done only to some extent. Teaching programmes which enable the users to make effective use of library materials is not conducted. No individual attention is given to the users by the staff. Responses shows that the users are not at all satisfied with the caring and help given by the staff.

Responsiveness

Responsiveness refers to readiness to provide services. Responses reveal that queries on the availability of a source requested are not answered accurately. Users have to wait for assistance at the reference enquiry desk and to use electronic resources which are against 4th law of library science. Majority of the users responded that the staffs are not showing readiness to provide services to them, but always pretending to be busy.

Mission, goals and objectives

It is a great importance in the management of an institution that the staff got a clear idea about its mission, goals and objectives. It is learned that the Kerala University Library doesn't have a proper mission statement which can be and should be a motivator to the staff. Staffs are having a general awareness and are of the opinion that the library should be fully automated to achieve the mission. But this is not sufficient to generate dedication and commitment to the ultimate goal of the library.

A clear cut mission, goal and objective statement should be developed and make it aware to all staff members.

Support of top management

84.9% of the staffs opined that they are receiving immense support from the top management and 15.1% responded that they are not supported. This shows that the support of top management, pre-requisite for quality services, is not rendered to all these staffs.

Staff-users relationship

Staffs are of the opinion that the library is user friendly. Knowing the information needs of the users is very important as it indicates the interest in the clientele and the readiness of the staff to serve them. Responses shows that though the staff is aware of the needs of the users, the quality delivery of services doesn't happen.

Competency in technological advancements

Analysis gives a clear picture that the library needs to improve a lot in the area of adopting new technologies. Around 50% of the staffs are of the opinion that they are not competent enough to handle new technologies and needs training.

Assignment of the staff in the library

84.9% of the staffs are happy with their assignments. 15.1% are not satisfied or given assignments in the area in which they are not proficient enough. Placing the staff in the areas where they are skilled, experienced and interested is an important aspect of quality management. Care should be taken to appoint staff in different sections where they are skilled.

In service training and need for improvement.

92.5% of the staff responded that they have not yet received any sort of training for updating their knowledge and skills. Providing sufficient in service training to the staff members enhances the quality in information delivery. Majority of the staff require training in computer, IT related services, library software etc.

Agreement to team values

Teamwork exist in the library only to some extent and needs to be improved for the total improvement in quality of the library. Other values - trust, commitment, shared vision, openness and non-judgmental participation also needs to be nurtured and built up more actively.

Staff empowerment

Responses depicts clearly the fact that majority of the staff had no chance for attending any training programmes or workshops. Authorities should make it a point that all the professionals get a chance to attend training and workshops in the field.

Quality Philosophy

Responses show that 56% of the staff are aware of the developmental plans of the library. The satisfaction level is less regarding the recruitment policy. Opinion on the result of the work and its contribution to library's success earned only 43.2% satisfaction to great extent and 30.2% staff are fully satisfied.

Faith in management

45.3% of the staff have faith in the managements competency only to some extent which reveals that they are not satisfied with the management. 43.4% are of the opinion that they are considered an asset to be developed and the remaining are not having the feeling that they are considered an asset rather than a commodity. Majority of the staffs are of opinion that all staffs are not treated equally.

Leadership

Majority of the staff are not fully satisfied with the leadership style. Areas like problems, needs and suggestions from the staff are always welcome by the authorities, maintenance of cordial relations in the library etc are only satisfied to some extent. The needs and grievances of the staff should be heard and answered by the authorities for the effective management of the library.

Customer focus

Staff are of the opinion that the users are satisfied with the services to a little extent only. Even though staff opined that the services, processes and practices are planned keeping in mind the users' needs and expectations, this is not a sincere response as they themselves know that the clientele are not satisfied with the services. Staff are not of the opinion that the users' who complaint. But the users are not getting remedy for the complaints on time. Also there is lack of promptness in answering the customers' enquiries.

Staff management

Responses reveals that the major decisions are not taken jointly in the library, which means the participatory management is not practiced in the library. Library staff is one of the most important components of the library service. To tap the potentiality and capability of the personnel, the management needs to possess the art of human resources management. The university library has got a good number of professionally qualified manpower. But what is lacking is satisfaction and contentment which may lead to lack of cooperation, dedication etc.

Job challenge

Staff agree that the re shelving of books is not done regularly. But they are not taking more time in the technical processing of new books. Staff members are personally loyal and they agree to the fact that they get pleasure in meeting customer needs.

Continuous improvement

Talks on current topics and problems related to information services are not at all done in the library. Also the staff are not in complete agreement to the statements on development of work process and delegation of authority and power to capable employees etc.

Process improvement

Only 50% staff are satisfied with the empowerment of the frontline staff. Staff orientation is not practiced in the library. There should be proper orientation/training to the staff, teamwork and empowerment political sufficiently in the library.

Mutual trust and confidence

More than 50% of the staff agreed that there is no feeling of mutual trust and confidence in the library. Festivals are celebrated jointly in the library. Also interdepartmental cooperation and communication are not satisfactory.

Commitment

41.5% staff are of the opinion that they are committed to service to a great extent. Library being a service organization must be fully committed to serve the clientele. Speedy service delivery, accessory in answering questions, willingness to accept assignments and extra work also need to be improved.

Job distribution/rotation

Job distribution/rotation is not effectively practiced in the library. Also the assignment of jobs and duties are not done to the full extent keeping in mind the suitability of the person.

Reward and recognition

50% of the staff are of the opinion that the target for individual performance is high and there is feeling of pressure to continuously improve personnel or group performance. Most of the staff disagreed that rewards are given in proportion to the excellence of job performed. Also they are not satisfied with the performance evaluation. The promotion criteria of seniority rather than merit even efficiency are also needs to be considered.

Adequacy of resources

Management should provide sufficient and up to date equipment for the processing/maintenance of documents. Management should also give enough encouragement to professional development. The equipments provided should satisfy the needs of the staff and the communication facility within the library should be improved.

Utilization of resources

Staffs should use the computers and other equipments provided effectively. The competency of the staff in handling problems related to information tracking is not satisfactory. Staff members are not making effective use of the resources in the library for their professional development. The user education programme rendered by the library is not sufficient.

Innovation of new techniques

Library website should be well managed and informative. Introduce new techniques in information services so that the users will be served better. OPAC is not updated on a regular basis. Also the electronic resources provided by the library are not up to user expectations.

Quality awareness and Quality Initiatives in the Library

Quality is determined by the user satisfaction and the extend of the usage of the various sources and services by the users. Though University Library is there to give quality services to its varied category of users, we cannot find any willful effort to give quality services to the users. Total Quality Management pre supposes the total involvement and cooperation of all the staff i.e. top to bottom. From the assessment through questionnaire it is understood that:

- There isn't any total quality policy.
- It is not defined the total quality values of the library.
- No step is taken to communicate the total quality values to the staff.
- There is no written plan and procedures to implement total quality in the overall services.
- The library has no strategic plan for TQM.
- There is no proper assessment of the quality of the service with the value incurred to provide the particular service.

11. SUGGESTIONS

Based on the above findings after analyzing the responses of the users and staffs the following conclusions are arrived at:

1. Absence of a leading personality adversely affects quality in the overall management of the library. Appointing a University Librarian may enhance effectiveness in the management of the library.
2. Adequate resources need to be procured to satisfy

users' information needs.

3. Open access in the reference section will be appreciated by the users and will result in more effective use of documents.
4. Stack room has to be renewed by weeding out unused items and rectifying the stock at least twice a week.
5. Cabins/study carols and group study rooms are to be provided to researchers and post graduates.
6. Prepare mission, goal and objective statements and distribute the same to the library staff.
7. Include the library under the list of university authorities and make the librarian as an ex officio member of any one of the authoritative committees, preferably syndicate.
8. Two scale salary systems under one roof is to get abolished. According to the status of the university, the post of Deputy Librarian, Assistant Librarian Grade I and Assistant Librarian Grade II are to be filled up by promotion according to the seniority and merit. Automatically, persons who have seniority get promoted without looking into NET qualification, but they are not given UGC scale where as their counterparts with NET qualification gets it. It is better to decide not to promote non qualified persons to this post and if no qualified person is there to promote to these posts better to go for direct appointment.
9. As far as library budget is concerned it is nowhere near the recommendations given by various committees and commissions. It needs a serious consideration and more money need to be allotted to the library for its developmental work which aims at quality services.
10. The funds allocated to the library by the various agencies should be utilized properly.

11. Books selection policy should be revised periodically.
12. It is heartening to understand that the library adopted a proper collection development policy. It is a need to build a healthy and effective collection.
13. Change the attitude of the staff towards the users; render enough support to the clientele.
14. Empower the staff and make them competent enough in the effective information delivery innovating new techniques.
15. Render personalized attention to the clientele.
16. Computerize all the sections of the library. Computerization help to avoid redundant manual work and it help to generate reports and statistics easily and more accurately. It is this report and statistics that direct the library to the future plan.
17. Improve the physical facilities provided to the users in a library.
18. Train the library staff to equip themselves with modern technologies and make them competent in their respective field to deliver quality services. Make it a point that every staff will be equipped with modern IT technologies which are found necessary for the delivery of library services in the age of digital libraries and virtual libraries.
19. Arrangements should be made for the effective orientation of the users.
20. A proper and regular feedback mechanism has to be chalked out and implemented. It will be good to put complaint boxes in various sections and some person of high authority other than librarian should be given the charge of going through the grievances and bring to the notice of the librarian if necessary or conduct regular user surveys.

21. Increase the working hours of the library on Sundays from 8.0 am to 8.0 pm.
22. Provision of in service training should be made effectively by the management.
23. Conduct staff meetings (can be section wise) regularly, discuss the recent advancements in information service and suggest solutions for the problems faced by the staff in information delivery.
24. Job rotation should be practiced effectively.
25. Excellence should be rewarded on the basis of performance and not on other grounds.
26. Provision for professional development should be provided by the management.

12. TENABILITY OF HYPOTHESES

The above findings of the study substantiated the objective formulated in the study. The study also tested fruitfully the validity of the hypotheses formulated in the beginning of the study.

13. CONCLUSION

In this era of Information Communication Technology research and development depend upon the quality of information provided and communicated by the Library and Information Centres. Present day libraries are more aware about the fact that their existence depends upon the satisfaction of the users and so aims to achieve hundred percent customer satisfactions. There may be some discrepancy between what libraries provided and what their customers actually need. This results in the failure of the library to meet customer needs. It is necessary to have a system through which the customer needs are heard and these must be used to improve the quality of service.

The university libraries are indebted to provide quality information to the clientele. As the customers of the library are educated community, the information required by them will be specific and nascent. The resources and services provided by the library should be planned in such a way to satisfy the information needs of the clientele.

Total Quality Management serves as an effective tool to achieve quality in services of a University library. TQM in the context of libraries is to provide the right information to the right user at the right place and time and also at the right cost. TQM offers a suitable framework within which libraries can re-think their service, objectives, delivery mechanisms and internal systems in order to meet user requirements and deliver quality services.

REFERENCES

Alemna, A.A.(2001) "The need for Marketing and Total Quality Management Strategies in Libraries in Ghana". Inspel, 35 (4)

Arora, K.C(2000) TQM and ISO 14000, Delhi, S,K.Kataria & Sons.

Aslan, G.(1999) "Quality Management Applications in Library and Information Services". Proceedings of the International Symposium held on the occasion of the 50th anniversary of the establishment of the Turkish Librarians' Association, Ankara, 17-21 November 1999. Edited by Ozlem Bayram and others. Ankara Turkish Librarians' Association,

Bascal, Robert., TQM in the public Eye www.escape. ca/rbacal/ tqm/htm

Basotia, G.R. (2001) Total Quality Management: modern methods of quality control and standardization, Jaipur Mangal Deep Publications.

Bavakutty, M. and Abdul Majeed, K.C.(2005) "Methods for Measuring Quality of Libraries". New Delhi: Ess Ess Publications.

Bernare, Sushon B. Implementing TQM: a model for Research Libraries, Integrating Total Quality Management in Library

Setting. New York: Haworth Press, 1993.

Bester field, Dale H. et al Total Quality Management. Ed. 3, New Delhi: Pearson Education, 2006

Bester field, Dale H., et al, Total Quality Management, Ed.3. New Delhi: Pearson Education, 2006.

Brophy, Peter and coulling Hate., Quality Management and Library science for information and library Managers Mumbai:. Jaico publishing House, 1997.

Budget estimates, University of Kerala, 2001 to 2007-08.

Chang, C.B. "Total Quality Management (TQM) and its Application in University Libraries". Bulleting of Library and Information Science, (40), February 2002.

Clair, Guy, Total Quality Management in Information Services. UK: Bowker-Saur, 1997.

Clair, Guy St., Total Quality Management in Information Services. UK: Bowker-Saur, 1996.

Cook, Cand Thompson, Bruce. Psychometric properties of scores. Library Trends, 49(4), 2001.

Creech, Bill, The Five Pillars of TQM: how to make total Quality Management work for you, New York; Truman Talley Books, 1994.

Dabas, K. C. and Gill, N. S. "Understanding the Essentials of Total Quality Management (TQM) for Library and Information Management in Academic Settings". Proceedings of the 5th National Convention for Automation of Libraries in Education and Research (CALIBER-98), Bhubaneswar, India, 4-5 March 1998. Edited by M.Mahapatra...et...al. Ahmedabad, India: INFLIBNET Centre, 1998.

Dabas, K.C. and Singh, S. "Application of Total Quality Management to the University Libraries in Punjab: a study". IASLIC Bulletin, 45 (3), September 2000.

Dabas, K.C. and Sewa Singh. Application of total quality management to the university libraries in Punjab: a study, IASLIC Bulletin 45(3), 2000, p.119-128.

Devinder K. Banwet and Biplab Datta. "Effect of Service Quality on Post-visit Intentions over time: case of a library". Total

Quality Management, 13 (4), 2002.

Dougherty, R.M. TQM - is it a real thing? Journal of Academic Librarianship, 18(1):3, 1992.

Garvin, D.A., Managing Quality: New York: Mc Millan, 1988.

Glowacka, E. "Library Marketing and Total Quality Management in Libraries". Przeglad Bibliotexzny, 69 (4), 2001.

Henner Jr., Thomas J. "Why we should establish a National System of Standards". American Libraries, 31 (3), March 2000.

India, University Education Commission (1948) (Chairman: S.Radhakrishnan) Report. VI p.110.

Ishwara Bhat, M and Sangam.S.L. Quality service in libraries : a customer based approach. Mumbai, Allied Pub. 2003, p.19-21.

Jain, S.L. and Gupta D.K. "TQM in Library and Information Services". Annals of Library Science and Documentation, 43 (2), June 1996.

Jayamalini G, An overview of TQM in Libraries http:/drtc.i.sibang.ac.in/bitstream/1849/99/2/pap-cb,pdf.

Johannsen, C. G. "A TQM Perspective on Interlibrary Loan Processes". Inter lending and document supply: resource sharing possibilities and barriers. Proceedings of the 5th Inter lending and Document Supply International Conference, Aarhus, Denmark, 24-28 August 1997. Boston Spa, West Yorkshire, UK: IFLA Offices for UAP and International Lending, 1998.

Johannsen, C.G. "Strategic Issues in Quality Management: 1. Theoretical Considerations". Journal of Information Science, 22 (3), 1996.

Jurow, Susan and Barnard Susan B., Introduction: TQM fundamental and overview of contents, in integrating Total Quality Management in a Library setting Howard Press, 1993. p.1-13

Kovel-Jarboe, P. "Quality Improvement: a strategy for planned organizational change". Library Trends, 44 (3), Winter 1996.

Kuhrner, E. "Is TQM Needed in Libraries?". Tudomnyos es Muszaki Tajekozetatas, 47 (3), March 2000.

Lakhe, R.R. and Mohanty, R.P.Handbook of Total Quality Management, Mumbai: Jaico Publishing House, 2000.

Lemieux, V. "The use of Total Quality Management in a records Management Environment". Records Management Quarterly, 30 (3), July 1996.

Library Association Information quality and liability. London: Library Association.

Line. M.B. "Managing Change in Libraries". Journal of Information, Communication, and Library Science, 2 (3), Spring 1996.

Livingston, David. "Total Quality Management for Library and Information Centres". SRELS Journal of Information Management, 42 (1), March 2005.

Manjunatha, K. and Shivalingaiah, D. "Customer's Perception of Service Quality in Libraries". Annals of Library and Information Studies, 51 (4), December 2004.

Masters, Denise G. Total Quality Management in Libraries. ERIC Digest.

Meera, B. M. "Total Quality Management: application to libraries and information systems". Proceedings of the 5th National Convention for Automation of Libraries in Education and Research (CALIBER-98), Bhubaneswar, India, 4-5 March 1998. Edited by M.Mahapatra...et...al. Ahmedabad, India: INFLIBNET Centre, 1998.

Mohammed, Z. "The Application of Total Quality Management to Library and Information Centres in Tertiary Educational Institutions". Focus on International and Comparative Librarianship, 33 (1), 2002.

Mohanty, R.P. and Lakhe, R.R, TQM in the service sector. Mumbai. Jaico publishing House 2002,

Mounissamy, P. and Rani, B.S. "Application of Total Quality Management in Library and Information Services". SRELS Journal of Information Management, 41 (3), September 2004.

Mukherjee, A.K. Librarianship its philosophy and history. Delhi, Asia Pub. 1966. Pp.185-186.

Parasuraman, A. et.al... 'SERVQUAL: a multiple item scale for measuring consumer perceptions of service quality', Journal of Retailing, 64, (1), 1994.

Poornima M. charantimath. Total Quality Management Delhi: pearson Education, 2003.

Prashanta Kumar Behra and Bibhuti Bhusan Sahoo. "Total Quality Management in Libraries and Information Centres: Some basic issues and implications". In Quest for Quality: Strategies and Applications in Libray and Information Services, ILA Seminar Papers, 46th All India Library Conference, Ahmedabad, 3-6 January, 2001. Edited by S.M.Dhawan, New Delhi: Indian Library Association, 2001.

Prichard, S.M. "Determining Quality in Academic Libraries". Library Trends Language, 44 (3), Winter 1996.

Rabinarayana Misra. "Indispensability of Total Quality Management in Library and Information Centre". In Quest for Quality: Strategies and Applications in Libray and Information Services, ILA Seminar Papers, 46th All India Library Conference, Ahmedabad, 3-6 January, 2001. Edited by S.M.Dhawan, New Delhi: Indian Library Association, 2001.

Raina, R. and Dayal, K. "TQM in Library Acquisitions: an approach at IIML". Annals of Library Science and Documentation, 46 (4), 1999.

Rajya Lekshmi, D. "Total Quality Management: Implications for Implementation in Libraries and Information Centres". IASLIC Bulletin, 43 (3), 1998.

Ramesh, L.S.R.C.V. "Role of ISO 9000 Standards in Obtaining TQM in Libraries: some problems and Prospects". Herald of Library Science, 39 (1/2), January-April 2000.

Reenen, J.A.V. "The Transfer of Learning from Continuing Education to the Job: an evaluation of the impact of total quality management courses on health sciences librarians". Bulletin of Medical Library Association, 84 (2), April 1996.

Rout R.K. Total Quality Management of University Libraries in India, In Mahapatra M...et al (eds) Information Management in Academic and Research Libraries: Papers presented at the fifth National Convention for Automation of Libraries in

Education and Research (CALIBER -98) at Bhubaneswar, 4th -5th March 1998, Ahmedabad: Inflifnet centre, 1998.

Rout, R.K. "Total Quality Management of University Libraries in India". Information Management in Academic and Research Libraries, Proceedings of the 5th National Convention for Automation of Libraries in Education and Research (CALIBER-98), Bhubaneswar, India, 4-5 March 1998. Edited by M.Mahapatra...et al. Ahmedabad, India: INFLIBNET Centre, 1998.

Rowley, J. "Implementing TQM for Library Services: the issues". Aslib Proceedings, 48 (1), January 1996.

Rowley, J. "Managing Quality in Information Services". Information Services and Use, 16 (1), 1996.

Sanville, Tom. "Defending and Expanding Library Turf: the need for scalable consumer research". Journal of Library Administration, 40 (3/4), 2004.

Selvi, G.T. "Total Quality Management (TQM) and ISO 9000 in the context of Academic Library Services". SRELS Journal of Information Management, 39 (1), March 2002.

Singh, A., Implementing TQM, Productivity, 34(1), 1993.

Singh, M.K. "Total Quality Management (TQM) in Library and Information Services". Herald of Library Science, 44 (3/4), July - October 2005.

Sreedhara Menon, A History of the University of Kerala, Vol.1 Thriruvananathapuram: Publications Division, University of Kerala, 1987.

Srivastava, Syam Nath and Varma, Subhash Chandra. University Libraries in India: their organization and administration, New Delhi: Sterling Publisher Pvt. Ltd., 1980.

Sureshchander, G.S...et...al. "A Holistic Model for Total Quality Service". International Journal of Service Industry Management, 12 (4), 2001.

Swing, Randy. "What Benchmarking Measures". About Campus, 8 (6), January-February 2004.

University of Kerala in the new millennium: a report of the development activities (2004) University of Kerala.

University of Kerala, Annual Reports, 2001 -2007.

Varatha Rajan, N. and Ravi, B. "Total Quality Management in Libraries - the reality". In Quest for Quality: Strategies and Applications in Libray and Information Services, ILA Seminar Papers, 46th All India Library Conference, Ahmedabad, 3-6 January, 2001. Edited by S.M.Dhawan, New Delhi: Indian Library Association, 2001.

White, Carl M. A survey of the Delhi University Libraries. Delhi: Delhi Planning Unit, University of Delhi, 1965.

8

Knowledge Management In Digital Age: Librarian's Perspective

Dr. Adarsh N Gokul
Dr. Ambily K S

1. INTRODUCTION

Knowledge management is emerging as a key concern of organizations, particularly those who have embedded a total quality management approach to manage organizations elegantly and effectively. Knowledge management is more than a buzz word and a new income stream for consulting firms. Knowledge is power, the competitive weapon and has become the driving force of the society. Advancement in information technology and global networking has increased the intensity of knowledge management in the linkage of information with information, activities and men for sharing and knowledge economy. This article explores the phenomenon of knowledge management from the viewpoint of professional librarian.

2. PARADIGM SHIFT FROM COLLECTION DEVELOPMENT TO KNOWLEDGE MANAGEMENT

In the perspective of library, there is a paradigm shift from "collection development" to "collection management" and to "knowledge management" which lead to the metamorphosis of Librarian to "Knowledge Managers". Print material, in the form of books, journals, and manuscripts were the predominant medium for library acquisitions during this "collection development" period. Later collection management emerged as a more complete and balanced approach to the collections field of librarianship. Major factors that influenced the evolution of 'collection development' to 'collection management' were the constricting budget provision and the escalating cost of library material, particularly the cost of journal subscriptions in science and technology, more quickly than library budgets; interdisciplinary research and changing use of library collections; and the information technology revolution. Librarians started to select and acquire new resources after conducting use and user studies, prepared careful collection policies to guide their work, and they participated in cooperation and preservation of collection to extend the scope and it's life. Librarians were early adopters of new information technology. Print, which held control in the collection development and collection management periods, is still the dominant format in many disciplinary fields, but digital formats are being quickly adopted by librarians and users.

A collection is too static and too limited a concept to fully describe the range of information resources offered in this digital age to the users. Digital information resources offered to our users by our libraries/Learning resource centers may or may not be actually housed in or owned by our libraries. In the new knowledge universe characterized by multiple networked accesses, and changing formats the term "collection" really does not convey what academic librarians do today. The databases and electronic texts we lease preprint archives and the Internet sites we link for our users through portals are not really the "collections" of our own library. The present generation librarians are shifting from collection management to Knowledge Management and personal knowledge is leveraged with explicit knowledge for the design and development of innovative processes, services, and products. This is possible through effective use of the information technology infrastructure capabilities of the organizations, successful management of knowledge processes, professionals, and sound knowledge work i.e. through knowledge management. Knowledge management is essential to deliver value to the library services and to achieve the goals and aspirations of organization. Identifying the relation, differences amongst data, information and knowledge, and understanding the field of information management are important in the knowledge management hype.

3. DATA, INFORMATION, KNOWLEDGE AND KNOWLEDGE MANAGEMENT - DEFINITION

3.1. Data (singular: datum) refers to a collection of natural phenomena descriptors including the results of experience, observation or experiment, or a set of premises. This may consist of numbers, words, or images, particularly as measurements or observations of a set of variables.

3.2. Information as a concept bears a diversity of meanings, from everyday usage to technical settings. Generally speaking, the concept of information is closely related to notions of constraint, communication, control, data, form, instruction, knowledge, meaning, mental stimulus, pattern, perception, and representation. According to the Oxford English Dictionary, the earliest historical meaning of the word information in English was the act of informing, or giving form or shape to the mind, as in education, instruction, or training.

3.3. Knowledge is defined by Oxford English Dictionary variously as (i) expertise, and skills acquired by a person through experience or education; the theoretical or practical understanding of a subject, (ii) what is known in a particular field or in total; facts and information or (iii) awareness or familiarity gained by experience of a fact or situation.

4. KNOWLEDGE MANAGEMENT

The e-knowledge centre depicts that knowledge management is a cross disciplinary practice which enables organizations to improve the way they create, adopt, validate, diffuse, store, and use knowledge in order to attain their goals faster and more effectively. The Gartner Group states that: "Knowledge Management promotes an integrated approach to identifying, capturing, retrieving, sharing, and evaluating enterprises information assets. These information assets may include databases, documents, policies, procedures, as well as the uncaptured tacit expertise and experience stored in individual's heads"

5. TACIT AND EXPLICIT KNOWLEDGE

Knowledge can be divided into two types. They are tacit knowledge and explicit knowledge. Tacit knowledge is cultivated in an organizational culture that motivates through shared vision and common purpose. Tacit knowledge consists of the hands-on skills, best practices, special know-how, heuristic, intuitions, and so on. Tacit knowledge is personal knowledge that is hard to formalize or articulate (Polanyi 1973). The transfer of tacit knowledge is by tradition and shared experience during apprenticeship or job training.

Tacit knowledge ensures creative intuition and task effectiveness to attain the objectives of an organization. Whereas tacit knowledge is implicit, explicit knowledge is rule-based knowledge that is used to match actions to situations by invoking appropriate rules. Explicit knowledge is used in the design of routines, standard operation procedures, and the structure of data records and enables the organization to enjoy a certain level of operational efficiency and control.

6. KNOWLEDGE MANAGEMENT IN LIBRARIES

Knowledge Management involves the identification and analysis of available and required knowledge, and the subsequent planning and control of actions to develop knowledge assets so as to fulfill organizational objectives. Knowledge management is not about managing or organizing books or journals, searching the Internet for clients or arranging for the circulation of materials. However, each of these activities can in some way be part of the knowledge management spectrum and processes. Knowledge management is about enhancing the use of organizational knowledge through sound practices of information management and organizational learning. Knowledge management in libraries should be focused on effective research and development of knowledge, creation of knowledge bases, exchange and sharing of knowledge between library staffs (including its users), training of library staff, speeding up explicit processing of the implicit knowledge and realizing of its sharing. Knowledge management in libraries is to promote relationship in and between libraries, between library and user, to strengthen knowledge internetworking and to quicken knowledge flow. In the knowledge economy era, libraries will carry out researches on development and application of information resources, construction of virtual libraries, protection of intellectual property rights in the electronic era etc., thus founding the base for knowledge innovation.

Davenport (1993) explains that knowledge management process is about acquisition, creation, packaging, and application or reuse of knowledge. Some examples of each of these types of knowledge management process are:

- Knowledge Acquisition: finding existing knowledge, understanding requirements, searching among multiple sources.
- Knowledge Creation: research activities, creative processes in advertising, writing books or articles, making movies, and so on.
- Packaging: publishing, editing, design work
- Applying or using existing knowledge : auditing, medical diagnosis;
- Reuse of knowledge for new purpose: leveraging knowledge in product development processes, software development.

Knowledge management is more than managing information flows. It rests on two foundations

- utilizing and exploiting the organization's information (which needs to be managed for this to occur) and secondly
- the application of peoples' competencies, skills, talents, thoughts, ideas, intuitions, commitments, motivations, and imaginations.
- Three pillars of knowledge management are users, knowledge professionals/ librarians, and technology experts. Users are those who are personally involved in the act of using and creating knowledge include the faculty staff, Research scholars, professionals, technologists, managers, and others possess and apply

the tacit knowledge and explicit knowledge. Knowledge professionals / librarians are the individuals who have the skills, training and know-how to organize knowledge into systems and structures that facilitate the productive use of knowledge resources. The knowledge technology experts include the system analysts, system designers, software engineers etc who develop knowledge based systems and networks with accuracy, reliability, and speed. Knowledge management can be achieved through strategic knowledge partnerships that combine the skills and the expertise of its users, knowledge professionals/ librarians, and technology experts. Through their coordinate effort library can acquire, create, package, exchange, apply and reuse knowledge. Knowledge management will inject new blood into the library culture. The main contents include: mutual trust, open exchange, studying, sharing and developing knowledge operation mechanism of libraries, enjoying the knowledge management process.

The library has to adopt a holistic approach to knowledge management that successfully combines tacit and explicit knowledge at all levels of the organization. Personal knowledge of librarian has to be leveraged with explicit knowledge for the design and development of innovative processes, services and products. Strategic vision and operational expertise has to be fused in creative action. Knowledge acquisition is the starting point of knowledge management in libraries. The application of information technologies enlarges the scope of knowledge acquisition, raises knowledge acquisition speed and reduces knowledge acquisition cost. It is impossible to accomplish such important tasks by using man's brains only in the modern society in which the knowledge changes with each passing day. It will be possible to link closely knowledge sources and knowledge workers by computer networks, thus constructing knowledge networks in libraries based on realization of single-point informatization.

In the 21st century, the Internet, with its mass information and extensive contents, will provide people with the main approach to searching knowledge and acquiring information. But now there emerge absurd, salacious, false and uncivil information resulting from seeking for commercial profits and political objectives on the Net. Therefore, it is necessary to strengthen knowledge dissemination management in libraries as follows:

1. uninterruptedly strengthening the creation of libraries' own document resources and deepening the development of document information resources;
2. continuously raising the quality of libraries' staffs and strengthening continuous engineering education of working staffs;
3. giving full play to the special role of the expert system in knowledge dissemination;
4. making comprehensive utilization of all media to ensure security of operation of networks, and prevent online criminal activities and online dissemination of inappropriate information.

The main information technologies relevant to knowledge management includes: Internet, Intranet and Extranet; storage architectures; database management systems; metadata; data acquisition and gathering; dissemination, messaging; push and pull; information retrieval; information resources sharing; groupware; middleware; on-line analytical processing; multidimensional analysis and data mining. How to convert data to the object of knowledge management - knowledge is also relevant to some basic information technologies, mainly including data processing, reporting, networked communication, document management, information search and retrieval, relational and object-oriented databases, electronic publishing, work flow and help desks.

The Chief Information Officer (CIO) is a conspicuously high management position that has emerged successively in the government departments and large organizations in Western countries since the 1980s. The Chief Knowledge Officer (CKO) is the highest-ranking person in charge of knowledge management, which has evolved from CIO along with the transition of information research management into knowledge management. The CKO system represents the latest development trends of the information management system of the organizations, and marks the transition of information management from the stage of information resources management to that of knowledge management[15]. Knowledge management is fundamental, where an organization's performance is heavily reliant on knowledge work. Knowledge work emphasizes the use of professional intellect in activities, which use individual and external knowledge. Human resource management is the basis of knowledge management in libraries and hence libraries have to give importance to vocational training and lifelong education of library staff to fit them to design and develop knowledge management system, to extract, filter disseminate vital knowledge and to train the users in information literacy to raise their scientific knowledge level and ability of acquiring and innovating knowledge. The level of technological sophistication and need of the user community emphasis the metamorphosis of librarian to knowledge manager/engineer.

7. CONCLUSION

"Knowledge Management is not so much the management of tangible assets such as data or information, but the active management and support of expertise" [16] which today's librarians has to practice. The future Libraries in addition to participate in the digital and network revolutions, in the creation, distribution and use of scholarly information, will have to carry out more integrated, customized and market-based, approach to the packaging and delivery of need based information. Future libraries under the control of well trained librarians/knowledge managers will not be just a consumer of scholarly information, but a campus hub for working with faculty on the integration of technology and electronic resources into teaching and research; an aggregator and publisher, and a provider of information services to academic, research and business communities and a center for social and cultural development and lifelong perpetual learning.

REFERENCES

1. Wikipedia, the free encyclopedia [Available at http://en.wikipedia.org/wiki/Data].
2. ibid. [Available at http://en.wikipedia.org/wiki/Information].
3. Newman, Wilda B. Knowledge Management Research and End User Work Environments 2010, INSPEL 34(2)2000, p.76.
4. Polanyi, Michael. Personal knowledge. London: Routledge, 1973.
5. Kim, Seonghee. The roles of knowledge professionals for Knowledge management. in INSPEL 34(1) 2000, p.3
6. ibid.
7. Shanhong, Tang. Knowledge Management in Libraries in the 21st Century. 66th IFLA Council and General Conference, Jerusalem, Israel, 2000. [Available at http://ifla.inist.fr/IV/ifla66/papers/057-110e.htm]
8. Cao Yi. The Reorientation of Libraries in the Knowledge Economy Era, Library Work & Research. (3) 1999, pp.24-26.
9. Davenport, T.H et.al. Improving Knowledge Work Processes, Sloan Management Review, Summer, 1996, pp.53-65.

10. Harari, O. The Brain Based Organisation, Management Review, 83(6) 1994, pp.57-60.
11. Chen Rui. Thoughts and Technologies of Knowledge Management, Information Knowledge in Libraries, (1)1999, pp.10-13.
12. Cao Yi. The Reorientation of Libraries in the Knowledge Economy Era, Library Work & Research, 1999(3), pp.24-26
13. Sheng Xiaoping. Knowledge Management of Libraries in the 21st Century, Library Magazine, 1999 (8), pp.29-32
14. Davenport, T.H., The Future of Knowledge Management. [Available at http://www.cio.com/archive/010196-dovenpor-content.html]
15. Chen Rui. Thoughts and Technologies of Knowledge Management, Information Knowledge in Libraries, 1999 (1), pp.10-13.
16. Blair, David C. Knowledge Management: Hype, Hope, or Help? Journal of the American Society for Information Science and Technology, 53 (12)2002,. p.1020.

9

Development of Knowledge Management Based Organisations: New Role of LIS Professionals

N. Suresh Kumar

1.0. INTRODUCTION

In the era of information explosion, every new generation organizations are becoming increasingly competitive, dynamic, innovative and productive. It is in this context, the Library and Information Centres need to innovate new practices/services to prepare its users to meet the challenges of modern times/present day requirements and to respond with technology and work environment/ requirement.

The innovativeness in LIS profession will have to become more strategic and proactive, the magnitude of innovativeness can be measured with respect to the results, which can happen only when proper LIS practices act as a catalyst in organizational/ users operations or activities.

Demand of Users

LIS Professionals need to develop competencies and embrace new roles as Information/ Knowledge managers, and act as service providers to both internal and external users. They need to have a comprehensive of the entire requirements / operations of his user groups not only within the organization but also to the potential users out side the organization too.

New Roles

First and foremost, there has to be a change in the mindset of LIS professionals towards modern technological changes. LIS professionals will themselves have to undergo specialized training in order to coup with the situation. In the ever changing world, LIS activities/services is undergoing massive transformation in the job title and roles. Future LIS jobs will be internal user service, managing external user requirements, networking stakeholders, transmission of organizational goals, making bottom line consequences and building learning / Knowledge Management organizations.

Internal use service

Services offered to various /other departments like faculty, placement/training/ promotion division, technology/information transfer, settlement of benefits/ customer care etc. LIS professionals have to ensure just-in-type internal user service, by taking internal service tenders from the user department / functions annually and mapping out the services accordingly for implementation. Cost/ benefit of services can be calculated for the contribution to bottom line of LIS department.

Managing external user requirements

The new generation organizations will simply transfer

the operational responsibility of the organization to an external agency in many of its present day activities. It is expected that in the coming days, all the staff functions will be outsourced. An organization will be run with three departments: Operation, commercial (buy & sale) and Administration. In such scenario, The job of LIS centre would to manage / provide the necessary Knowledge/information services to not only the parent organization but to market the LIS services to the potential user companies such as identification of agency, making standard terms of reference, provide MIS services to monitoring the work and providing information about legal problems arising out of such activities etc.

Networking with stake holders

The persons/ bodies who have stake in the organizational profit and loss are called stake holders, such as, share holders, contractors/ vendors/ suppliers, customers, employees, Administration department, Production department, marketing department, Public relation department, Govt. bodies etc. LIS department has to network with the external stake holders on a regular basis through meeting and visits, sending annual report, news letters, gifts, conducting conference and seminars, participating in exhibitions, organising cultural programs etc. Proper networking will help in brand positioning and image building of the parent organisation.

Transmission of organisational Goals

Organisational goals are the targets of the institution, set at the corporate/management level. LIS department can work as liaison to transfer the goals of the management to the hands of the users/customers/ employees at different levels and functions through workshops and presentations, bulletins, newsletters etc along with conventional LIS activities.

Making Bottom line consciousness

Bottom line of the parent organisation is achieving its goals. Organisations calculate what is the investments and what is the return. LIS department has to make skill audit and competency mapping periodically and work out LIS programmes appropriate in each level. The coverage would be total i.e. top to bottom. Through bottom line consciousness programs, the quality and productivity will be increased and there by achieving the organizational goals of the institution.

2.0 BUILDING LEARNING / KNOWLEDGE MANAGEMENT ORGANIZATION

Organization of tomorrow will be staffed by knowledge employees only. There is need for developing and retaining performing employees. Organisations can be made performing institutions through knowledge- creation, knowledge-acquisition, knowledge-integration and knowledge- sharing. LIS departments have to plan purposefully, prepare carefully, process positively and pursue persistently. In the process, the organisations will be learning organizations to cope up with ever changing world. Leading organistion of the world attached the highest important to learning/ research and development, Knowledge Management Systems enabling alignment of individual aspirations with organizational plan/goals.

3.0 THE ROAD AHEAD

Conventional information system works logically as depicted in Fig 1.

Process, Computer System and people form MIS system. Collecting data, generating information to knowledge for taking an action, to create values (results) forms an MIS system. The system grows in terms of volume of useful and other data for the regular operation of the organization and the knowledge generated is not captured in the computers and over a period of time the ogranisation will become less depended on the MIS system and become more depended on the people rather than process and system. This makes the performance of the organization poor in customer satisfaction / organizational performance. In brief Knowledge move with people and that is not a good practice for any successful organization / research project.

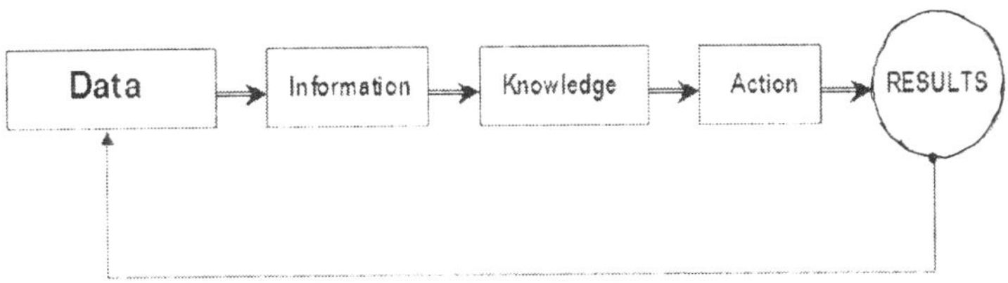

Fig. 1. Conventional Information System

Computer based knowledge management system is designed as shown in Fig 2. Actionable information is within the system rather than within the people. Knowledge to execute the actions are arrived by the people who are the main source of knowledge. From knowledge required for an action, the right information set is derived by the performing team. Then right quantity and quality of data is collected to arrive at the information as the last phase in the flow as shown in the fig 2. Action, knowledge, information and data are optimised to control the nature and quality of the system.

KMS is designed in reverse order of conventional MIS systems and implemented like the MIS system. Main difference is the volume of qualified data input and storing process. In the case of KMS the system will have only the right quality data for the right purpose in the system. But the conventional MIS, the required data is filtered from the huge volume of data stored in the databases.

Prime purpose is to collect right amount of qualified data and capture and reuse the actionable information and knowledge for improving the performance of the organization in the immediate future. People driven organization will get transformed into a system and process driven one.

People get an environment where they discuss, share, publish, accept, and/or learn right actionable information with right members for right purpose at the right time making everyone involved to grow in his own field of knowledge event-by-event and day-by-day of his/her stay in the organisation.

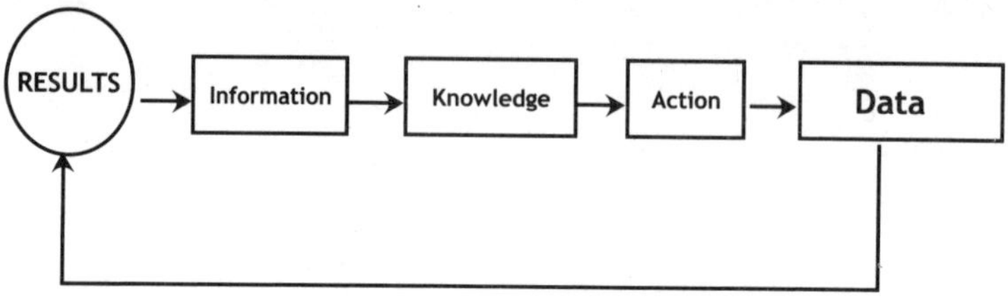

Fig. 2. Knowledge Management System

4.0. HIGH LEVEL DESIGN(HLD)

Knowledge networks are commonly defined as formally set up mechanisms, structures, and behavioural patterns that connect knowledge agents who were not previously connected because of functional, hierarchical or legal boundaries between organizations. Inter organizational knowledge networks provide the setting for knowledge management under cooperation. The identification of key resource capabilities or critical knowledge areas are an essential step in defining competitive forces and determining strategy. A critical knowledge area is another critical success factor that can be used in conducting situational and competitive analysis, formulating differentiating strategies, making strategic decisions, and aligning the organization infrastructure for a strategical KMS fulfilment. The consideration of critical knowledge areas in management deliberations in a variety of scenarios can enhance competitive advantage and the potential for positive performance result. The structure of an organization, its processes, systems, policies, and practices can be examined and adjusted to achieve greater leverage with the critical knowledge areas selected for KMS.

The critical knowledge areas can also used as a benchmarking measure for comparison of practices. Asset valuation and ownership policies can be more intentionally applied to the critical knowledge areas. All of these are ways in which the identification and measurement of critical knowledge areas, that can impact management decision making and contribute to the economic value / performance of a firm / organization.

Fig 3 shows the high level conceptual design of KMS for an organisation. The design shows the KMS server at the center of the architecture and the knowledge agents (Sources, Users or both) communicating through the KMS server.

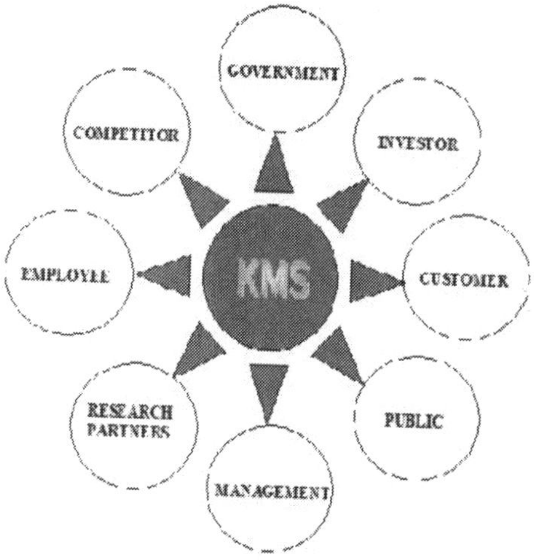

Fig. 3. KMS Design

In this design, KMS is the Knowledge Server which works 24 X 7 hours a week, helping the people in every members of the agents in capturing actionable information or data that could be transformed into actionable information and insights, storing and making that available to members for future activities in the projects or process to develop product and service for the global customers of organisation.

Secure internet connections are treated as main communication channel for members of the PUBLIC, CUSTOMER, COMPETITOR, RESEARCH PARTNERS (other research institutes, universities etc., working with the organisation in various projects) and GOVERNMENT. Intranet of the organization creates the link between others through the KMS server.

Technical design shall be created upon approval of the HLD by the management of organisation. This will be based on the investment plan of organisation for the KMS. The hardware, software and other computer resources shall be decided for desired size and quality of the KMS system.

5.0 IMPLEMENTATION PLAN

First step is to identify and appoint THE CHIEF KNOWLEDGE OFFICER (CKO) for creating, supporting and maintaining the KMS environment of that particular organisation. The Best practice to make The Head of organisation to play the role of CKO. The Pilot system has to be implemented within a time span of 12 months, starting from the date of approval of High Level Design.

Implementation team needs to be formed by CKO within a week time. The team size shall not exceed 5-members including the CKO. One Member from Library &Information Department, One from IT department, Main functional Head, and Brand Manager of organisation shall be the right choice to be part of the implementation team. CKO should be trained by experts on KMS systems & practices along with conventional Library and Information activities/ services

Creating an awareness across the staff of organisation is the next important step, in the implementation process.

Third step before the project start is to take stock of the IT systems and components and evaluate the purpose and utilization of each unit, or equipment under IT dept. Standard structured plan and control of the Project shall be as proposed in section 5.0.

6.0 PROJECT MANAGEMENT

KMS team shall work with the Principal Consultant (External/internal KM expert) and his/her expertise shall create a Project management plan (PMP). Normally PMP shall be for 12months of KMS design, development and pilot system implementation and shall consider the formation Operation and Support Team (OST).

There are Five Phases in this project,

1) Project Definition
2) Design
3) Development
4) Testing
5) Implementation.

Around 50% of the time is required to do Phase 1, in which what need to be achieved, when, where and who need each source of knowledge etc. and researched and decided based on the Mission critical processes of organisation and where organisation wants to reach towards the end of third year from now. The Life Cycle of KMS is 3-years, and major upgrade and change need to be done on KMS towards the end of the life cycle. Rest of the time out of 12 months is for the other four phases.

Normally Testing & Implementation would take 20% of the time. Every staff shall be working as Knowledge node and need to be trained while implementation is being done. First impact and benefit are for the customers/users of organisation and the employees interacting with the customers. Training plan shall be focused on this factor as well.

7.0 CONCLUSION

To successfully implement knowledge Management System, it is important to understand the infrastructure required to support the acquisition, generation, transfer, and storage of tacit and explicit knowledge resources. Knowledge management involves the coordination and integration of multiple knowledge based activities, structure, systems, processes, and individuals with diverse roles in the organization. These elements are frequently grouped into three categories- People, Process and Technology. Reliable, Scalable and User-friendly Computer based knowledge leadership environment has to be conceptualized based on expertise/experiences and the information collected through the interactive sessions with KM team members.

Knowledge creates value when it is incorporated into products and services. Driving force of this effort is that "Process drive IT" rather than "IT drive the process". IT enables, enhance, motivate every step in the process of knowledge management in an organisation optimizing the time to achive!. Every one can successfully execute this KMS project to harness the power of actionable- information.

LIS professionals have to read the winds of changing the world. The days of only conventional Services and systems are numbered. The challenges before the profession are unpredictable and highly competitive in the era of Information technology. Scope for innovative ideas/ services is in abundance. The very existence is performance liked/

based. LIS professionals have to change their mind set and to take up action plans in building learning/ knowledge Management based organization for tomorrow and contribute to the bottom line. It is not enough that you innovate something. It is even more important that you know how to implement it, and you do implement it.

"Scenarios are not predictions. It is simply not possible to predict the future with certainty. An old Arab proverb says that *he who predicts the future lies even if he tells the truth*. Rather, scenarios are vehicles for helping people learn."

REFERENCES

1. Coakes, E.(2004) Knowledge management :A primer, Communication of Information System, 14(article 21),406-489
2. Davenport, T.H & Prusak, L(1998) Working knowledge: How organizations manage what they know. Harvard Bussiness School Press, Boston.
3. Grant, R.M (1996) towards a knowledge based theory of firm. Stralegie Management journal, 17(winter spl. issue) 109-122.
4. Hayek, F.A.(1945) The use of knowledge in society. American Economic Review, 35,519-532.

   Nonak, I & Takenchi, T.(1995) The knowledge creating company. Oxford University Press, New York.

6. Schwartz, D.G (2006) Encyclopedia of knowledge Management, Idea Group Reference, Hershey.
7. Schwartz, D.G (2005) The emerging discipline of knowledge Management. Intl. Jonl. of knowledge Management.,1(2),1-11.
8. Sveiby, K.E, (1997) The new organizational wealth: Managing & measuring Knowledge based Assets. Berrett Koehler publishers, SanFrancisco.

10

British Council Libraries in India- Policy & Performance: An Analysis With Special Reference to Higher Education

Dr. Lalitha M

1.0. INTRODUCTION

The British Council was set up to promote a wider knowledge of the United Kingdom abroad, to promote the knowledge of the English language and to develop closer cultural relations between the United Kingdom and other countries. But unlike some of the other cultural institutions of diplomatic representations, it has embraced a broader definition of what culture is than its founders ever envisioned.

The setting up of a library network in India bears testimony to this. The analysis of the Council's policies suggests that the British Council libraries in India, in spite of being a public library by virtue of its collection and membership norms, have increasingly- and perhaps unintentionally- acquired a slant towards higher education in general and students (i.e. the Council's T3 category) in particular, despite the frequent and often abrupt changes in policy direction. Moreover, in India, the Council's libraries have increasingly become the visible face of the Council's activities. This phenomenon is in contrast with the Council's operations elsewhere (for example in countries like Egypt, Africa or Europe) where the thrust is seen to be more on the Council's stated objectives of propagating English culture and language rather than on library-related activities. This can be attributed to certain unique characteristics of the Indian academic environment, especially in larger Indian cities, viz., i) clarity about their needs, ii) the wide prevalence of English language as a medium of instruction in higher education and also iii) the Council's unwavering customer focus and innovation.

1.1. British Council's Library Policy

Few libraries exist in a vacuum, accountable only to themselves. There is thus always a large context for assessing library quality, that is, what and how well the library contributes to achieving the overall goals of the parent organization. In the case of the British Council Libraries, its parent body, the British Council, states its country aim for India as: 'to win recognition in India for the UK's values, ideas and achievements and nurture lasting, mutually beneficial relationships between India and the U.K. For this, the 'strategy' developed by the British Council Libraries is: 'to develop and expand both off and online services to reach much larger number British Council target audience in more cities in India'. For the libraries this reaching out means reaching out to 1, 04,197 members[1]. In 1992, this was 1, 07,000. There was a drop but it was natural since two libraries were closed (Ranchi and Patna). But in their place, Chandigarh's information centre was opened and there is the Knowledge and Learning Centre in New Delhi.

In the same Country Plan, the Council defines its target audiences. T1 (Influence), T2 (Engagement), T3 (Appreciation) and T4 (Awareness) are what they are called. The researcher does not want to go into the categories but what is important here is how the Council perceives the needs of its targets, especially T3, which is the group in focus for the purpose of this study as well.

According to the Council, the users belonging to T3 are in need of:

- information for study and for professional updating through books, journals, websites, lectures, workshops etc;
- access to a well-managed IT environment;
- access to relevant high quality tailored content, (eg. personal development modules), which will enhance their chances of securing a top job;
- opportunities to improve their English, including their presentation and communications skills;
- educational opportunities overseas;
- access to online and managed leaving opportunities which are affordable and work-related;
- information on and access to UK qualifications; and
- exciting and fun events which portray contemporary UK.

Most of the services and products are aimed at meeting these needs. "In the context of a US- obsessed youth culture and of our desire to extend our services to much larger numbers of people, it is important that the young decision-makers and change agents who are India's future are aware of and appreciate what the UK has to offer."

The Council has three areas of activity, viz, creativity, learning and society. Libraries come under 'Learning'. The Country Plan says the Council will continue to provide learning opportunities for specific groups, developing tailored programmes and services, both on and offline meet their requirements. It hopes to "develop its role as an enable and facilitator by bringing people together, helping young professionals.....as access the very best UK resources-both online and offline-through the British Council Library Network."

This is the Council's side of the story, about what it thinks the targets need and about what it has done to meet these needs. But there is another side to it: that of the user, or, customer, as he has been called from the 1980, when the focus shifted to customer care. What he/she thinks of the services and products and their usefulness, adequacy and appropriateness also matters a lot. Definitions of library effectiveness have ranged from technical efficiency measures to vague statements of goodness but most have focused on goal achievement, efficiency, user satisfaction, personnel management and ability of the organization to survive.

The present study tries to bring out all these factors by focusing on the users' side of the story. The British Council Library has organized certain things anticipating their use and appreciation by the customers. How the customer, the King, assesses it and what he thinks about it will point to the effectiveness and efficiency of the library policy.

1.2. Objectives of the Study

In this study the researcher tries to analyze the policies being followed or adopted by the British Council Libraries and also to find out (1) whether the aims are designed to meet developmental needs of India and the regions; (2) how the basic aims behind establishing the library network and the Indian needs are balanced; (3) whether there is an apparent prominent shift to any side; (4) whether the aims reflect policy orientations in terms of developmental priorities, economics, operational modalities and subject priorities and finally (5) the changes that have come, over the years, in the category of target groups.

1.3. Methodology

Not many studies have been done so far on the British Council Libraries in India and studies at a country level are few and far between. Besides no studies have been undertaken recently concerning the British Council Libraries alone, in spite of the fact that the last two decades have witnessed tremendous changes with regards to library policy, book collection, book selection, range of services and even the target audience. Research and reports on British Council Libraries in India have so far restricted themselves to the marketing of their services or something in general about the services. Hence the present study was undertaken to study the library policy of the British Council and find out how far the library network in India has succeeded in implementing it. For this purpose perceptions and responses of a stratified sample of more than 350 users from the higher education sector (teachers, students and researchers from educational and research institutions) in a British Library were analysed.

Questionnaire was administered only in British Library, Thiruvananthapuram, taking it as the representative of the 11-library British Council Network. For the purpose of this survey, teachers and students in the colleges and university departments in the Thiruvananthapuram City who also hold valid membership in the British Council Library, Thiruvananthapuram were contacted. Since the study is about the users in the higher education sector, the junior students of degree courses were excluded but those in their final year of degree courses were brought under the study. This was because it was felt this group would have a better understanding of their chosen subjects and would exercise better judgment and a keener sense of direction while using the library. The majority of the population was from professional courses, postgraduate courses and those doing research in the various departments. Teachers were also included. In all, 500 questionnaires were distributed and 351 responded (70.2%). Out of this, 231 were students including 49 Research scholars, 109 employed including 62 teachers and 11 were unemployed.

Questions were formulated in such a way as to make the user assess the various aspects of the British Library like collection and services and overall rating was also done by the user himself based on his own experience.

Statistics not cited in this section come from internal British Council Library and Information Services documents (unpublished). The analysis is based on the Corporate Plan (British Council Worldwide), Country Plans (India), Code of Practice, reliable information and materials gathered from interviews with former British Council officers and other internal documents.

A mention has to be made here about the limitation of this study: the facts and figures correspond to the period only upto the year 2006. The library in Thiruvananthapuram has also become a thing of past, with its closing down in 2008.

2. HOW THE BRITISH COUNCIL OPERATES

The British Council seeks to achieve maximum impact in fulfilling its purpose and strategic objectives by supplementing its core funding of the government grant through the Foreign and Commonwealth Office (FCO) - through paid services. Such services include teaching English and administering, British examinations through the overseas network of offices (Enterprises work) and managing development and training contracts for a wide range of clients (Development and Training Services (DATS). These overseas operations are supported by corporate services including finance, HR, Resource Planning, Communications etc.

The British Council's network of overseas offices draws on different sources of income and different modes of delivery to achieve country and regional objectives. Almost all offices have operations that utilize more than one mode of delivery and individual staff jobs often reflect the overall mix in the office. As for corporate planning, a hierarchy of plans governs all Council activities. The Council's planning year runs from April to March. At the higher level, the British Council has a corporate plan, updated every year and it covers a four-year period. It sets out the strategy that the Council intends to follow and all staffs are encouraged to contribute to improving the procedures. Offices in individual countries and headquarters departments follow the planning cycle and provide the operational detail summarised in the corporate and regional plans.

All plans contain performance indicators, both quantitative and qualitative, as appropriate, to allow performance to be measured against agreed targets. Performance indicators at the corporate plan level are developed according to the balanced scorecard devised by the Council. Strategic objectives support overall Council objectives meet the requirements of Regional frameworks.

Though there is a corporate plan, each country will have a plan of its own, concentrating on its priorities. In India, the thrust is upon information provision to help the developmental needs of the country. Thus the libraries occupy the centre stage and DFID has collaboration with various agencies in the fields of primary education and health. Since English is almost the first language in India, English language teaching which is a money spinning and the most sought after activity of the British Council in countries like Iran, Hong Kong, China, Russia and Japan, is not given the priority. This will be clear when we look at the stated country aim for India.

3.0. British Council's Library Policy: Historical Perspective

The history of the British Council Libraries shows that Flood was uttering a potent half-truth when he once claimed that the Council has never had a conscious policy in library and printed word matters. "What it has achieved is the total of individual initiative by the professional librarians on its staff." It is certainly true that one will look in vain, in this sphere, for a statement of objectives agreed with sponsoring departments, together with financial targets and appropriate resource allocations.

However, the Council does have a 'printed word policy', which has been maintained with notable consistency ever since the days of Ann Ormrod. There is more than one strand to this policy. The first takes the form of giving precedence to the Council Libraries as the preferred means of cultural projection by way of the printed word. Secondly, there has been the provision of assistance to the book trade in the 'promotion' of British publications. The other has been assistance to library development in the Third World. Like the building up of the library network, the Council's deep involvement in such activities originated from deliberate policy decisions. The move to give pre-eminence in 'printed word' projection to Council libraries came from headquarters but participation in library development resulted initially from pressures from overseas.

During the immediate post-war years, it seems to have been 'policy' to establish at least one Council library in each representation. But this was never achieved. However, this aim was taken off the agenda and for many years, the Council had operated with some success in such countries as Norway and Sweden without having its own libraries and without feeling the need for them. In the developing world, this was different. Libraries provided greater visibility to the Council, as they did in the days of Barnicot's 'second-growth libraries'.

A feature of British Council Libraries over the years has been perhaps an 'unconscious policy' of flexibility, of a readiness to adapt them within reason to meet customer demand. But there are those in the Council who feel that undeniably the ultimate object of the Council is not to satisfy customer demand but rather to 'promote an understanding and appreciation of Britain in other countries through cultural, educational and technical cooperation.

The nature, problems and defects of the various library development programmes with which the Council has been associated like those in Jamaica, the Eastern Caribbean, the Gold Coast and Nigeria, show that these are the results of adverse national or international economic developments. Another reason is that it failed to give direct assistance to the library needs of rapidly developing educational systems. Such assistance would have been more likely to ensure effective and continued support from host governments. British aid to public library development has often been offered on condition that the recipients establish a public library service which would operate in accordance with British ideas of what a public library service should be.

3.1. British Council in India

The British Council's main target audience in India is seven million young professionals spread over 25 identified cities. The extensive market research and opinion surveys carried out have shown that the target audience attitudes to the UK are mixed, but, overall positive. There is a high level of appreciation for the UK education and active promotion of UK higher and further education has translated into a large increase in South Asia students going to the UK. This is reflected in the number of educational queries received at the British Council's libraries in India and the number of students going to UK for higher studies.

For the British Council, the challenge in this region is to find ways to scale up its engagement and its publications. To do this the British Council needs the support of its physical network, which is the library network, through which it can extend its services to a wider audience. For this the British Council has to find and negotiate licenses for appropriate content and develop reliable online delivery systems. Through its KLC, New Delhi, it is expected to lead the region on developing innovative online services providing language and work place skills, degree level online study and high quality information. This is being offered alongside an upgraded library network which is benchmarked with best UK practice. That India is the only country in the region to have had an increase in the allocation - it has been increased to £563 million shows the strategic importance and relevance of the British Council operations in India.

3.2. Country Aim & Strategy

Country Aims & Strategies, 1992 & 2003/04

(1) South India Regional Management Plan 1992/93*: To sustain and reinforce Indo-British relationships by collaboration between institutions and individuals, especially in education, Science and Technology, the Arts and Humanities by managing joint projects for ODA (now DFID) which directly meet India's developmental needs and by providing access to British ideas and achievements.

The regional aim derived from this is effectively to deploy the resources of the Madras office and library and of the British Libraries in Bangalore, Hyderabad and Trivandrum in support of the Country Aim. Priority subject areas in South India include medicine, natural resources and English studies.

(2) Draft Country Plan for India 1999/00 to 200/02: To enhance the reputation of the United Kingdom in the world as a valued partner providing the best network for information and knowledge exchange in India as a gateway to international opportunity.

(3) India Country Plan 2003 -04 : To win recognition in India for the UK's values, ideas and achievements and nurture lasting, mutually beneficial relationships between India and the UK by

- developing and expanding both off and online services to reach much larger numbers of a target audience in more cities in India;
- by increasing opportunities for engagement with our target audience by developing our offline services in 11 cities as well as an online membership offer for young professional people living in 25 first and second cities in India; and,
- by continuing to research the needs and requirements and of these people, develop appropriate new products and services but at the same time focus on providing excellent customer relationship management.

3.3. Strategy 2005 & India

A key feature of the strategy is a reduction in the overall size of the Council's overseas estate in order to free up funds for the operational activities. Many offices were closed down. The second key element is the development of new and expanded programmes and services. This means that the Council will be giving increased emphasis to targeting the successor generation especially those who are expected to be in positions of influence in future - such as young professionals and post graduate students, at the same time not neglecting the authority generation either.

This change in policy has resulted in significant changes both to the nature of the Council's activities and to the way in which it operates. The changes include an increase in work in governance and human rights and in education especially the education promotion, distance learning and vocational education and the reshaping of information services in response to the changing requirements of target audiences with emphasis on the electronic delivery of information services. Strategic partnerships have also been developed with the organizations that have similar objectives like the British Broadcasting Corporation (BBC) and World Bank. This has resulted in mutual advantage like KLC, a joint programme developed with World Bank in support of the global knowledge agenda.

For the last four or more years, the single most important area of investment in programmes and services has been the development of new IT services which have been used to complement and enhance the Council's core people to people activities like the library and the information centres. The internet is a particularly important vehicle for the Council's work in information provision and this has enabled the Council to reach a much larger audience than what conventional programmes can. Another offshoot of this shift has been the establishment of KLCs that provide a range of facilities including internet access, support for distance learning courses, video conferencing multimedia and book collections. This is again targeted at the young professionals giving them access to resource materials from the UK and supporting the development of professional networks both with UK contacts and with similar groups in other countries.

The implementation or the strategy has involved a substantial amount of change for all Council offices - changes to programmes, to the delivery of the services and to the way in which the Council operates. Given the scale of change, some adverse reaction is inevitable especially from those who are users of services or who have participated in programmes which were discontinued as a part of the policy change. Still the British Council of the future strategy represents an ambitious programme of change and modernisation. Building on the Council's recognised strength, it aims to ensure that the Council is equipped to meet the opportunities and challenges of the 21st century. It is hoped that over the next few years, the Council's operations around the world will be reshaped to create a stronger more effective organisation capable of achieving significantly greater impact for the UK.

Accordingly in India, the country aim is to sustain and reinforce Indo-British relationships by collaboration between institutions and individuals, especially in education, science and technology, the arts and humanities, by managing joint projects for DFID which directly meet India's developmental needs and by providing access to British ideas and achievements". From this the Regional Aim is further derived. For e.g. for South India it is "effectively to display the resources of the Madras office and library and of the British Libraries in Bangalore, Hyderabad and Trivandrum in support of the Country Aim".

This is in fact narrowing of the Country Policy relating it to libraries and education. The policies are thus to contribute to India's development in the fields of education, health, natural resources, management, public administration, science and technology; to provide target groups with what they need and wish to know about Britain through the maintenance of a visible and widespread library network, in itself a prime access system for British information and ideas and through projects and exchanges activity; to increase the number of Indian students in Britain who will, on return, effectively promote Indo-British relations; to promote the use of English for the purpose of technological, economic and social development and to encourage an appreciation of English literature; to satisfy a desire for contemporary interactive British drama, music, painting and sculpture and film events as a means of demonstrating and publicising Britain's cultural vitality to influential Indian target groups. Of these policies stated above, only (2) concerns itself directly with the Council's most successful library network with over 1,00,000 members but constrained by resources like finance, space and present number of locations in the face of potentially limitless demand. The general objectives of the British Council libraries in India and be stated as:

- to provide a ready, comprehensive, up to date book stock for reference and lending service of subjects falling properly in the Council's field in a developing country
- to keep students, postgraduates particularly, in priority areas such as medical services, technology, management, behavioural sciences etc, who use libraries, in touch with recent British development in their fields and
- to support the Council's important work in the teaching of English, conducting British examinations and Indo-British collaborative programmes

The country objective in relation to the libraries is to provide target library with a professionally acceptable level of service by the completion of a stock replenishment programme; concentrating resources on libraries where they are most needed and used by priority groups; to be funded by increased subscriptions, the size of the annual increase depending on an assessment of market opportunities.

From this it would appear that the general objective is to provide a service useful to a developing country. Though the aims of library activities are described satisfactorily in this sort of generalised statement, it does not provide a sufficiently practical tool for the setting of objectives in relation to needs because of insufficient knowledge of these elements and the difficulty in distinguishing between them when allocating resources. In the case of India, the British Council has always misjudged initially but once their assumption is proved incorrect, all steps are taken to set it right. For instance, in the 1980s, when there was a drastic change in the policy, it was decided to close down children's section and downsize the collection in sections like fiction. It was pointed out then that this would not be received well by the Indian users and it was wrong to suppose that the satisfaction of needs could be measured adequately in simple terms such as the number of requests for information or the number of books borrowed.

This takes us to the policy regarding membership and who the target audiences are. From the beginning, there were worries about the nature of readership. Smeaton, who was the Librarian at the initial stages, felt that the target in Delhi should be senior civil servants and specialists and membership subscriptions were fixed at a level deliberately intended to discourage the general reader and the student population.

Even so, Council libraries proved to have a magnetic attraction for both these categories; in 1965, almost a third of the Bombay membership were 'students' and more than a third were 'employed white collar' a category which can be equated with 'general readers'. Teachers and technical professionals were counted separately.

But by 1975, a shift in emphasis has began to be felt - from a general library to a specialist library, with importance to postgraduate and research material, which meant the number of books under fiction would be cut down gradually. Another change was the winding up of the children's section. But around this time a sample of the membership of British

Council Library, Chennai shows that out of the total membership of 13,032, 20% were students 25.4% from the technical and professional class and employed white collar, 23.3%.

3.4. Objectives Relevant To Libraries & the Targets

Library Objectives & Targets, 1992 & 2003/04

Objectives Relevant to Libraries

(1) South India Regional Management Plan 1992/93, prepared by A N Sanderson (MAD/680/6 26 March 1992)

   i) To provide target library members with a professionally acceptable level of service by the completion of a stock replenishment programme, concentrating resources on library where they are most needed and used by priority groups, to be funded by increased subscriptions, the size of the annual increase depending in an assessment of market opportunities

   ii) To increase library or membership by target groups to 80% Target categories to be attracted and retained by usage of IT and distance membership.

   iii) To increase by 20% the number of Indian students in Britain through the proactive education counseling service by the Council and to build and educational promotion element into 20% of incoming exchanges.

(2) Draft Country Plan for India 1999/00 to 200/02

   i) To project the UK's creativity, cultural diversity and recent achievements and to challenge outmoded stereotypes of the UK abroad. For this the Library and information network is to provide access to latest information from and about Britain to the present and future leaders in India's department (Targets library service to 80,000 personal members and 4000 corporate members in Year 1, 75% of personal members from the target audiences by end of Year 2, proactive information service to reach 2000 key contacts in Year 1)

ii) To build the UK's role as a leading provider of educational opportunity for people overseas; for this, to sustain the 20% increase in student recruitment through counselling etc. (**Target 2000**: 6000 Indian students in UK); to expand the range of BEC and other ELT exams in India through out India; to fully administer PLAB for the GMC throughout India, to deliver exams for at least 2 more professional bodies.

iii) To position the UK overseas as a committed partner in tackling key reform agendas and promoting sustainable development. For this library and information network to provide comprehensive access to development information pertaining to India.

Targets & Strategies

(3) India Country Plan 2003 -04

(It is known as strategic theme)

i) To reach more target audience information services on and offline by marketing the newly T3, particularly in colleges and universities, who are the prime focus and by offering online membership to remote users in 26 premier Indian cities

ii) To work with HQ, partners and suppliers in India to develop and refine this offer which will be the primary means of reaching and influencing much larger numbers of the T3 audience in India.

iii) To market services in 11 centres (libraries) to increase membership and renewal rates

iv) To refocus book collection in 11 centres

v) To improve customer service and enquiry management.

3.5. Library Policy in a Nutshell

1. All Council Library and Information Services (LIS) support the Country Plan (CP) policies and thereby the interests of the Council's clients/target audiences. No services or materials are provided which do not support CP policies.
2. All Library and Information Services activities are aimed at some or all of the CP priority groups devised in accordance with Management services Department on specifying priority groups. Initially the libraries were used to capture more partner countries. Later the students were the targets. Then it changed to people in key positions and occupational groups. Now the importance has shifted back to the youth in the 18-35 age group and almost all the services that are provided are aimed primarily at these groups. It will be seen from the Corporate and Country Plans that there is no list of Library and Information Services - Specific priority groups.
3. Some Library and Information Services activity is likely to be aimed at users/Customers of other Council activities. This is clearly evident in the case of ECS and Examinations. When the Prime Minister's Initiative was launched and targets were set, the libraries were also expected to lend support to these activities in those geographical areas with no British Council presence. In such cases, the Library and Information Services support is regularly reviewed by the respective managers of the two services.

4. This also means that Library and Information Services is the main information service for other members of the Council staff whenever it is needed. But care is taken to ensure that there is no service overlap. Though there is co-operation and mutual support, each division has a clear understanding of what is expected and what it is. This kind of demarcation is what has helped the British Council maintain and sustain good relation with Indian Council for Cultural Relations (ICCR) in India. The British Council in India respects the ICCR's role in the British Libraries and is careful not to mix Council activities like exams and distance education with the BL activities in those cities where there is no diplomatic representation. This speaks for the perfect professionalism exhibited by the Council.
5. Regional directors carry out some form of Library and Information Services market analysis annually to improve user profiles, explore customer needs and benefit aspects, identify service weaknesses and promotional opportunities. Survey questionnaires are administered on library users and 'enquirers' and the latter are informed of the findings and of action taken as a result. Similarly period market analysis is done to explore, for instance, the impact of a new service or the needs of non-user priority groups. Before re-introducing the children's section in the British Council Libraries, market analysis was done to test the ground. The information centre at Chandigarh was opened only after getting a very positive feed back and assurance about the need and necessity of such a centre in Chandigarh.
6. From the earlier days, the British Council has realised the importance of cultivating good customer care and for this, continuous contact with user groups is encouraged, particularly through meetings with

segments of the clientele or through newsletter. In order to achieve this, open houses and focus group meetings are organised in the library on a regular basis on the basis of its outcome, changes are made in their services. If there is to be a policy change, the matter is discussed at SLIM (South Indian Librarians Meeting) and the Regional/British Librarians' conference (now known as Library Manager's Meet) and a decision taken.

7. Both the information and recreational needs of priority groups are regularly identified/established and then the managers determine how many of these can be met through Library and Information Services activity and if so, what resources are needed and can be made available. These decisions are later made explicit in internal policy documents and in promotional materials. As for marketing of the Library and Information Services of the priority user groups target audiences is concerned, promotional materials like Library brochures with stress on the benefit of services to the user are produced. These are distinct from the library rules and regulations.

8. The resources allocated to individual library and information centres are also related to Country Plan policies and to performance and are regularly reviewed on these bases. 'Use' is a crucial performance measure for all stock and the aim is to acquire those materials that will contribute to Country Policies and be well used. There is a written collection department policy for each region. The acquisition of materials is planned and budgeted in advance, with allocations relating to the regional priorities.

9. Services provided by the Council Library and Information Services are normally drawn from a list of possible library and information services, which consists of video CDs and home videos, lending of books

and periodicals, enquiry answering services (educational and general), promotion of UK educational opportunities, current awareness bulletins, CD Rom searches of databases, online searches of databases, IT corners, and reservation facility and photocopying. The service mixture depends upon several factors like relevance to CP policies, the findings of market analysis, performance and the availability and effectiveness of local Library and Information Services. For example, in the four regional libraries in Delhi, Kolkata, Chennai and Mumbai home videos are popular where as this service is not available in the British Council Libraries. In the initial stages, video cassettes were lent out only to institutional members. Now, with the advent of CD, the service is offered to individual members as well.

10. As part of customer relations, the full range of Council's Library and Information Services available locally is made known to all members through 'Know Your Library' sessions. Formerly the British Council Libraries used to have a video presentation, 'What is your library?' before KYL but now the library is introduced to the newcomers through power point presentations. This helps the user to shed his/her inhibitions in knowing more about the library services on offer and this leads to more utilization of library materials and also to customer satisfaction.

11. There is also a procedure for users to suggest improvements to services and even a complaints procedure. All the British Council Libraries in India have a Complaints and Suggestions box displayed at a very prominent place in the library and all are looked into. This is a very effective feedback mechanism and by attending to this, the user/consumer is also made to feel that he is important to the library/British

Council and also that it is his library. This identification with the library goes a long way in promoting the British Council Libraries in India.

12. Library opening hours also reflect user needs as identified in market analysis. The British Council Libraries used to have a lengthy lunch break in the 1970s but this was found to be very inconvenient for the users especially students. As a result, the library came to be kept open continuously from 11am to 7pm on five days a week, from Tuesday to Saturday. The five-day-norm has again been changed now due to the persistent demand from library members and now the libraries in India are open from Monday to Saturday. But in Bangalore, Delhi and Mumbai the timings are different because of the weather conditions and the distance factor. This has forced them to open and close early.
13. As for Council stock, till very recently, it was essentially restricted to British materials. All the materials were expected to have a substantial British contribution in them. But now, again, owing to the demand from users, the British Council Libraries in India have strong 'India collection' sections stacked with books in subjects relevant to India, by Indian authors and published in India. This is also a part of the British Council strategy to attract more young people to the Council and to increase the membership which again is an objective in the CP for 2004 - 2005. BookFind is recommended for book selection and publishers' catalogues are not normally recommended as basic selection tools.
14. Policy recommends that each year a number of stock revisions be planned in subjects related to interests of priority user groups. Multiple copies are ordered only in those cases where there is a constant and continuous

demand for standard work; Reference books are also included in subject stock revisions. Similarly, materials in poor condition or that are obsolete or have not been loaned in the previous two years, are withdrawn from the stock and this weeding and trimming of stock is also a continuous process. Another policy is that annual withdrawals should roughly equal annual additions. In a library which contains absolute stock or where use rates are very low, annual withdrawals can be double annual additions. This means that while the British Council Libraries will always have a fixed number of books in the collection at the same time, due to stringent stock editing, the library will always be stacked with up-to-date information, a factor which is very much appreciated by the library users. This also saves physical space.

15. The weeded out materials were formerly presented to nearby library or educational institutions. Now, they are being sold at a much subsidised rate to the members. This has been the result of a reassessment of the former policy in view of funding shortages. It was decided that the practice of making large-scale presentations of books and periodicals using British Council operational money was not a good one especially when there were financial crunch every year and it was finally decided to sell them to interested members, bringing in revenue for the Council that could be utilised for buying more materials for the library itself.

16. Performance measurement is another key aspect of the British Council policy and it is applied to the library as well. A large amount of library statistics is compiled locally, including local records of membership and use, broken down in a way which relates to priority user groups / targets audiences.

Library and Information Services performance indicators are divided into effectiveness and efficiency. The indicators for the former are the number of library members from priority groups; % of CP priority groups who are library members; average number of loans per item per annum; % of total enquires received from priority groups renewal rate of priority group members, number of key contact library members, by name and status, average number of current awareness uses per periodical per week; column inches of publicity about British Council LIS in newspapers/professional journals; its amount of time of publicity received TV/radio and average number of users in the library. Efficiency is gauged on the basis of net cost of library service per library member, number of enquiries handled per staff hour on enquiry points, % of library and information service costs recovered from revenue, % of enquiries answered in two working days of receipt and book stock withdrawals as a % of book stock additions. Such regular and systematic assessment forces the libraries to maintain certain standards all the time.

17. Fee levels and charges for all Library and Information Services are also periodically reviewed to ensure that they maximise revenue while not damaging the delivery of services. In fixing fees, charges are compared other local indicators and fees are normally increased annually in tune with increases in local inflation rates. Similarly charges for photocopies are also fixed at the top of local commercial rates. A sliding scale of fines is also imposed for late return of library books and other materials is fixed at a rate high enough to later non-return.

In the past, the Council had tried to provide a surrogate lending service for the general reader educated in English.

The core collection over the years has been adapted to serve the needs of the student. It has also tried to reflect the various strands of Britain's department aid to India. In his report, Cavaliero gives an accurate self-analysis: "It [The British Council] has tried to do too many things and has ended by doing none of them very well. We have to admit that membership is random. There has been scant liaison with other major British Council programmes, the department of reference collections has been differently pursued in the regions, book exhibitions have pre-empted too much time in relation to results, there has been very little interaction with the public sector library scene in India and we do not know very clearly what its resources are. We have by our very oasis-like qualities allowed the libraries to settle into not very impressive simulation of public libraries in Britain".

4. POLICY AND PERFORMANCE: FINDINGS

As for how policy formulation was shaped by changing needs in Higher Education sector in India, it was necessary to critically analyse the policy of the British Council in general and that with regards to its libraries in particular. On the basis of this, the roles played by the British Council Libraries in promoting higher education in India could be studied. In addition to this, the Code of Practice for libraries as formulated by the British Council was also studied and the findings are given below. It shows what the Code of Practice / Country Plan want to achieve with respect to various facets of library and information services and what the survey says. Policy stipulated in Code of Practice / Country Plan with regards to each aspect is given in bold letters and the corresponding survey finding is given in italics.

- **All Council LIS to support Country Plan (CP) policies and thereby the interests of the Council's client.** The users, T3 and T4 of the Country Plan, get what they want.

- **Number of library members from priority groups should be more and LIS activity is to be aimed at some or the entire CP priority groups.** There are more from the priority groups and their percentage is more. They are satisfied with the LIS but want more services.
- **LIS should meet the needs of priority groups.** Satisfied but need to be educated on how to utilize them to the maximum.
- **There should be continuous contact with user groups through user education and focus group meetings.** But respondents do not seem to be very familiar with these programmes.
- **Resources allocated should be related CP policies and performance.** They are used very extensively by students and to a lesser extent by teachers in higher education.
- **LIS should be continuously and systematically promoted to priority user groups.** There are more new members among the priority user groups. Renewal rate of Priority Group members is also high and there are many members with long duration of membership
- **Materials that contribute to country policies should be acquired.** Library materials are well used.
- **There should be a written collection development policy.** Collection well-used and this is proof of its effectiveness
- **Comfortable environment should be provided.** Satisfied; Rating high
- **A checklist of possible library and information services is given.** Satisfied; but they want more services to be introduced
- **In non-educational counselling service centres,**

libraries should handle the queries. But this does not seem to be very effective; not much demand

- **Libraries to have a consistent policy for the use of back numbers of periodicals.** Use of journals is satisfactory ; students use them more
- **Use of CD-Rom and / or online services should be considered in subject areas when existing use or market research has revealed a demand for information in this form.** CD use high especially among students; online services yet to pick up; meaningful internet use is yet to take place.
- **Reservation service is an essential feature of a good Council Library.** Facility much used and appreciated by the users
- **There should normally be a library photocopier for providing copies but without violating copyright laws.** Users are satisfied; use percentage is high.
- **The full range of LIS services available locally should be made known to all new members.** Not enough awareness about the programme. More user education needed for better use of resources and services.
- **Library opening hours should as far as possible reflect user needs.** Users are still not satisfied.
- **Council stock (books, periodicals, videos etc.) should essentially be restricted to British materials.** Demand for publications from other countries.
- **Stock should reflect the customer's needs.** Satisfied with the collection as evidenced by their borrowal pattern and rating; still want more non-British and Indian books
- **Weeding of stock should be a continuous process.** Users not happy; shows British Council Libraries have to be more careful - not seem to know the demand.

- **The premises should meet the standards required by British or local health and safety legislation, whichever are the more stringent.** Given excellent rating
- **Plans for LIS premises should ensure that there is easy user access to resources and equipment.** Users do not agree. Congestion is cited as one of the problems hindering easy access; Libraries should separate busy areas from quiet areas (for study and reading)
- **In the Council libraries, there should be some tables and seating for study purposes and some casual seating, the proportion that of will depend upon their respective use by priority groups.** Users do not feel it is adequate - suggest more seating and more 'quiet' and more space for internet browsing.
- **Catalogues for library books and other holdings should be obtained through OPAC.** OPAC is there but use of OPAC is not much.
- **The usual Council loan for books should be 3 weeks and the average loan period for home videos should be not more than one week.** But the users want more time (4 weeks.)
- **A sliding scale of fines should be imposed for late return of library books and other materials and be fixed at a rate high enough to deter and non-return.** But users feel it is high and want it to be reduced.

It is clear that British Council Libraries contribute to India's development in the field of education

- by providing students and teachers in the Higher Education with what they need; this is done through the maintenance of a visible and widespread library work in India. Appropriate resources are concentrated on libraries where they are most needed and used by priority groups that include students from the Higher Education sector.

- by providing the students, especially postgraduate and professional students, with a stock designed to meet their education and information needs; the stock is replenished and updated regularly for this purpose.
- by providing quality information for study and for professional updating through books, journals, CDs, websites etc;
- by providing library members, which include students of higher education sector, with a professionally acceptable level of service; In addition to the traditional services like reference and lending, online services are also provided to them through the network which are beneficial to students, especially those doing postgraduates and research;
- by making services more user- oriented;
- by developing library resources as identified through various surveys and other feed back mechanisms; information and thought content (primarily of British origin) are made accessible to the right people (including postgraduate and professional students) at the appropriate time and are adequate and up-to-date enough to be effective; and
- by providing access to online and managed learning opportunities which are affordable and work - related.

The findings evolved out of the study have thus substantiated the objectives derived and tested logically the tenability of the hypotheses formulated at the beginning of the study.

5. SUGGESTIONS FOR IMPROVEMENT

The study reveals some areas the British Council has to pay special attention to.

1. The British Council Libraries should have a clear vision about what they are supposed to do and what they can do. Going by the aims and goals presented in the Country Plans and Corporate Plans, the picture that emerges is that of a library which tries to do so many things at the same time. It is true that now it at least seems to have a clear definition about its target groups. The libraries should be given enough time to consolidate their gains due to a particular change, evaluate and modify them before they are pushed on to another change.
2. Though almost all the members have a high opinion about the British Council Library, it is seen that many of them do not have a holistic picture of the library. Effective user education is the only solution to this problem. Upholding their image as information providers and keeping in tune with their educational role, the British Council Libraries can think of starting information skills programmes for their student members. Even research and postgraduate students have doubts about their skill levels in word processing, knowledge of application software packages and they are overwhelmed with the range of databases, e-prints, e-text and e-journals. This programme can be evolved to remove such misgivings and also meet the changing skills requirements. Strategies adopted in the sessions can include keeping up-to-date with new services and instruction in the use of bibliographic software packages. This can be an advanced version of the present 'Know Your Library session'.
3. Even the 'Know Your Library' sessions can be made more frequent, say, once in two weeks and the attendance at these sessions has to be monitored. The session's content can be improved and modified to include tips on internet searching, effective search

strategies and how to use OPAC effectively. This will lead to maximum utilization of library facilities and resources, thus justifying the 'tax payers' money spent in procuring them.

4. The evolving information and technology environment is creating many changes and opportunities in higher education. Being a provider, shaper and generator of knowledge, the British Council Libraries in India can utilise their IT environment, to set up something along the line of the Global Enquiries Project[1]. This will facilitate enquiry handling via bulletin boards, similar to the bulletin board currently run by British Council, China[2].

5. More publicity has to be given to the online databases the British Council Libraries offer to their members. The online services provided by the British Council Libraries seem to be underused or it may be that one never knows what are being used by remote access. Such services were introduced due to the realisation that students of today do not have the mindset to browse among books for reference. But they are to be educated properly on how to use them. British Council Library has to help the students gain the skills necessary to negotiate an increasingly complex digital maze.

6. If the British Council Library really wants to support and facilitate the information and education needs of its T3 user group in Higher Education, it has to become more student-friendly. This can be done by (1) using the website to communicate news about collections and exhibitions, including recommended and new items; (2) by creating constantly changing small exhibitions (for eg. books of the week, website of the day etc.), particularly when these create opportunities for dialogue with users; (3) by video conferencing with

some 'high achievers'; and (4) by developing a proactive information service like e-news alert service being done in British Council, Pakistan[3]

7. Creativity and personality of the students can be developed by the British Council Library by making the already - existing culture cafés, poetry clubs and readers clubs more active. This will help to promote the reading habit among students. Chat clubs can be floated under its leadership. A presentation by one of the library staff, a teacher or a guest speaker can be arranged. Students and even outsiders can attend and participate in the lively discussions based on current affairs, political and other topical issues. This will be very useful to students especially those preparing for competitive exams and will also help them sharpen their critical thinking skills.

8. In Knowledge and Learning Centres (KLCs), the Distance Learning Zones already exist through which the British Council Libraries offer learning support on behalf of selected UK Universities with distance education programmes. But this benefits only a small section of students in Higher Education sector due to the joining cost, insufficient databases and the limited number. of 'free' resources. To overcome this problem, new services can be thought of like developing the general service for students (like Internet and electronic journals) into a more focused and modern research service for the growing number of postgraduate students. This can be done by delivering the resources to the student's own home by databases, websites, e-mails, telephone and even by post. The libraries can this way act as virtual libraries, not bound to bricks and mortar and off-site database will be very popular with students. This service can be two-fold: an initial induction and training on research methodology

and use of databases can be followed by personalized support to the students research needs. Information profiling of the members/users of the service can be updated by e-mail.

Assistance can be offered to individuals for keyword searching based on e-mail request forms. The British Council Library, Kuala Lumpur (Malaysia) has already introduced a similar service and this can be tried out in India also for the benefit of the students in Higher Education here.

9. The membership of the British Council Libraries shows a smaller figure when compared to University Library and Public Library. But it has been seen that with limited resources and limited members, the British Council Library still has more number of issues to its credit. The low number may be attributed to the wilful measures adopted by the British Council to keep it that way. But the Country Plan as well as Strategy 2005 has come out with clear definitions about target groups. In order to reach more people from these groups, the British Council Library should take the initiative to publicize the library and its services among the academic and student communities. Visits to colleges should be arranged and personal interaction with students should be established to achieve this.

10. Study in Britain should also be given enough awareness and publicity among the students.

11. An oft-repeated complaint against the British Council Libraries is that they are urbanized and cater only to 'high society' people. It is true that the British Council Libraries are all located in important cities in India. Because of this, the libraries' out reach is limited and they may not be reaching as many people as they should, especially from the Higher Education sector. Academic libraries are there all over India whereas

there are only 11 British Council Libraries that aim at the users of academic libraries. This can be solved by opening new centres along the lines of the British Council USA Education Service which has 5 members of staff and no public access. 99% of their target audiences are online. These centres can offer services like the Virtual Study Abroad Adviser, the FAQ Knowledge Base Application and a targeted monthly e-zine which can combine advice, useful information and links to website. These centres can be linked to local academic libraries and the British Council Library can thus benefit many a student.

12. One group that has been left out owing to the importance placed on T3 is T4, to which teachers belong. Higher Education covers both the teacher and the taught. It has been found that the teachers still depend on other sources to satisfy their education and information needs. The British Council Libraries can make it more useful to the teaching community by strengthening and supplementing the collection accordingly.
13. British Council is an international organization that places much value on customer care and feedback. In its endeavour to improve the performance; the British Council / British Council Libraries always administer a minimum of three questionnaires on its members. They have been doing this for long and for the same reason, it has become a ritual now. To connect needs to resources and services, the questionnaires have to become more effective.
14. British Council should also keep in touch with the universities in the locality / area, study the curriculum and provide what is relevant. Libraries and librarians are key players in facilitating student learning in higher education. This makes it imperative that the libraries

resources and services should be effective in aiding students learning and supporting the research activities of staff and students. Thus there should be a fruitful partnership between library and academic staff to foster students' information literacy. If British Council Libraries were to serve T3 user groups well, British Council should have its pulse on the Higher Education curriculum. Since the librarians have the freedom to choose their materials, they can build their collections according to the local needs. This is possible only if the British Council Libraries have a fairly good idea about the Higher Education scenario of their part of India. They can also establish closer links with libraries Higher Education sector, thus becoming learner - centred rather than institution-centred.

6. AREAS FOR FURTHER RESEARCH

1. There remains a glaring lack of research on the effect the library environment has on students' educational gains or outcomes. Most studies on libraries are related to the effectiveness of the services provided and not designed **to assess how the services affect students' cognitive and affective outcomes. Such a study can be taken up in the context of British Council Libraries to assess their actual contribution to education and students.**
2. Electronic resource provision is clearly the most significant are for future research. This is seen to link to the key issue of supporting teaching and learning which is becoming increasingly important, due to the number of new developments such as personalised e-learning and managed learning environments. Since British Council Libraries have introduced these new concepts through the KLCs, this will be an apt area of

research. One of the main issues surrounding electronic services and resources is their expense and librarians are keen to make sure that they are using their budgets effectively. There is a concern about **the impact of electronic resources, particularly in comparison to traditional library resources.** How many people are using these, what effect this will [illegible] on libraries, usage patterns, especially access from off-site, student preferences and digitisation of special collections are all important areas for research in this respect.

3. British Council Libraries have only British books and only English books in its collection. This is the physical manifestation of the BC's 'cultural diplomacy'. In this context, it will be worthwhile to study the sharing of cultural experiences as promoted through the physical manifestation of the British Council's 'cultural diplomacy'. In this context, it will be worthwhile to study **the sharing of cultural experiences as promoted through the physical manifestation of the British Council's cultural diplomacy'.** Though a comparison of previous figures shows a decline in the number of users of British Council Libraries world wide, the number is on the increase in India.

7. CONCLUSION

Policy is about choice. Policies are deliberate choices or decisions that guide actions and influence outcomes. Organizations have policies, which guide such matters as personal decisions and interactions with the media. Libraries typically have internal policies, which guide collection development and service priorities. Library policies are traditionally informed by principles or intellectual freedom and by their own facet or implicit mission statement. In other words, choices made by library decision-makers are presumed to facilitate, rather than restrict access to information and to advance the library's ability to serve its clients.

By its very nature, the Council has offered library development with both cultural and material 'strings' attached. Its aim, after all, is to project the values of the former imperial power and it has a quite undisguised interest in promoting relevant British goods and services. Still it is remarkable that the Council should have played the part that it has in post-colonial library development. It is a tribute to the decentralized 'flexibility' of the Council that such practical assistance to library development can continue to be given not as part of a fomal aid programme but within the context of its own library work. The overall picture of this work is neither small nor simple, involving as it currently does the running of around 220 overseas libraries and information centres. This is system which is the biggest of its kind in the world today. To combine the running of a worldwide operation of such a size with the ability to respond to widely differing local needs and opportunities presents a considerable challenge but it is one to which the Council has risen with conspicuous success in the past.

As the present day corporate and Country Plans show, things have changed now when compared to the British Council of earlier days. There is a clearer vision about what the Council stands for, how the various units have to function without encroaching into one another and though the word 'libraries' is missing from the plans, information work has taken pre-dominance and whether it is openly admitted or not, libraries still have a special place in the academic and administrative psyche in India. This shows that the libraries are much more than what meets the ordinary eye. By providing quality service and by being selective and specific about its target audiences, the libraries have naturally become the vibrant, local points for the Council to interact with people who matter and to promote Britain unobtrusively.

REFERENCES

1. LISMIS. Annual Report for India. 2003/2004.
2. Sanderson, Arthur N (1992) to Kevin Spears. MAD/3130/3/ 23 March,. 2.
3. Edmund Marsden in Country Plan, India.2003-2004
4. www.britishcouncil.org
5. Flood, R.A.(1974) Official organizations. Proceedings of the International & Comparative Librarianship Conference, Scotland,. 53-7.
6. www.britishcouncil.org retrieved on 25 January 2006
7. Coombs, D.(1988) Spreading the word: the library work of the British Council. London: Mansell Publishing, (Information Adviser Series). 275.
8. Parker, J.S. The overseas library consultant. Library Review no. 28, pp.214-25
9. Sanderson, A.N. (1992) MAD/680/6 26 March
10. www.britishcouncilindia.org retrieved on 20 June 2007
11. The British Council - 2005 Strategy. British Council, 2003.
12. Sanderson, Arthur N.(1992) South India Regional Management plan, 1992/93. MAD/680/6. 26 March.
13. Devanally, D.K.(1981) 'MBO Techniques in British Council Libraries'. A paper presented at the Staff Training Course, New Delhi, 16-27 March. 4.
14. Chief Librarian's Reports, 1965, 1966 and 1967. IND/260/20, vol. V.
15. Silver Jubilee celebration: Yeoman Service of the British Council Libraries. The Mail 6 Oct 1975
16. British Council. Strategy 2010. British Council, 2003
17. Country Plan (India) 2003-04. British Council, 2003
18. DATS Quality Manual Version 4 issue 1
19. Coombs, D.(1988) Spreading the word: the library work of

the British Council. London: Mansell Publishing, (Information Adviser Series). p.275

20. Saunders, W.L. and Broome, E.M.(1977) The Library and Information Services of the British Council: a review undertaken by Professor W. L. Saunders and E. M. Broome. London: British Council.
21. Chief Librarian's Reports, 1965, 1966 and 1967. IND/260/20, vol. V.
22. British Council Archives. Libraries - policy. GEN/265/1, vols. I - III.
23. Book selection. DEL/265/1 from Minister, Cultural Affairs, India. 20 Feb. 1989
24. Spears, Kevin (1989) Book Selection. DEL/265/1, 20 Feb.
25. Suseela Kumar (1998) Five decades of the British Council Libraries in India. In: Fifty Years of Library and Information Services in India. Ed. by Rajaraman.-Bangalore: Institute of Advance Information Studies, 107-124.
26. Bhat, M.Ishwara.(2002) Effectiveness of marketing of information in British Council Library network. PhD Thesis, Karnataka University, Dharwad.
27. Subramoni, T.K (1992) Discarding library collections. ILA Bulletin, vol.xxvii, No.4 Jan-March 157-160.

11

Role of Library Associations for the Professional Development of Librarians

Dr. A Gopikuttan
Hima P R

1. INTRODUCTION

Associations are powerful forces representing the voice of the professional community to solve the problems related to the welfare, status, working conditions, physical facilities, education and training including the research and development activities. They act as a backbone of the professional development. Social, political, economic and educational factors have a major share in the flourishment of the Associations. Associations are considered as a yardstick for measuring the problems and needs of professionals.

Library Association's are professional organization that aims to bring together library and information professionals to share ideas, interest and any other related matters.

Library associations help the librarians and information professionals to build up themselves time befitting for the century. In every country, there are many professional library associations to promote the library education and library related activities in that country. Many library associations play a vital role in the growth and development of the profession. Very often they arrange different types of seminars, conferences, training programs etc. Indeed the growth of librarianship is closely concerned with the development of professional library associations.

Pervaiz and Rehman (2007) points out that library organization connect library profession and professionals. These organizations include associations, groups and forums. Punjab Library Association is the first library association in Pakistan. At present there are 11 such organizations in the Punjab province of Pakistan. The paper concludes with their contribution for the foundation of librarianship in the province and the country.

Karisiddappa (2002) argues that professional associations, societies, academies and foundations form a backbone of the professional development. He points out that the social, political, economic and educational factors have a major share in the flurishment of associations. This paper presents a brief outline of the existing scenario of the library associations in India. It is seen that, in the recent years the associations at the national level are striving hard to make their presence felt and convincing the professionals that they have some role to play in the library development programme.

They bring together librarians providing them an opportunity for:-

- intercommunication of ideas through conferences, congresses, symposia and workshops and its publications

- serve as a platform for general discussion of problems related to library theory, practice and teaching
- wake it possible to crystallize ideas in relation to library and society
- help to build up library movement
- take steps towards professionalism
- interaction with society
- co-operate with other organizations for the advancement of Library and Information Science
- popularize libraries
- conduct research to advance frontiers of knowledge
- provide financial support for research in Library and Information Science
- confer distinctions / fellowships / prizes etc on its members in recognition of their contribution to librarianship
- organize continuing education programmes
- support professional causes
- lay down standards for various aspects of librarianship
- do everything possible for the status and welfare of its members.

The library associations are professional associations, the basic purpose of which is to speak and act for the profession as a whole in the fields of common profession as a whole in the field of common professional interests such as the question of revision of grades and enhancement of professional status; formulating library legislation; publication of library journal; compiling, maintaining, updating and publishing library directories; creating library consciousness and awareness among the people; organizing educational programmes, training courses, conferences, symposiums and committees on topics of general interests etc.

2. ROLE OF LIBRARY ASSOCIATIONS FOR THE DEVELOPMENT OF LIBRARY PROFESSION

A single person or an institution cannot do much to deal with wider and far reaching issues of concerned profession. For this, a collective action by interested group is necessary. These collective actions can only be done by associations, which are called Professional Associations. These association serve as a forum for coordinated efforts for their concerned professions. Professional associations are made up of by and for the professionals of the concerned field.

Library Associations are also professional associations, the main objective of which is to foster a spirit of public service among their members, promote library services, project the interests of their members and build up the image of the library profession. They indeed assist in clarifying concepts of libraries and also present appropriate proposals to right quarters. Because the library associations are formed for all side development of libraries and library personnels, these associations play a vital role regarding library profession as follows :-

1. The main aim of library association is to promote library movement in the country to spread knowledge and information .For this, they interact with governments from time to time for the development of library system by advising, representing and helping in drafting legislation, policy statements, guidelines etc.
2. Library associations make the people conscious towards the utility of the libraries .So the people may demand their rights for accessing to public library services and may mobilize social pressure for healthy development of library services.
3. These associations strive for an evolution of an integrated library and information system at national

level based on the national policy.

4. These associations bring the attention of authorities to defects, distortions in the existing library infrastructure.
5. They also provide a common forum for library professionals for the exchange of their information, ideas, experiences and expertise etc.
6. These associations work for the betterment of salaries, grades, service conditions of library staff and also for improving their status in the society.
7. These also work towards sharing of resources and avoiding duplication of efforts among the libraries.
8. These also contribute towards the development of manpower for library and information work, for which they arrange education and training programmes for library personnels.
9. These hold the image of library profession high in the society and promote cooperation among libraries and among the professionals of the libraries.

3. BRIEF HISTORY OF THE LIBRARY ASSOCIATIONS

According to the literature library associations dates as far back as nineteenth century, with the establishment of The Library Association (LA) on 5th October 1877, to extend and improve library service and librarianship in UK.It is said to be the first one in the world, which was formed as a result of the first International Conference of Librarians held at the London Institute. Later its name was changed in 1896 to Library Association. Since that time other associations developed gradually as the need arise in different regions of the world. However, some developed faster while some are still lacking behind. Now again the name of the association was changed after the merger of LA with Institute of Information Science and adapted the new name from 2002 onwards as CILIP: the Chartered Institute of Library and Information Professionals.

There are a number of library associations at international level that are engaged in the promotion of library and documentation services. A few of these have earned high reputation due to their wide range and qualitative activities. A few well known international library associations are:-

1. The Library Association(Later Changed the name as CILIP) (1877)
2. American Library Association(1876)
3. International Federation for Information and Documentation(1895)
4. Special Libraries Association(1909)
5. International Federation of Library Associations and Institutions(1927)
6. American Society for Information Science and Technology(1937)
7. Canadian Library Association(1946)

4. LIBRARY ASSOCIATIONS IN INDIA

Development of library associations in India is different from that of development of such associations in other countries . In other countries, national level library associations developed first, but in India some state level associations emerged prior to the formation of the first national level library association namely Indian Library Association(ILA).

4.1. Prominent Library Associations in India with cite address

1. Indian Library Association(ILA)
   http://www.ila-india.org/

2. Indian Association of Special Libraries and Information Centers(IASLIC) http: / /www.iaslic 1955.org/
3. Society for Information Science(SIS) http: / /sis-india.netfirms.com/
4. Developing Library Network(DELNET) http: / /delnet.nic.in/
5. Information and Library Network(INFLIBNET) http: / /www.inflibnet.ac.in/
6. Kerala Library Association http: / /www.keralalibraryassociation.org/
7. Gujarat Library Association[Gujarat Granthalaya-Seva Sangh-GGSS] http: / /ggss.org.in/
8. Madras Library Association http: / /www.accel-india.com/ mala/
9. Bengal Library Association http: / /www.blacal.org/
10. Delhi Library Association[DLA] http: / /www.dlaindia.org/
11. Ahmedabad Library Network[ADINET] http: / /www.alibnet.org
12. Bombay Science Librarian's Association[BOSLA] http: / /www.bosla.org.in/
13. Mysore Library Network[MYLIBNET] http: / /www.mylibnet.org/
14. Indian Theological Library Association http: / /www.geocities.com/ itla_in/home.html
15. Society for Advancement of Library and Information Science[SALIS] http: / /autolib-india.net/ salis.html

Library Association is recognized as a Professional Association. They undertake a variety of activities to take a review of the professional needs, advancement of knowledge and to contribute to the advancement of Library and Information Science. With the view of these things, we can say that a library association could be treated as a professional Association working for the professional development of its members.

Membership in Professional Library Association

Opinion	No: of respondents	Percentage
Yes	81	73.64
No	29	26.36
Total	**110**	**100**

5. STATEMENT OF THE PROBLEM

Title of this study is "*Role of Library Associations for the professional development of Librarians*".

6. DEFINITION OF KEYTERMS

6.1. Library associations

Library Associations are associations which work for the better organization of libraries and also for the advancement of librarianship.

6.2. Professional Devalopment

Professional development can be defined as adopting new attitudes and skills in the field to become effective and efficient.

6.3. Librarians

One who has the care of a library and its contents, selecting the books, documents and non-book materials which comprise its stock, and providing information and loan services to meet the needs of its users.

7. OBJECTIVES

The study has the following objectives:

1. To find out the present strength of library professionals in the library associations
2. To examine the extend of professional development programmes organized by the library associations.
3. To check whether the library associations work for the betterment of salaries, grades, service conditions, status etc of library professionals.
4. To find out whether the associations succeeded in bringing out the attention of authorities regarding professional issues of librarians.
5. To ascertain whether the library associations succeeded in bringing its members into close relation with one another.

8. METHODOLOGY

For the purpose of the study, data were collected from three categories of libraries such as academic, public and special. For convenience 65 questionnaires are circulated among the academic libraries and 59 (90.76 %) responses are received; 30 questionnaires are distributed among the public libraries and 25 (83.33%) responses are received; 30 questionnaires are circulated among the special libraries and 26(86.66%) responses are received.The details of the rate of response related to the collection of data under this study was given in Table on next page.

The methodology chosen for conducting this study consists of questionnaire method and literature survey.

i. Questinnaire

A questionnaire is a written document listing a series of questions pertaining to the problems under study, to which the investigator requires the answers. It is given,send or

Rate of response

Type of library	Questionnaires distributed	Responses received	Percentage
Academic	65	59	90.76
Public	30	25	83.33
Special	30	26	86.66
Total	**125**	**110**	**88**

mailed to respondents.

ii. Literature Survey

A bibliography relating to a specific subject and listing a material either in a given collection, or in more than one library, or of literature on the subject is called a literature survey.

9. HYPOTHESES

The hypotheses related to this study are:

1. Professional associations are very much helpful for the betterment of service benefits and to improve the status of the library professionals.
2. Professional associations are useful to provide co-operation among library professionals.

10. SIGNIFICANCE OF THE STUDY

The present study is intended to get a clear idea about the role played by the library associations for the professional development of librarians. No such study has so far been conducted recently. In such a context the present study is more relevant.

11. LIMITATIONS

Due to time limitation the study is focused on some of the selected libraries in the Thiruvananthapuram district of Kerala

12. FINDINGS AND CONCLUSION

The study has revealed a number of useful findings. The major findings are summed up here. These findings are significant indicators of the role played by the library associations for the professional development of librarians.

The analysis of data collected has brought out a number of useful findings. The major findings are summed up here.

12.1. Membership in Professional Library Association

Membership in Professional Library Association

Sl.No:	Name of Association	No: of respondents	Percentage
1	KLA	69	56.09
2	KELPRO	23	18.69
3	ILA	4	3.25
4	IASLIC	10	8.13
5	IATLIS	1	0.82
6	SALIS	6	4.88
7	Others	10	8.14
	Total	**123**	**100**

From the table it is seen that 69 (56.09%) of the respondents have membership in KLA; 23(18.69%) of the respondents have membership in KELPRO; 4 (3.25%) of the respondents have membership in ILA;10 (8.13%) of the respondents have membership in IASLIC; 1(0.82%) of the respondents have membership in IATLIS; 6 (4.88%) of the respondents have membership in SALIS; and 10(8.14%) respondents have membership in other professional associations

(1) Most of the library professionals are members in one or more of the professional associations.

(2) 73.64% respondents have membership in any of the professional library associations.

(3) 26.36% respondents did not have membership in any of the professional associations.

(4) 56.09% of the respondents have membership in Kerala Library Association (KLA)

(5) 18.69% of the respondents have membership in KELPRO

(6) 3.25% of the respondents have membership in ILA

(7) 8.13% of the respondents have membership in IASLIC

(8) 0.82% of the respondents have membership in IATLIS

(9) 4.88% of the respondents have membership in SALIS

(10) 8.14% respondents have membership in other professional associations.

12.2. Membership in any LIS User's Group

(1) 64.55 % of the library professionals does not have membership in any of the LIS User's Group.

(2) 35.45 % are users of any of the LIS User's Group.

(3) 32.87 % are users of LIS-FORUM

(4) 21.92 percentage are users of nmlis

(5) 21.92 percentage are users of iatlis

(6) 20.55 percentage are users of oadl

(7) 2.74 percentage are users of other LIS User Groups.

12.3. Betterment of salaries, service benefits and improving the status of librarians

(1) 62.73% respondents are of the opinion that library association's work for the betterment of salaries, service benefits and improving the status of librarians.

(2) 37.27% respondents feels that associations fails to work for the betterment of salaries, service benefits and improving the status of library professionals.

12.4. Organization of educational programmes

(1) 73.63% are of the opinion that most of the library associations organize educational programmes

frequently

(2) 26.37% of the respondents disagree with this.

12.5. Professional development programmes

Out of the 110 respondents, 73(66.37%) had attended the professional development programmes organized by the associations and the rest of them, that is 37(33.63 %) had never attended any type of professional development programmes in their professional life. Given below

Professional development programmes

Responses	No: of respondents	Percentage
Yes	73	66.37
No	37	33.63
Total	110	100

(1) 66.37 % had attended the professional development programmes organized by the associations

(2) 33.63 % had never attended any type of professional development programmes in their professional life

(3) Majority of the respondents that is 37.96% attend seminars and conferences and its attendance is greater than other professional development programmes.

(4) 22.22% respondents attended workshops

(5) 11.57% respondents attended refresher courses

(6) 20.37% respondents attend training programmes

(7) 7.88% respondents attended other professional development programmes including lectures organized by the library associations.

Participation of members in the professional development programmes organized by the library associations is given in table 4.13 . It is seen that majority of the respondents that is 82(37.96%) attend seminars and conferences and its attendance is greater than other professional development programmes. 48(22.22%)

respondents attended workshops; 25(11.57%) respondents attended refresher courses; 44(20.37%) respondents attend training programmes and 17(7.88%) respondents attended other professional development programmes including lectures organized by the library associations.

Participation in professional development programmes

Sl. No.	Type of programmes	Attendance 1-5 times	6-10 times	11-15 times	More than 15 times	Total	Per-centage
1	Seminars/ Conferences	58	18	4	2	82	37.96
2	Workshops	39	9	0	0	48	22.22
3	Refresher Courses	17	7	1	0	25	11.57
4	Training Programmes	34	9	1	0	44	20.37
5	Others	9	6	2	0	17	7.88
	Total	**157**	**49**	**8**	**2**	**216**	**100**

12.6. Ranking of usefulness of the professional development programmes

(1) Among the various programmes, the respondents gave first place to Seminars

(2) Second place to Refresher Courses

(3) Third place to In-house training

(4) Fourth place to Workshops

(5) Fifth place to Formal Courses

(6) Sixth place to Vendor demonstration

(7) Seventh place to Conferences

(8) Eighth place to other professional development programmes.

12.7. Usefulness of the programmes organized by the professional associations

(1) 75.45% respondents feels that the Programmes organized by the professional associations are useful in nature

(2) 19.09 % of the respondents finds that these programmes are not at all useful for their professional development

(3) 5.46% of the respondents did not respond to this question.

12.8. Sponsorship / Financial assistance from the library association for acquiring professional qualification

(1) 2.73 % professionals got financial support from the associations for acquiring professional qualifications

(2) But 97.27% didn't get any financial support.

12.9. Publication of the association

(1) 53.63% respondents got journals/newsletters published by the associations

(2) But 43.63% of them agreed that they didn't get any journals /newsletters

(3) 2.73% of them did not respond to this question.

12.10. Managing the Professional issues

(1) 54.54 % respondents are of the opinion that the professional associations fails to bring out the attention of authorities regarding the professional issues.

(2) But 40% of the respondents are satisfied with the current working of associations regarding the professional issues

(3) 5.46% of the respondents are not responded to this question.

12.11. Co-operation among the library professionals

Co-operation and professional respect are essential among the members of library association. Most of the associations helps to sustain good relations among the librarians and library professionals .Associations role in promoting co-operation among the librarians and library professionals is clear from table 4.19. It is seen that 77 (70%) respondents are of the opinion that associations are helpful in promoting the co-operation among the library professionals but 29(26.37%) disagree with this and 4(3.63%) members have not responded to this question.

Co-operation among the library professionals

Responses	No: of respondents	Percentage
Yes	77	70
No	29	26.37
Not responded	4	3.63
Total	**110**	**100**

(1) 70% respondents are of the opinion that associations are helpful in promoting the co-operation among the library professionals

(2) But 26.37% disagree with this.

(3) 3.63% members have not responded to this question.

12.12. Role in providing latest developments in LIS field

(1) 18.18 percentage of the librarians are of the opinion that professional association's role in providing latest developments in LIS field are good

(2) 30 percentage are satisfied

(3) 32.72 percentage opined that the associations need improvements

(4) 16.37 percentage of the respondents expressed their dissatisfaction.

(5) 2.73 percentage did not give any opinion against this question

12.13. Development of extra-curricular / co-curricular activities of the librarians

(1) 42.73 percentage of the respondents are of the opinion that library associations are very much helpful for the development of their extra - curricular/co-curricular activities.

(2) But 55.45% are against this view

(3) 1.82% respondents did not respond to this question

12.14. Necessity of library association

(1) 89.09 % of them suggested that they need library associations for their professional development

(2) But 10.91% of them are against this opinion.

12.15. Attitude of librarians towards Library Professional Association

Attitude of librarians towards Library Professional Association is clear from table 4.23. It is found that 12(10.91%) of the library professionals are very much satisfied with the current functioning of the associations; where as 27(24.55%) have reported that they are satisfied. 42(38.18%) are opined that they are somewhat satisfied and 29(26.36%) are not at all satisfied.

Attitude of librarians towards Library Professional Association

Sl. No.	Responses	No. of respondents	Percentage
1	Very much Satisfied	12	10.91
2	Satisfied	27	24.55
3	Somewhat Satisfied	42	38.18
4	Not Satisfied	29	26.36
	Total	**110**	**100**

(1) 10.91% of the library professionals are very satisfied with the current functioning of the associations

(2) 24.55% are satisfied

(3) 38.18% are somewhat satisfied

(4) 26.36%) are not at all satisfied.

13. SUGGESTIONS

(1) In addition to the traditional services, most of the librarians need various sophisticated information services such as repackaging of information, current awareness services, selective dissemination of information, referral services etc. So associations have to take initiative in providing necessary training to library professionals in these areas.

(2) Frequent programmes are needed in the current developments such as techniques, concepts, terminology etc.

(3) Associations should take more initiative in publishing

(4) Standardization of courses in different Universities and institutions

(5) More Workshops/ Training Programmes to be conducted by the associations for introducing new tools and techniques.

14. VALIDATION OF HYPOTHESES

1. Findings No 12.3 revealed that 62.7 percentage are of the opinion that the Professional associations are very much helpful for the betterment of salaries, service benefits and to improve the status of the library professionals. So hypotheses 1 is satisfied

2. Finding No 12.11 indicates that 77 percentage of the respondents are opined Professional associations are useful to provide co-operation among library professionals. Hence the Hypotheses 2 formulated at the beginning of the study is also substantiated.

16. CONCLUSION

The role played by the library associations for the professional development of librarians has been analysed and the result would help to understand the attitude of librarians towards the professional associations. It revealed the involvement of librarians in professional activities for their professional development.

REFERENCE

1. Karisiddappa,C R .Role and importance of national and state level associations in library development in India.68th IFLA Council and General Conference. August 18-24,2002
2. Nafiz Zaman Shuva. History of Library Association of Bengladesh and present scenario. Department of Information Science and Library management. University of Dhaka. Karisiddappa,C R .Role and importance of national and state level associations in library development in India.68th IFLA Council and General Conference. August 18-24,2002
3. Prakash B.Jain. Role of Library Associations in India. In Library and Information Profession in India.vol.2.Ed. Vashishth,C p and Satija, M P. Delhi: BR publishing Corporation,2004:192-5
4. Khanna,J K.Library and Society.2nd rev.ed. New Delhi:Ess EssPublications,1994:309-36
5. Prakash B.Jain.Role of Library Associations in India . In Library and Information Profession in India.vol.2. Ed.Vashishth,C p and Satija, M P.Delhi:BR publishing Corporation,2004:192-5
6. Jain, C T. Professional Associations and development of Librarianship:case studies of the Library Association and the American Library Association . Delhi:Metropolitan Book Co,1971:2-4
7. Librarianship and Professional development :An evaluation. In Professional Librarianship.Ed . Devarajan, G. et al .New Delhi:Ess Ess Publications, 1991:34-43

8. Harrod's Librarian's Glossary. Ed.5.England:Gower Publishing Company,1995:444
9. Krishan Kumar. Research methods in Library and Information Science.Ed.2.New Delhi:Har-Anand Publications,1999:120
10. Harrod's Librarian's Glossary. Ed.5.England:Gower Publishing Company,1995:468

12

Information Needs and Information Seeking Behavior of Ayurveda Information Users

Dr. Joshi George P.

INTRODUCTION

Ayurvedic information sources and information seeking behavior of Ayurveda information users have some peculiar features which differ from modern medicine and other subject fields. In Ayurveda the old classics are still the most commonly used literature. There was a tendency to keep the Ayurvedic information sources and research outputs to as secret data. But there is a gradual change in this situation and now experiment results are coming out in journals. The exhaustive indexing/abstracting and reviewing type of periodicals are not published in Ayurveda. Very few patents are registered in Ayurveda. In this context this study aims to find out the various features of information needs and information seeking behavior of Ayurvedic Information Users. For the study to be effective the users are categorized as shown below.

- Scientists working in the various research institutes of Ayurveda
- Practitioners of Ayurveda, in which there are two categories: the qualified practitioners who have studied in Ayurveda colleges and similar institutions and conventional practitioners who have no formal degree in Ayurveda who have learned the Ayurveda treatment methods from the Gurus, parents, relatives and from books and other documents etc.
- Teachers of Ayurveda who are teaching in various Ayurvedic institutions
- Ayurveda Students. There are undergraduates, postgraduates, house surgeons and research scholars in this category.

The scientists, teachers, students and qualified practitioners are the categories which use mainly libraries and different types of information sources. Among the different sources, books are found to be used by all the members in these categories. Table 1 shows that while cent percent of the teachers and scientists use current and back volumes of periodicals 64% of the doctors and 93.73% of the students use current periodicals and 47.88% of the doctors and 93.42% of the students use back volumes of periodicals. When 78.94% of students use the dissertation/theses only 7.04% of the doctors use it. Conference/ seminar proceedings are used by 68.42% of the students, 40.29% of the scientists, 32.43% of the teachers and 19.71% of the doctors. Research reports are used by 47.76% of the scientists, 33.78% of the teachers, 31.57% of the students and 16.9% of the doctors. The use of indexing/abstracting/

reviewing periodicals are less in all categories of users. In all these categories of users the first preference among the types of information sources goes to books followed by periodicals.

Table 1 : Different categories of users (shown in percentage) Vs Different types of information sources

Information sources	Scientists	Teachers	Doctors	Students
Books	100	100	100	100
Current periodicals	100	100	64	94.73
Back volumes of Periodicals	100	100	47.88	93.42
Indexing/abstracting/ Reviewing periodicals	4.47	2.7	4.22	3.94
Dissertations/theses	17.91	28.37	7.04	78.94
Conference/seminar Proceedings	40.29	32.43	19.71	68.42
Research reports	47.76	33.78	16.9	57.89
Technical reports	23.88	17.56	15.49	15.78
Patents	14.92	00	2.81	2.63
Standards	2.98	0C	2.81	1.31

Table 2 : Different categories of users using non book materials

Users Category	Percentage
Scientists	61.19
Teachers	45.94
Doctors	39.43
Vaidyas	60.65
Students	42.10

The data given in Table 2 show that members of all categories use non- book materials. Scientists (61.19%) and Vaidyas (60.65%) are the two categories of users which use non-book materials, especially manuscripts, heavily. The data show the importance of manuscripts and other non-print media in Ayurveda.

The majority of the users opined that the collection in their library is inadequate to meet their information needs. Table 3 shows that 91.04% of scientists, 75.68% of teachers, 71.42% of doctors and 48.68% of students opined that collection is inadequate. The data shows the importance of strengthening document collection in Ayurveda libraries.

Table 3 : Different categories of users who found their library collection inadequate

Users Category	Percentage
Scientists	91.04
Teachers	75.68
Doctors	71.42
Students	48.68

Table 4 : Different categories of users who face difficulty in getting the right information in right time

Users Category	Percentage
Scientists	100
Teachers	93.24
Doctors	81.69
Vaidyas	45.9
Students	60.52

Data given in table 4 show that all the scientists, 93.24% of the teachers, 81.69% of the doctors, 45.9% of the traditional practitioners and 60.52% of the students face difficulty in getting right information at the right time.

Scientists, teachers and students are the three categories having the privilege of using the library attached to their parent institution. Table 5 shows that among the various ways to find the source of a new piece of information the most used means are directly searching the library shelves and discussion with the colleagues. The use of methods like consulting the catalogues, seeking the help of library staff and practitioners are comparatively less among various categories of users.

Table 5 : Different categories of users (shown in percentage) Vs Approaches to find the source of new information

Approach to find inf. Sources	Scientists	Teachers	Students
Searching the library shelves	95.52	97.29	97.36
Consulting the catalogue	28.35	31.08	30.26
Asking the library staff	10.44	14.86	47.36
Discussion with colleagues	94.02	94.59	68.42
Asking the practitioners	29.85	21.62	21.05

Table 6 : User's opinion regarding the services offered by their libraries shown in percentage

Opinion	Scientists	Teachers	Students
Adequate	7.46	20.27	30.23
Partially adequate	49.25	56.75	32.89
Inadequate	43.28	22.97	32.84

Data given in table 6 show that the majority of the users in all the three categories having library facilities are not satisfied with the services offered by the libraries at present. This data points to the need of revival of the libraries with the addition of new information services.

Table 7 : Different categories of users Vs Use of journals

Users Category	Percentage
Scientists	91.04
Teachers	75.67
Doctors	67.6
Students	69.73

Table 7 shows that the majority of the users viz. scientists, teachers, doctors and students are regular readers of journals. The rate is very high among scientists. This data show the importance of journals in information transfer in

Ayurveda.

Table 8 : Different categories of users and use of literature from other Indian systems of medicine

Users Category	Percentage
Scientists	64.17
Teachers	25.67
Doctors	25.35
Vaidyas	11.47
Students	22.36

Table 8 shows that when a major share of the scientists (64.17%) shows interest in reading the literature from other Indian systems of medicine only a small group from other categories shows interest in reading literature on other Indian systems of medicine. This shows the importance of collecting literature on other Indian systems of medicine in Ayurveda research libraries.

Table 9 : Different categories of users Vs Use of allopathic journals

Users Category	Percentage
Scientists	71.64
Teachers	36.48
Doctors	35.21
Students	44.73

Data given in table 7.26 show that there are regular readers of allopathic journals from different categories of users. Scientists are the group in which a majority of them (71.64%) reads allopathic journals regularly. This table shows the importance of literature from modern medicine in Ayurvedic libraries and information centres.

Table 10 shows that seminars are attended by members from all the categories of users. The seminars are very important media for information transfer among users in Ayurveda.

Table 10 : Participation of different categories of users in seminars

Users Category	Percentage
Scientists	79.1
Teachers	58.1
Doctors	69.01
Vaidyas	42.62
Students	88.15

Table 11 : Different categories of users who consult traditional practitioners for practical information

Users Category	Percentage
Scientists	56.71
Teachers	33.78
Doctors	47.88
Vaidyas	75.4
Students	43.42

Table 12 : Different categories of users who consult qualified practitioners for practical information

Users Category	Percentage
Scientists	50.74
Teachers	37.83
Doctors	64.78
Vaidyas	24.59
Students	51.31

Data given in tables 11 and 12 show that both the qualified and traditional practitioners are consulted by members from all categories of users for practical information. Table 11 shows the importance of the practical knowledge acquired by the traditional practitioners and the importance of sharing it with others for the benefit of the Ayurveda medical system.

Table 13 : Different categories of users who are the members of some formal or informal forum for sharing practical information

User category	Formal forum	Informal forum
Scientists	97.01	53.73
Teachers	68.91	32.43
Doctors	73.23	43.68
Vaidyas	73.77	78.68
Students	28.94	11.84

Table 13 shows that personal communication to share practical information is a commonly used medium in Ayurveda. Both formal and informal forums are used for this purpose. Informal communications are very prevalent among the traditional practitioners.

Table 14 : Different categories of users who are interested in practising some specific treatment methods (ottamoolies etc.)

Users Category	Percentage
Scientists	40.29
Teachers	28.37
Doctors	25.35
Vaidyas	72.13
Students	23.68

It is clear from table 14 that there are members from all categories who are interested in practising some specific treatments like ottamoolies etc. which are not commonly practised by every practitioner. The information about these treatments is generally kept secret. The traditional practitioners are more interested in these kinds of treatment than others.

Table 15 shows that members from different categories claim that they have developed some new drug formulations for treating their patients. But in most cases they are not manufacturing it on a commercial basis. This rate is relatively high among traditional practitioners.

Table 15 : Different categories of users who developed new drug formulations for treating their patients

Users Category	Percentage
Scientists	26.86
Teachers	12.16
Doctors	14.08
Vaidyas	40.98

Table 16 : Different categories of users who have collection of rare books/manuscripts/ medical formulae etc.

Users Category	Percentage
Scientists	20.89
Teachers	20.27
Doctors	25.35
Vaidyas	59.01
Students	10.52

Table 16 shows that members from all categories, especially the traditional practitioners possess rare documents with them in their personal collection.

FINDINGS AND CONCLUSION

The analysis of the responses by the different categories of users leads to the following inferences. The information sources generally used by the Ayurveda users are books, periodicals, seminar volumes, theses and manuscripts. Technical reports, patents and standards are not popular among them. Practitioners of Ayurveda commonly use books and current periodicals. Depending on the availability, the members of all the categories of Ayurveda users are making use of manuscripts and rare books. Scientists, teachers and students are generally making use of the libraries attached to their parent institution. But most of them are not satisfied with the collection as well as the services provided by these libraries.

A majority of the practitioners both qualified and conventional do not use libraries regularly, they depend mainly on personal collection of books and periodicals. All categories of Ayurvedic personnel are faced with difficulty in getting the right information at the right time.

A small group of the Ayurvedic personnel are interested in other systems of medicine, especially the systems like Siddha and Unani. A good number of Ayurveda users use periodicals in allopathic medicine also.

All categories of users attend Ayurveda medical seminars. As the library and information field and primary publication field are not so active in the field of Ayurveda, seminars become an important media for communication in this field. Even the conventional practitioners conduct a number of seminars and study classes under the auspices of their associations. These seminars and study classes are well attended by the members of these associations. The scientists, teachers, practitioners and a small number of students consult other qualified and conventional practitioners for getting practical information. Many of the Ayurvedic personnel are members of some forum either formal or informal for the sharing of practical experiences. Among the traditional practitioners, informal sharing of practical information is very prevalent.

Even though there are many seminars conducted separately by the qualified and traditional practitioners, formal communication between these two categories is very little. There is no common forum for the sharing of experiences between them. Both these categories are reluctant to recognize each other. This is a very severe draw back in Ayurveda. If they are willing to share the information freely then there will be lot of advancement in Ayurveda.

Many of the practitioners, especially the traditional practitioners have specialized in some specific treatment methods not commonly practiced by other practitioners. This is also a peculiar feature of Ayurveda where a lot of special treatment methods like 'ottamoolies' are possessed by the practitioners through their ancestors and kept secret as personal properties. Similarly, a good share of the respondents to the study, claimed that they had in their possession rare books/manuscripts/medical formulae etc. Many of the eminent Ayurveda personnel opined that there was secrecy and reluctance to publish the information in Ayurveda and this was the one major obstacle in the growth of Ayurveda. The general tendency of Ayurveda practitioners is to hide the rare information, especially about ottamoolees and other specific treatment methods, from other practitioners. For the growth of Ayurveda there should be a change in this attitude for which there should be some awareness programs to be conducted among these practitioners.

Lack of sufficient number of well-established libraries, poor collection and services provided by the existing libraries, weaker publishing media, reluctance of the Ayurvedic personnel to reveal the rare information they posses etc. warrants the need of a well-established National Information System for Ayurveda. Such a system will help in the collection, storage, processing and dissemination of information in this field, which is the need of the hour for the revival of this great medical system, which is the cultural heritage of our country.

REFERENCES

1. India,Ministry of Health and Family Welfare,(2000) Department of ISM and Homoeopathy. Indian Systems of Medicine and Homoeopathy in India 1998. Delhi: Controller of Publications.

2. Svoboda, Robert E.(1992) Ayurveda: Life, Health and Longevity. New Delhi: Penguin Books.
3. Sharadini Dahanukar (1989) A. and Urmila Thatte, M. Ayurveda Revisited. Bombay: Popular Prakashan. .
4. Raghavan Thirumulppadu, K.(1995) Ayurvedaparichayam. Kochi: Nagarjuna Foundation, Krishnankutti Variar (1980) Ayurvedacharithram. Kottakkal: Kottakkal Aryavaidyasala.

13

Learning Object Repositories in Higher Education: A Survey

Jayaraj J. R.

INTRODUCTION

The application of Information and Communication Technology (ICT) in Education has made progressive and revolutionary changes. These changes have enabled the education sector to become more efficient and cost effective. In fact, these changes led to the development of the phenomenon called 'E-learning'. Here teachers, students and academicians are increasingly adopting the internet and related technologies to effectively accelerate their activities. These technologies and related applications are proving themselves to be highly effective for academic purposes. Nowadays computer-based instruction is being proposed as the preferred technology to improve learning, increase access and raise productivity in Higher Education.

ADVANTAGES OF E-LEARNING

The significant advantages of E-Learning have been extensively studied by Joint Information Systems Committee of United Kingdom. These features of the E learning make it a potential and highly effective tool for using it in Higher Education. The following features of E Learning enhance the effectiveness of both self learning and class room learning.[1]

a) Interactive
b) Learner-centric
c) Participatory learning
d) Democratic
e) Flexible
f) Readily available
g) Supports multimedia
h) Create access to abundant information
i) It can be accessed from any part of the world overcoming geographical limitations
j) Access to latest information as it facilitates latest updating of data, information and knowledge
k) Student can learn at his own pace
l) The technology is user friendly
m) The debates are the hall mark of the system
n) 24 hr access to the system
o) The system promotes openness
p) The networking inculcates the sense of sharing and giving
q) Continuous feedback
r) Opportunity to improve or modify the process of learning
s) Excellent means for life long learning

LEARNING OBJECTS

E-learning is facilitated by the use of Learning Objects. Learning Objects act as the building block of E-learning. A Learning Object is a digital entity that is used to support the learning process and it should have a specific learning objective. The definition of learning objects put forth by Institute of Electrical and Electronics Engineers' Learning Technology Standards Committee (2005) is ' Learning Objects are defined as any entity, digital or non digital, which can be used, re-used or referenced during technology supported learning. Examples of technology - supported learning include computer based training systems, interactive learning environments, intelligent computer aided instruction systems, distance learning systems and collaborative learning environments. Examples of Learning Objects include multimedia content, learning objectives, instructional software and software tools, and persons, organizations or events referenced during technology supported learning'.[2]

There are different terms used for the Learning Object interchangeably. One such term used by David Merril is 'Knowledge objects'.[3] Merril also addresses the term as instructional components. The ARIADNE project uses the term 'Pedagogical Documents'.[4] Educational Software Components of Tomorrow (ESCOT) project uses the term 'educational software components'.[5] The Apple Learning Interchange uses term as "Learning Resources'.[6] Multimedia Educational Resource for Learning and On-Line Teaching (MERLOT) refers to them as 'Online Learning Materials'.[7] Even though all of the above terms have got slight variations in meaning, they all conform to the definition of Learning Technology Standards Committee.

The learning objectives, assessments and other instructional components differentiate a learning object from an information object. An information object is simply a digital entity which does not hold any instructional components. An information object holds information about a thing or phenomena while a learning object is the combination of information object with learning objective and instructional strategies and learner assessment mechanisms.

MAJOR LOR INITIATIVES

Internationally, many countries have developed open source software based e-Learning programmes that include the use of various types of digital repositories. These resource services usually need to exchange data with other parts of the programme or in some cases other parts of the world. Due to the diverse services and resources that typically exist within such e-Learning programmes, there is a need to ensure as high a degree of interoperability as possible.

CANARIE

CANARIE (Canadian Network for the Advancement of Research in Industry and Education) e-Learning program which has invested close to $30 million in online learning projects was launched in 1999. The design and development of Learning Object Repositories (LOR) constituted a major research theme of the program. There have been LOR-based projects producing valuable research in software, standards, community building and infrastructure deployment. A typical example is the CanCore application profile, the eduSource Communications Layer (ECL) for interoperation between distributed repositories. The Canadian initiatives have made internationally recognized contributions to the creation of open source tools that, added together, bring closer the possibility of a fully open sourced infrastructure of LOR systems.[8]

CAREO

CAREO (Campus Alberta Repository of Educational Objects) is a project supported by Alberta Learning and CANARIE (Canadian Network for the Advancement of Research in Industry and Education) that has as its primary goal the creation of a searchable, web-based collection of multidisciplinary teaching materials for educators across the province and beyond. CAREO takes a distributed approach to the location of "educational objects" in its architecture. CAREO is probably the best-known of these systems to date. The repository contains just over 4000 objects at the moment, which are loosely defined as modularized educational resources, educational objects or learning objects. The system is designed to be part of a larger networked repository system that displays XML document records based on IMS metadata. CAREO uses the CanCore Application Profile for metadata tagging of objects.

The CAREO application is designed to allow the search, retrieval and display of IMS metadata records in a web browser. Apart from tools supporting resource discovery (e.g. search, retrieve) it enables publication, aggregation and sharing of online materials. CAREO implements IMS Content Packaging to allow users to aggregate content. These compound aggregations may range from simple collections of images into a single package, to electronic representations of physical books, to highly structured online courses. The University of Calgary Learning Commons repository uses CAREO as do several other repository systems.[9]

COLLOR

COLLOR - the institution known as the Commonwealth of Learning (COL) have created an OSS/FS LOR which integrates two OSS/FS packages, pakXchange and eRIB. pakXchange implements a document repository system, providing comprehensive role-based administration, and version control, of publications whereas the eRIB provides the repository functionality. The COLLOR demonstration system is configured to access the eduSource network of repositories. The system includes the ability to add information about the learning objects with 'meta tags'. The system is able to federate-search other repositories when the user is looking for learning materials. Along with the OSS/FS developed by the eduSource and CANARIE projects COL has worked with Vancouver-based waynet Inc. to develop some complementary OSS/FS that, when used together with the project software, could provide a fully functioning learning object repository. In co-operation with COL, waynet created all the programming "connective tissue" to make these systems work together and provide an easy-to-use webpage to access content. COL is hosting the software and is collaborating with the African Virtual University, headquartered in Nairobi, Kenya, that will upload and make available open source courseware that Commonwealth countries can access free of charge. COL anticipates partnering with other groups as awareness of the LOR grows.[10]

CONNEXIONS

Connexions at Rice University is an environment for collaboratively developing, freely sharing, and rapidly publishing scholarly content on the Web. This system is based on the Plone Content Management System, which runs on Zope, an open source application server. The system's collections are made up of modules, each an XML document meeting specific criteria allowing their use and reuse in various contexts. Each item is written in cnxML, a format that contains both the metadata for a material and the content itself. Connexions is focused on the web-publishing of shareable modules (instead of learning objects) with the aim of building up non-linear courses out of these modules. The Connexions project at Rice University is a collaborative, community-driven approach to authoring, teaching, and learning. A group of authors work together to pool their expertise in the form of knowledge modules by collaborating both within and across disciplines. These modules form the basis for building courses that are authored by many, with each author receiving attribution for his or her contributions. Information can be modified under an open license to tailor the material for the audiences of learners.

A global community of authors continuously converts raw knowledge from the continuum into small, self-contained modules of information, the equivalent of a page or two in a textbook. Modules can be imagined as special web pages with hyperlinks pointing to prerequisites, applications, and supplementary material. Modules are placed in the Content Commons (a database repository) to be used, reused, updated, and adapted. Instructors use a Course Composer software tool to weave modules into customized courses that can be placed on the Web, presented in class, or printed as a paper text.[11]

DLEARN

DLearn is a learning object repository of shareable, digital, learning materials developed at the University of Arizona that is based on the DSpace model. The University of Arizona has retooled DSpace as a LOR to become "DLearn". They retained Dublin Core (DC) metadata in favour of Learning Object Metadata. Like other repositories following the DSpace model, DLearn content is organized around communities which correspond to University of Arizona administrative entities such as schools, departments, labs and research centres. Within each community there can be an unlimited number of collections. Within each collection there can be an unlimited number of items.

Content will consist of lectures, journal articles, book chapters, syllabus, music recordings and data sets in various digital formats.[12]

EDNA ONLINE

In the Australian e-Learning context, Education Network Australia (EdNA Online) is one their largest education and training resources and since 1996 it has been providing the education and training community with online access to quality assured information and tools and services to support teaching, learning and research. The new generation EdNA Online search centres provide access to other quality assured repositories of education and training resource information: both Australian and international. A visitor to EdNA Online can search just one repository, or they can mix and match repositories.[13]

E-GYANKOSH

Indira Gandhi National Open University (IGNOU) has taken a major initiative to produce self instructional study materials for various programmes in an open source repository called e - Gyankosh. IGNOU has initiated the establishment of a national digital repository of learning resources which facilitate instant access to study materials. The depository envisages to store, index, preserve, distribute and share the digital learning resources of open and distance learning institutions in the country. These materials can be accessed by general public also. The repository would support seamless aggregation and integration of learning resources in different formats - self-instructional material, animations, simulation, graphics, interactive multimedia; archives of radio broadcast, TV telecast, teleconference sessions, interactive radio chats; classroom notes of teachers. The repository would facilitate just in-time access to its collections 24 × 7 × 365 offering interoperability and federated searching facility. The decentralized model of the repository supports multiple submission points facilitating submission of contents from remote locations. The collection can be searched and browsed by subject, title, author, etc.[14]

MATDL

MatDL is the Materials Digital Library, and is part of the National Science Foundation (NSF). MatDL is a collaborative effort of the Materials Science and Engineering Laboratory at the National Institute of Standards and Technology (MSEL/NIST), Kent State University, Massachusetts Institute of Technology (MIT), University of Michigan, and the University of Colorado at Boulder.[15]

MERLOT

MERLOT - Multimedia Educational Resource for Online Learning and Teaching is a free and open resource designed primarily for staff and students in higher education. Anyone can contribute descriptions of learning materials to the catalogue, or use MERLOT material subject to licensing and rights agreements. MERLOT conducts structured peer reviews of online learning materials carried out by editorial boards. Links to online materials are collected here along with annotations such as peer reviews and assignments. The quality of learning objects being deposited in the repositories is a major concern. Peer review of learning objects are done in MERLOT to ensure the quality of learning objects.[16]

PLANET

PLANET Digital Repository is an e-Learning project led by the University of Rovira Virgili in Tarragona; their digital repository implements the open source ECL protocol using web services. This provides search submit and request services, with search being based on LOM metadata. PLANET

Digital Repository is Java-based, runs on Jakarta-Tomcat and uses the open source MySQL database.[17]

SPOKEN WORD PROJECT

As part of the international JISC/NSF Digital Libraries in the Classroom Programme led by Glasgow Caledonian University, North-western University and Michigan State University in partnership with the BBC explores the use of digital audio in the humanities. The Spoken Word proposes to transform undergraduate learning and teaching through integrating the rich media resources of digital audio repositories into undergraduate courses. Fedora is one of the repositories used and was chosen for several reasons, including its support for preservation activities such as content versioning and its ability to meet their pedagogical objectives. The OSS/FS nature of the product, plus its interoperability, rights awareness, scalability and ability to allow content repurposing were the main attractions of using Fedora for the project.[18]

TILE

TILE - The Inclusive Learning Exchange is a revolutionary learning object repository service that responds to the individual needs of the learner. TILE provides the authoring tools, repository architecture, and preference schema needed to support this learner-centric transformation, particularly to allow learning objects to be accessible to those with disabilities. TILE is now evolving to become a service layer that can sit on top of learning object repositories and allow users to search and access them in a responsive way.[19]

CONCLUSION

It was observed that major learning object repository initiatives aimed at higher education are taken by countries like Canada, USA, Australia and some European countries. Countries like India have great potential for developing LOR systems. Some initiatives have already started in India to utilize the advantages of Learning Objects.

Majority of the Learning Object Repositories have been implemented in open source based learning content management systems. Most of them are aimed at providing interoperability and portability among various systems and browsers. LOR systems are highly efficient and cost effective. Sharing of learning resources among various institutions having similar academic interest is possible in open source learning management systems.

REFERENCES

1. Advantages of e-learning. Retrieved from www.jisc.ac.uk/uploaded_documents/elearning_advantage_v2.doc on 4 May 2008
2. Learning Objects. Learning Technology Standards Committee. Retrieved from http://ltsc.ieee.org/ on 7 April 2008
3. Knowledge Objects and Mental Models. Retrieved from www.reusability.org/read/chapters/merrill.doc on 16 May 2008
4. Pedagogical Documents. Retrieved from http://www.ariadne-eu.org/ on 12 May 2008
5. ESCOT. Educational Software Components of tomorrow. Retrieved from http://www.escot.org/ on 16 May 2008
6. APPLE. Resources. Retrieved from http://ali.apple.com/edres on 08 May 2008
7. MERLOT. Multimedia Educational Resource for Learning and Online Teaching. Retrieved from http://www.merlot.org/ on 16 May 2008
8. http://www.canarie.ca/
9. http://www.careo.org/
10. http://www.col.org/col

11. http://cnx.rice.edu/aboutus/
12. http://www.dlearn.arizona.edu/index.jsp
13. http://www.edna.edu.au/edna/page1.html
14. http://www.egyankosh.ac.in
15. http://www.matdl.org
16. http://www.merlot.org
17. http://ants.etse.urv.es/planetdr/
18. http://www.spokenword.ac.uk
19. http://www.inclusivelearning.ca/tile/index.html

14

E-Book Aggregators

K. Ravindran Assari

1. WHAT IS E-BOOK AGGREGATOR?

When we had only the print media, purchase of books and journals was done through booksellers and subscription agents. In India such practice is still being followed as the major method for acquiring books and other information sources. The trend of publishing digitally became vigorous by the turn of the present decade. Now leading publishers like the Oxford Universiy Press, Elsevier, Blackwell, Kluer Academic and Springer Verlag publishes most of their books and journals in the digital format along with the print format. For distributing printed books internationally there are booksellers, which come under two major categories - whole sailors and retailers. Users and libraries can purchase direct from publishers also. But the process is cumbersome because there are hundreds of publishers and each have different terms and conditions. To deal independently with different publishers in different countries and accepting different terms and conditions and making payment in a variety of foreign currencies make the process unmanageable. Therefore for purchase of printed books we depend on booksellers. Just like printed books and journals are acquired libraries, now e-books can be acquired. Acquiring e-books have become an established practice in developed countries. In developing countries like India, although, subscribing e-journals has become a practice purchasing or accessing e-books on payment has not become common.

To purchase e-books direct from publishers, you have to contact a variety of publishers and you are confused by the different licensing agreements, platforms, and pricing models. Use an e-book aggregator for solving this problem. Aggregators connect with multiple publishers to supply content (e-books, audio books, other media) and provide a platform for libraries and end users to search, order, access, and download the content on the Web. Just like booksellers and subscription agents provide books, journals and other printed information sources, eBook aggregators provide the platform for accessing eBooks, e-Journals, and other electronic media for libraries and other electronic content users.

The major advantage of an aggregator is having a single platform or interface to host countless titles, with international coverage, and typically no special players or plug-ins. Furthermore, because aggregators partner with hundreds of publishers, librarians can centralize their selection and acquisitions processes, ordering print or electronic content direct from the aggregator or through one of the many book wholesalers, such as YBP, Blackwell, or Baker and Taylor. As a result of this centralization, only one contract or licensing agreement is needed.

There are several pricing models, but the most popular are purchasing title by title for either single-user or multiple-user access or purchasing an entire e-book subject collection for multiple-user access. Subscription or perpetual-ownership models are available as well. Prices vary depending on the aggregator and number of users but are generally at or above the print list price. Additional benefits of using an aggregator include federated search compatibility, 24/7 access to full text, free MARC records, usage statistics, and the ability to customize the interface or offer it in multiple languages. In contrast to the printed books e-books are not physically sent to the libraries, on the basis of permission granted by the e-book aggregator the required books are downloaded to the customer's computer, either in part or full. Sometimes the e-books are downloaded permanently or for temporary use. With e-books and e-journals, the traditional concept of book and library will change.

2. AGGREGATORS PROLIFERATE

As the number of e-books platforms has proliferated, and as the models which allow access to them grow in variety and complexity, publishers and librarians have become increasingly interested in knowing the different types of e-book aggregators. Therefore, studies have been undertaken to explores in depth the attributes and features of the main aggregator platforms, and evaluate their performance. The commercial and pedagogical advantages and drawbacks of e-books are also described from the different perspectives of publishers, librarians and academics.

Five distinct aggregator groups of e-book providers are examined in detail:

1. 'General' aggregators;
2. 'Specialist' aggregators;
3. Online journals aggregators who also host hosting e-book collections;
4. Digital warehouses; and
5. Library suppliers.

3. MAIN CONSIDERATIONS

When we select an e-book aggregator, we have to take into consideration, the following aspects:

1. The technologies on which the platforms are based and their precise attributes and functional features.
2. Precise purchase/licensing models that each operates.
3. Sets out how DRM and encryption is managed, and how securely.
4. How many titles the aggregator holds.
5. How many customers the aggregator deals with, and in which geographical regions.
6. Pricing models, and how publishers are paid.
7. Financial stability.

The market for e-books has taken off, particularly in the world of education. Aggregators provide easy access to large collections of titles from many publishers, through a single interface. Consultants Ray Lonsdale and Chris Armstrong compare the offerings of the largest providers, and point to emerging trends.

During the last decade, e-books have grown to become a significant library resource; a 2007 international e-book survey showed that 88 per cent of respondents 'answered that they own or subscribe to e-books' and nearly half of the respondents (45 per cent) have had access 'to more than 10,000 e-books'. Although annual US wholesale e-book sales rose by 23.6 per cent in 2007, the situation remained uneven in the UK. Higher and further education continue to dominate sales, with a number of public and special libraries also committing themselves to the format. Other sectors such as schools are only just becoming aware of the possibilities.

In the same way that some years ago aggregators developed platforms of e-journals, now they have become an important means of access to e-books, providing large collections of titles from many publishers under a single contract and through a single interface. They constitute a major source to which UK libraries turn for the provision of e-books, as reported by Jisc: 'Until 2005 roughly 50 per cent of higher education institutions had been buying e-books from aggregators, but this figure has risen to 63 per cent in the last 18 months. This is the situation in US and Europe. In India an organized move for the supply of e-books has not started so far. This can be attributed to two reasons: First the publishers still give importance to print books and journals and the second reason being the libraries give prime importance to printed sources.

In order to understand the nature and functioning of e-book aggregators the following aggregators are considered.

Credo Reference (re-badged xreferplus) http://corp.credoreference.com/

Dawsonera www.dawsonera.com/

Ebook Library (EBL) www.eblib.com/

ebrary www.ebrary.com/corp/

Gale Virtual Reference Library (from Gale/Cengage Learning) http://gale.cengage.com/

Knovel www.knovel.com/knovel2/default.jsp

KnowUK (from ProQuest) www.knowuk.co.uk/

MyiLibrary (from Ingram Digital) www.myilibrary.com/company/home.htm

NetLibrary (from OCLC) www.netlibrary.com/

OverDrive: Leading Digital Media Service, http://www.overdrive.com/

Questia www.questia.com/

Safari Books Online (available via ProQuest) http://proquestcombo.safaribooksonline.com/home

VitalSource (from Ingram Digital) www.vitalsource.com/

All offer information on their websites, and two - Knovel and Questia - allow searching from non-subscribers. It should be noted that what follows deals with the main aggregations for each company. Some companies, for example Ingram Digital which offers vital source for textbooks, may offer additional products. It is envisaged that the new Gale Directory Library will extend to include titles from other publishers and will thus become an aggregator product. The major factor to be considered in detail are licensing and a comparison of software features.

Possibly one of the most difficult areas for librarians faced with collecting e-books is that of licensing and charging models. As the Jisc report stated, 'It is clear from our discussions with library staff that there is a considerable amount of ignorance and misunderstanding about e-book marketing and what terms can be obtained from aggregators and publishers.

Licensing is a complex subject. There are probably, as many licensing policies as there are aggregators. Some e-book aggregators offer a model in which the library owns books that have been purchased - ownership, in this case, meaning a fixed number of accesses each year. This model may incorporate a small overhead for the platform and in some cases also offer a rent-to-buy approach.

The other main model is the concurrent-use license, with an annual subscription to a collection or part of a collection. Some models allow users to download e-books to a laptop for a limited loan period; others allow library users to view titles in the aggregator's master collection to which the library has not yet subscribed. Finally, MyiLibrary has a pilot 'inter-library loan' system developed with the Canada Institute for Scientific and Technical Information (CISTI), which allows users to purchase one month's access to an e-book by way of a credit card payment.

Academic Database Assessment Tool is a separate site of JISC <**www.jisc-adat.com/adat/home.pl**>This site aims to help libraries make informed decisions about future subscriptions to bibliographic and full text databases. The most recently added area concerns e-book platforms, and five aggregators are compared on the basis of important criteria, which include: Access Control, Search, Indexing, Search Results, Restrictions and Usage Statistics. This comparative study revealed more novel features of aggregators.

4. AGGREGATOR CHARACTERISTICS

One of the very important characteristics is the provision of large collections of e-books from a range of publishers, all of which may be used on a single software interface. Often the full text of the entire collection can be searched in one go. There will be a range of features such as the ability to search in-book, and to have password-specific book-marking, highlighting and note-taking; for the most part, books are intended to be read online, although a few aggregators may allow the e-book to be downloaded to a laptop. All aggregators offer free trials, either full text of books or part of it. The majority work with consortia as well as with individual institutions.

5. COLLECTION CONTENT

With respect to subject coverage, EBL claims an STM (Science Technology and Medicine) emphasis. GVRL has focused on the humanities, and literature in particular. While Gale gives importance to science and health, Dawsonera, MyiLibrary, NetLibrary, Questia and ebrary are truly multi-disciplinary. Only NetLibrary includes fiction and children's fiction. Reference collections tend to be smaller and the four aggregators included here vary from around 120 titles (KnowUK) to some 2,000 (Knovel); the general aggregators vary from around 48,000 (Dawsonera) to 170,000 (ebrary). Typically each aggregation includes titles from 60 to several hundreds of publishers. Safari, which specialises in online IT and business/management, has a smaller collection of around 6,000 titles from 26 publishers.

Four aggregators - Credo Reference, Knovel, KnowUK (a UK-related collection) and GVRL, concentrate on reference sources including encyclopedia, dictionaries, atlases, yearbooks, and guides. Knovel focuses specifically on science and technology while the rest give importance to all reference sources.

The majority of aggregators update collections as new editions become available. GVRL is moving towards dynamically updating the online content of certain of its titles, including The New Catholic Encyclopaedia and Grzimek's Animal Life Encyclopedia parallel to the process of continuous revision.

It brings together rich content in one place in response to a search query, certainly, which users find helpful. More than 80 per cent of respondents to ebrary's Global eBook Survey stated that integration of multiple online resources is 'very important'. Questia offers journal, magazine, newspaper and encyclopedia articles; ebrary does not include newspapers, but adds sheet music, maps and reports. NetLibrary offers eAudioBooks, databases and e-journals; and Safari also has non-e-book documents and articles, and some 600 hours of video instruction.

MyiLibrary is moving in the same direction and has noted an increase in demand for certain of these formats, while Dawsonera has on its website 'new media', and audio. GVRL, KnowUK, Credo Reference and Knovel - the four reference aggregators - vary. Knovel has also moved beyond the e-book to include 'databases and other e-content', while Credo Reference and KnowUK focus only on reference books.

6. MARKET TRENDS

Historically, e-book publishers and aggregators focused on the academic library sector, initially within higher education and later on to post-16 education. Public libraries and special libraries too have, in recent years, benefited from a broadening of the range of e-book titles offered by aggregators. These sectors still constitute the principal market, as typified by Ebrary which sees its users as 'based in universities, further education colleges, corporations and public libraries'.

However, studies reveal that aggregators are now exploring the potential of children's and school library sectors. For several years, NetLibrary has expanded considerably its collection for North American school libraries so that it now constitutes a critical market.

7. GEOGRAPHICAL COVERAGE

Several aggregators, such as MyiLibrary, are UK oriented, and are now looking to extend their international content. However, one of the early criticisms levelled by UK libraries at some of the general aggregators which were established in North America concerned the predominantly US bias of their collections. Our study suggests that there is a discernible move towards offering a significant quantity of e-book titles from non-US publishers.

The move towards internationalism is also reflected in the development of multi-lingual interfaces and multi-language content. A few aggregators offer non-English-language material. NetLibrary has been conscious of this issue for some years, and now offers approximately 7,500 non-English-language e-book titles in more than 20 other languages. Critically, there is a move towards serving the markets in China, Japan and India.

8. DEVELOPMENTS IN PLATFORMS

Aggregator platforms offer some very sophisticated means of access to e-book content.

In addition to the conventional searching facilities, some aggregators offer more innovative approaches. Safari - because of its IT specialism - has developed the search facility to specify computer and programming code, and has cleared copyright on this content as well.

Some aggregators offer referencing help by providing citations, sometimes in as many as half a dozen styles, and Knovel automatically exports a citation with any text or table. Ebrary also offers automatic citations when text is copied and pasted and printed. Ebrary's citations, available in several different formats, also include a URL hyperlink back to the source.

9. BIBLIOGRAPHIC ISSUES

A perennial problem that has been articulated for the past decade in research into e-books is the issue of bibliographic control of the format. Given the lack of a single national bibliographic source for the foreseeable future, the identification of new titles can be a difficult and time-consuming activity. One important development has been the integration of e-book titles within several international bibliographic sources, such as Global Books in Print and WorldCat. Some aggregators recognised the significance of this issue, and acknowledge the need to be more proactive in exploring the implications of bibliographic control. Several aggregators do put their titles in these bibliographies. For example, NetLibrary and Knovel have their titles within OCLC WorldCat, and GVRL within Global Books in Print.

10. IMPACT OF NEW TECHNOLOGIES

All the aggregators are very conscious of new developments, particularly the increase in interest over e-book readers and mobile technology. EBL noted that titles were 'already available on handheld readers - the books can be transferred to a PDA, and the aggregators are working with some device companies to provide more sophisticated devices.

11. CONCLUSIONS

Overall, aggregators represent a major, perhaps the major, source for e-books in libraries, bringing together vast collections of general academic titles and quite large reference collections for easy access. While English collections dominate, there is a discernable move towards developing multilingual access and content. Markets are focused in academia and public libraries, but schools and special libraries are increasingly represented, and all aggregators acknowledge their needs.

Aggregators provide access to, and the ability to interrogate, the digitized texts in innovative and helpful ways using an array of software features. While marketing models are complex, most of the aggregators believe that they can evolve a fair deal to both the publishers and the libraries, both of whom have to be accommodated in negotiations.

REFERENCES

1. Ebrary's Global eBook Survey. 2007 (www.ebrary.com/corp/ collateral/en/Survey/ ebrary_eBook_survey_2007.pdf).
2. David Rothman. 'U.S. 2007 wholesale e-book sales: $31.7M, or 23.6 percent over 2006 - but should they have been still higher?' TeleRead, 18 February 2008 (www.teleread.org/ blog/2008/02/18/us-2007-wholesale-e-book-sales-317m-or-236-percent-from-2006-but-should-they-have-been-still-

higher/).

3. A Feasibility Study on the Acquisition of e-Books by HE Libraries and the Role of Jisc. The Higher Education Consultancy Group, 2006 (www.jisccollections.ac.uk/workinggroups/ebooks/studies_reports.aspx).
4. http://cat.cisti-icist.nrc-cnrc.gc.ca/screens/myilibrary_e.html
5. www.jisc-adat.com/adat/home.pl
6. John Cox. 'Making sense of e-book usage data.' The Acquisitions Librarian, 19 (3/4), 2008 (www.library.nuigalway.ie/coxebooks.pdf) (Archived by WebCite(r) at www.webcitation.org/5WRHRWnKO).
7. 2004 Information Format Trends: content, not containers. OCLC, 2004 (www.oclc.org/reports/2004format.htm).
8. Chris Armstrong, Ray Lonsdale, and Dave Nicholas. 'SuperBook: planning for the e-book revolution.' Library & Information Update, 5(11), 2006, pp. 28-30.
9. C. J. Armstrong and R. E. Lonsdale. Initial analysis of SuperBook qualitative survey [unpublished], 2007-08.
10. C. J. Armstrong and R. E. Lonsdale. The Publishing of Electronic Scholarly Monographs and Textbooks. Ukoln, May 1998; and Report G5, Library Information Technology Centre, April 1998 (www.ukoln.ac.uk/models/studies/).
11. Chris Armstrong, Louise Edwards and Ray Lonsdale. 'Virtually There: e-books in UK academic libraries. Program 36(4), 2002, pp. 216-227.
12. Promoting the Uptake of E-Books in Higher and Further Education. Gold Leaf, 2003 (www.jisc-collections.ac.uk/workinggroups/ebooks/studies_reports.aspx).

15

Impact of 'Theory Y' Assumption on Superior Subordinate Relation in Academic and Public Libraries in Germany

Dr. B. Mini Devi

0. INTRODUCTION

No library can succeed without highly motivated and committed team of employees. It is only through them all the resources of the library are got to be used for the accomplishment of predetermined goals. We have sent hat some people work hard. Some avoid work. To certain others work is worship. To many work is a necessary evil. Some take work as a challenge. A few works if paid well. To some others nice words are better than few rupees to improve their work output. A certain work interest some but to some others the same work is boring. "We can take the horse to water, but can not make it to drink", so goes a saying. A motive is a drive or desire that causes a person to act. Motivation refers to the degree of readiness of an organism to pursue some designated goals and implies the determination of the nature and locus of force including degree of readiness. Understanding human motivation is crucial for managing people.

Douglas McGregor, late Professor of Industrial Management at Massachusetts Institute of Technology, in his thoughtful treatise titled, "The Human Side of Enterprise" [1] described Theory 'X', as the conventional view of direction and control, and Theory 'Y', as the integration of goals of individuals and of organisations of creating such conditions in which the members of an organization can best achieve their goals by directing their efforts toward achievement of the organizational goals. Douglas McGregor observed two diametrically opposing viewpoints of managers about their employees, one is negative called 'Theory of X' and another positive called 'Theory of Y'.

Theory of X

The following are the assumptions of managers who believe in the 'Theory of X' in regard to their employees:

- Employees dislike work; if possible avoid the same.
- Employees must be coerced, controlled or threatened to do the work.
- Employees avoid responsibilities and seek formal direction.
- Most employees consider security of job, most important of all other factors in the job and have very little ambition.

Theory of Y

Following are the assumptions of mangers who believe

in the 'Theory of Y' in regard to their employees:

- Employees love work as play or rest.
- Employees are self-directed and self-controlled and committed to the organizational objectives.
- Employees accept and seek responsibilities.
- Innovative spirit is not confined to managers alone, some employees also possess it.

1. OBJECTIVES

1. To find out the relation, if any, between librarians' assumptions about human beings in general, particularly subordinates, and the frequency and the nature of problems they experience with their subordinates.
2. To explore the significant differences, if any, in the assumptions held by librarians at different level in the organization.

2. HYPOTHESIS

More acceptance and commitment to 'Theory Y' (high Y) at higher levels of library leads to less problems with the subordinates at all levels where as more acceptance and commitment to 'Theory X' (low Y) at higher levels leades to more problems with the subordinates.

3. METHODOLOGY

For data collection e-mail questionnaire method is used. The questionnaire has two sections. The first section deals with the assumption of people about human beings in general and these second section aims to seek information regarding the problems librarians face with their subordinates.

About 100 questionnaires were e-mailed among the

managerial librarians of academic libraries and another 100 questionnaires were e-mailed among the same of public libraries in Germany.

The questionnaire returned from the first category was 44% and from the second was 63%. The data collected are statistically analysed and interpreted using 't-test' and the non-parametrical 'sign' test.

4. DATA ANALYSIS AND DISCUSSION

The questionnaires returned back are first analysed to find out the assumptions librarians hold about their fellow employees and studied in detail. From librarian's direct acceptance of Y statements or from the non-acceptance of X statements, the Y assumption of the librarian is found out. Taking this method the Y score of every librarian is expressed as a percentage of the total number of the statements.

The Table I shows the percentage of Y content of managerial assumptions. It is clear out from the data that pure 'Theory X' oriented librarian are rare today. The analysis showed that there is none among the respondents with a Y content less than 50%. The 'Low Theory - Y managers Vs. High Theory - Y managers' aspect is analysed. If the % of Y-content of a librarian is below the level of median he is categorized under 'High Y' librarians. At the same time librarians with 'Low Y' content in their assumptions have more number of problems with their subordinates when compared to those having 'High Y' content is presented in the Table 2.

4.1. Y assumptions and nature of problems

The nature of problems experienced by the librarians with their subordinates were categorized into

i) job performance

ii) commitment and involvement

iii) communication

iv) personal relations.

From the analysis it is evident that 'low Y' librarians have more problems with their subordinates on all categories except on the last one. In a nutshell the differences between 'low Y' librarians and 'high Y' librarians are more on the competence, responsibility and involvement of the subordinates. This is a clear evidence that 'high Y' librarians do have problems on communication with their subordinates.

Table I: Percentage of Y content among the library managerial personnel

Percentage Y content	Total frequency SS	Frequency in Library A	Frequency in Library B
100	5 (4.64%)	2 (4.44%)	3 (4.84%)
95	13 (12.14%)	7 (15.55%)	6 (9.68%)
90	9 (8.41%)	6 (13.39%)	3 (4.84%)
85	18 (16.82%)	8 (17.77%)	5 (8.06%)
80	13 (12.14%)	8 (17.77%)	10 (16.13%)
75	20 (18.69%)	4 (8.88%)	16 (25.81%)
70	6 (5.61%)	2 (4.44%)	4 (6.45%)
65	11 (10.28%)	3 (6.66%)	8 (12.9%)
60	7 (6.54%)	2 (4.44%)	5 (8.06%)
55	0	0	0
50	5 (4.7%)	3 (6.66%)	2 (3.23%)
Less than 50%	Nil	Nil	Nil
	107 (100%)	45 (100%)	62 (100%)

The sign test is used to compare two sets of figures to see if there is significant difference. Here the sign is considered as positive if the observation under low Y group exceeds the observations under high Y group and viceversa. The signs of the difference between two corresponding observation of positive signs is compared with the number of negative signs.

Table 2: Frequency of problems experienced by librarians with low and high Y content: Sign test to find out the significance of difference.

Item No.	Nature of problem	Low Y Group Group size 62	High Y Group Group size 62	Sign
1	Lack of learning	5	4	+
2.	Lack of intelligence	7	3	+
3.	Lack of experience	9	10	-
4.	Not competent in work	12	8	+
5.	Not enthusiastic	5	4	+
6.	Not committed to library's objectives	8	7	+
7.	Lack of initiative	7	5	+
8	Lack of involvement in work	10	9	+
9.	Hesitation to take responsibility	2	1	+
10.	Inconsistent	5	7	-
11.	Insubordination	2	20	+
12.	Group instinct rather than logical thinking	7	3	+
13.	Not co-operative with the superior	4	2	+
14.	Violation of rules and regulations	5	3	+
15.	Not co-operative with equals	8	6	+
16.	Waste materials and resources	5	4	+
17.	Easily annoyed by criticisms	4	3	+
18.	Prefer to work less if they can manage	7	3	-
19.	Tries to justify actions though there can't be justifications	6	5	+

20.	Conscious of privileges but not on duties	16	15	+
21.	Resistant to change	20	19	+
22.	Take away superior's time discussing personal problems	20	24	-
23.	Too radical outlook in views	4	5	-
24.	Can't communicate properly	3	2	+
			Total (+) =	19
			Total (=) =	0
			Total (-) =	5

Number of positive signs = 19

Number of negative signs = 5

For significance at 5 percent let

19-5 should be <2√ Sum of the observations

Since 14<2, the higher values under low Y group is significantly greater than the values.

under high Y group

The formula $\left[\frac{\text{Twice sum}}{\text{difference}}\right]^2$ will give the 'sufficient data' required.

$$\text{Here} = \frac{(2 \times 24)^2}{14} = 11.75$$

∴ 24 observations are sufficient to justify the conclusion drawn.

The extracted reasons are:

i) The subordinate staff of the library are incapable of communicating their feelings to their superiors.

ii) The subordinate staff keep up the traditional superior-subordinate relationship.

4.2. Y-assumptions and levels differences

The 'low Y' group and the 'high Y' group are further classified on the basis of the level they occupy in the libraries. The variation in 'Y content' for each level was tested using t-test and it is evident that there is no significant difference in the Y assumptions at different levels except at the level of senior librarians, where 'high Y' content is predominant. Table 3 shows that the significant difference at the level of senior librarians is the result of major contribution from Library A alone.

Table 3 : Low and High Y group libraries at different levels in Library A and B

Level of librarians	Library A		Library B	
	Low Y Group	High Y Group	Low Y Group	High Y Group
Top Management	-	-	-	1
Senior Management	2	10	6	2
Middle Management	4	3	18	17
Junior Management	8	7	7	10
First line supervisor	7	1	-	-

From the table it is evident that the percentage of 'Y-content' in library A is higher than library B and also the 'Y content' librarians at the level of senior librarians is more in library A when compared to library B; but the reverse is true with the junior level librarians. The library A creates a better working atmosphere by the model provided by the Senior librarians and the immediate superior of every subordinate, whereas in library B the senior level librarians and the immediate superior of each subordinate are not probably accepted as a model by their subordinates.

5. CONCLUSIONS

1. Librarians with pure 'Theory X' assumptions are on a declining state today. In a democratic socialistic setup,

the pure 'Theory X' is viewed by librarians as an unsophisticated set of ideas.

2. Librarians are in a process of conversion from 'Theory X' to 'Theory Y'.
3. The less 'Y-content' librarians have more the problems they experience with their subordinates. In the information technology era for producing better feed back the profession needs more Y-oriented librarians.
4. Librarians with Y assumptions are found to be dominant at all levels.
5. To reduce the problems caused by 'low Y' librarians, periodical appraisal of the superior by his subordinates should be done.

REFERENCE

1. McGregor, D. (1960) The Human Side of the Enterprise, New York, McGraw Hill.

16

Preservation and Conservation of Library Materials

Vasudevan T M
Jineesha V

INTRODUCTION

Few years ago the preservation of library materials was mainly concerned with a few rare books. Books were rolling off the presses faster than libraries could absorb them. Materials in all media were proliferating and libraries were purchasing. Soon libraries no longer could afford to develop their collections on a cosmic scale and librarians were compelled to take a hard look at the material already on their shelves. Today preservation is recognized as a vitally necessary component of collection development.

Today preservation not only the conservation of the books or other objects in their original formats but also quite literally the preservation of the intellectual content of library and the maintenance of the physical plant where library materials are housed.

Importance of preservation and conservation in libraries

The two important things of preservation of library materials are:-

1) The preventive measures which include all forms of indirect methods aimed at increasing the life expectancy of undamaged or damaged elements of cultural property. It comprises all the methods of good house-keeping, caretaking, dusting, periodical supervision and prevention of any possibility of damage by physical, chemical, biological and other factors.
2) The curative measures consist of all forms of direct actions aimed at increasing the life expectancy of undamaged or damaged elements of cultural property. It includes repairing, mending fumigation, lamination and other jobs which are required in considering the physical condition of the individual document.

Preservation and conservation play a vital role and has assumed much importance because a large number of institutions do not have proper conservation facilities. In fact if diagnosis in time is followed by proper preventive measures many problems can be solved.

VARIOUS CONSERVATION METHODS USED IN LIBRARIES

Permanence and durability are two characteristics of documents. The main cause of decay of these documents is the degradation of cellulose fibers. Restoration of documents is a complicated problem and its repair and restoration is done in various institution depending upon their facilities available and the nature of the condition of documents. The important measures and techniques used all over the world are mentioned below:-

a) **Lamination:** It is a process of protecting and strengthening paper by covering one or both sides with transparent tissue paper, and / or cellulose acetate foil using heat or acetone solvent. This process is only partly reversible because solvents can't remove all of the film from the pores of the paper.

b) **Encapsulation:** Enclosure of a document between two sheets of polyester film sealed with pressure sensitive tape, by ultrasonic welding or sewing. Two layers support the sheet and allow it to be handled and seen from both sides. Encapsulation is reversible.

c) **Fumigation:** Gaseous treatment of materials to destroy micro-organisms and infestation by insects. Killing or deactivating mould or insects by exposure to poisonous fumes or vapor, usually done in a vacuum air tight chamber.

d) **De-acidification:** A process that neutralizes the acidic components in paper and usually provides an alkaline buffer to counteract acidic buildup in the future. It is the treatment to the paper or other library materials to neutralize acidity in order to improve durability.

e) **Binding:** Book binding is the process of collecting printed pages of a book together in correct sequence and putting them between covers. Binding of library books' and 'library binding' are two terms having different connotations. The former term consists of different types of binding used for different types of materials, having different physical forms and intrinsic value. But the later is a specific type of binding which adopts typical binding process, using materials of specific standard.

f) **Minor repairs:** Minor repairs are affected on documents which are only slightly damaged or torn. An adhesive in the form of a synthetic (polyvinyl acetate) paste, a solution of cellulose acetate film in acetone, or flour paste is applied to the damaged or torn portion and tissue paper is laid over the tear and pressed down. The process is repeated on the other side of the document. When the paste dries, the excess tissue paper is scrapped off. Alternatively, strip of tissue paper impregnated with acetate may be employed.

PRESERVATION AND CONSERVATION

Preservation is concerned with maintaining or restoring access of artifacts, documents and record through the study, diagnosis, treatment and prevention of decay and damage. The various preservation techniques include stabilizing, marinating and monitoring temperature, humidity, light exposure, air pollution, dust and dirt. In short, preservation is an indirect method of treatment in which the environment around an item is changed.

Conservation is an aspect of preservation activity. It refers to the treatment and repair of individual items to slow decay or restore them to a usable state. It normally implies the active use of preventive measures, or processes of repair of damaged material. In short it is a direct method of treatment in which an item is physically/chemically changed.

NEED FOR PRESERVATION OF LIBRARY RESOURCES

Library as a social institution has the responsibility to acquire knowledge and disseminate it to those who are in need of it. It enjoins the obligation to protect the library property with an aim to preserve it for posterity.

The normal degradation of present generation people, their anti-social behaviour and lest effort an attention paid by the library staff also affect preservation of library materials. As a large part of genuine library user's suffer due to lack of documents for their studies, preservation is needed for library resources.

LIBRARIAN'S RESPONSIBILITY

In so far as librarians are concerned, they have moral responsibility of preservation and conservation vested in them. Books and other media in a library preserve facts, thoughts, fantasies, and accomplishments in a word, the record of human civilization. The records which are being created and accumulated in our libraries today will turn as records of the past achievements tomorrow. If, therefore, today's librarians do not pay adequate attention to preservation, not only of the old documents but also of the current ones, of which they are the custodians, they will be answerable to the future generations for having failed in one of the most important responsibilities entrusted to them by the present society.

STRATEGIES FOR PRESERVATION:

Strategies for the preservation of library materials are now being activity developed. These are basically concerned with the following areas:-

a) Determination of Preservation priorities

It is realized that we cannot preserve all items in our libraries for all time. Priorities for what can or should be preserved and for how must be judiciously established.

b) House keeping

The house keeping methods include;

i) Introduction of preservation principles into all aspects of library;

ii) Orientation of library staff;

iii) Training programme for the users;

iv) Publication of posters, pamphlets etc. and holding of

exhibitions and other mass awareness programmes from time to time, to educate the users;

v) Implementing a regular maintenance programme which should include maintenance of appropriate physical and environmental conditions;

vi) Disaster response planning - assessment of the causes of disaster like fire and water;

vii) Lessening the likelihood of occurrence of such disaster.

c) Transfer of information from deteriorated items

Transferring the contents from deteriorated items in library collection to other more durable media-microfilming and transfer to a digital form (stored on optical discs or computer tapes) are the main techniques used at present.

d) Co-operative Action

There are certain areas where co-operative efforts are called for. Some of these are:-

i) Mass de-edification of books in the library collection within a particular region.

ii) Newspaper microfilming projects;

iii) Establishment of preservation laboratories and centers which offer their services within a particular region.

FACTORS OF DETERIORATION OF LIBRARY MATERIALS

Deterioration is a change of original state of any material by interaction between the object and the factors of destruction. The following situations are responsible for the decay and deterioration of the library materials because of one or more situations acting simultaneously.

i) Natural ageing of paper is an inevitable phenomenon since the major constituents are of organic nature.

ii) In the manufacturing of paper sometimes fibers with low cellulose content or sometimes non-cellulose of the lignin type by which paper degenerates very soon.

iii) Mineral and chemical compounds used for sizing of paper affect durability of paper.

iv) Impurities in the ingredients used as basic constituents of paper cause inevitable deterioration.

v) Presence of excess acidic sizing materials such as alum, rosin etc. cause the acidic effect.

vi) Oxidizing agents present in the constitutions of paper make it weak by demising the mechanical strength as well as by discolouring and disintegrating the paper.

vii) Alkali used in manufacture of paper affect the paper if used in a higher quantity. Fungi grow very easily on such paper.

viii) Chemicals present in a-v materials, ingredients of base elements and processes of production can't withstand any adverse condition because these are very delicate.

ix) Because of the nature and characteristics of basic elements, physical and chemical changes may occur within the materials under adverse environmental conditions.

The causes of deterioration of library materials may be grouped broadly under three categories;

1) Natural ageing

Natural ageing indicates the gradual degradation or deterioration of the material. Obviously it affects the durability of the material and it is inevitable that each material is subject to natural decay.

2) Intrinsic or internal factors

Intrinsic or internal factors refer to the basic ingredients used in the manufacture of physical entity of library materials as well as in the manufacturing process.

3) External condition

External conditions are different physical, chemical and biological factors that cause and aggravate deterioration and damage to library materials.

Generally library materials are susceptible to deterioration by the following external factors;

1. ENVIRONMENTAL FACTORS

The environmental factors causing the physical deterioration are given below:-

a) Light

Light is a form of radiant energy and it may be natural or artificial. Natural light is the sunlight and artificial light may be fluorescent tube light or electric bulbs. Both in natural and artificial light several kinds of rays are present. They cause deterioration to bleaching ink, dyes and color in illustrations and maps. They also bleach coloured paper, leather and textiles. Paper of low quality become yellowish because the non cellulose material, lignin break down into acid compound. The modern inks, dyes, colour and pigments become fade, decoloured or dark by U.V. ray.

b) Heat

Heat is an insidious agent of deterioration which is generally measured in terms of temperature. If the books are exposed to high temperature for a short period, the paper becomes yellow and brittle. It causes dehydration and paper closes its usual strength. In general, the lower the temperature is, better it is for the collection. Room temperature of 200C-250C and relative humidity of +55% creates the ideal condition for the preservation of paper documents. Heat accelerates photolysis, hydrolysis and oxidation.

c) Relative humidity

RH is defined in terms of temperature as, the amount of water vapor in a volume of air expressed as the percentage of maximum amount that the air could hold at the same temperature.

Library materials well or shrink as RH changes, since the organic materials are hygroscopic (that is, they expand and contract as moisture level rise and fall). Very high humidity level turns many materials brittle, so that paper breaks when handled.

d) Moisture

As to heat and light, moisture works both for and against the preservation of library materials. Even though a certain amount of moisture is necessary for flexibility in paper, excessive moisture in paper encourages mould growth and makes paper brittle.

e) Darkness

Direct sunlight and excessive light are harmful to library materials but light is required in storage areas. Darkness creates a condition for breeding of biological enemies and makes their hide-outs.

f) Dust and dirt

Fine dry particles of any matter in the air are known as dust. The harmful action of sulphur compounds are aggravated by dust and dirt, which are sources of both physical and chemical degradation.

g) Gases

The burning of fossil fuels (coal, petroleum, oil and natural gas) causes concentration of gaseous air pollutants in cities and industrial areas. The notable deleterious substances in the library are sulphur dioxide is the brown, brittle edges of books.

h) Water

Water acts as a physical agent of deterioration by causing hydroscopic materials to undergo dimensional changes. The effect of water are stained paper, rotted leather, and smeared ink, weakened adhesives, sustained fungi and vermin, hydrolysis cellulose, softening of gelatin on film and tape.

2. BIOLOGICAL FACTORS

The deterioration caused by biological agents such as micro organisms, insects and rodents is generally known as bio-deterioration. The biological agents do harm fast. They are totally external factors and they have no relationships with the constituent of materials.

The biological agents can be subdivided into:-

a) Micro organisms
b) Insects
c) Rodents

a. Micro organisms

Micro organisms include fungus and bacteria. Both are present in the environment in every habitat. They remain in a dormant state for long period. But they appear as brown/ black vegetative growth on paper.

b. Insects

Common insects that are responsible for attacking and damaging paper and other book components are silver fish, book lice, cock roach, termite, book worm which are recognized by their characteristic appearance.

c. Rodents

These gnawing biting animals, which are occasional visitors to the library which are found all over the globe include rats, rabbits and many other species. They are very quick in their action. Even in a single night they collectively can cut a part of the library collection into pieces.

3. CHEMICAL FACTORS

Chemical deterioration is the most damaging and destructive condition for the library materials. It is caused both by internal and external factors.

The internal factors are inherited by intrinsic conditions existing within the elements of the physical composition of library materials. External factors for chemical deterioration occur so slow depending on various internal and external conditions.

The major causes of deterioration are:-

a) Acid

The most common acid deterioration is caused by Sulphur dioxide present in small amount in the atmosphere. Acid of acid reactions makes the paper brittle and crumble and the paper loses the readability. The minute trace of acid can destroy the entire document in course of time.

b) Foxing

Foxing is a common phenomena on paper in the from of brown spots. Forcing stains are the result of chemical action between the iron impurities present in the paper'

c) Disasters

The term disaster may be defined as any occurrence that threatens human safety and/or causes damage to library facilities and materials. It may be natural or man-made depending on their origin and is unpredictable.

Let us first examine the various kinds of disasters that library and information centers face.

a) Fire

Fire related disasters are very destructive and produce

enormous amount of heat, smoke and toxic gases. Causes of fire include natural phenomena such as lightning and earthquakes, as well as old or defective wiring.

b) Water

Floods and storms that cause wind or water related damage are typical natural disasters for libraries and information centers.

c) Earthquake

It is a natural catastrophe that may effect the collection in a library or museum.

5. HUMAN FACTORS

In the history of mankind it is a fact that man caused the maximum damage and merciless destruction to the libraries. Library staff and patron may cause inadvertent damage by misuse of library materials. Much harm has been done to innocent volumes by careless or thought less or ignorant or indifferent handling.

PREVENTIVE MEASURES FOR THE FACTORS OF DETERIORATION

Environment Control

1. Selection of site should be done with care
2. Libraries must have cross ventilation facilities for free air circulation with in the building.
3. Construct the building away from traffic to avoid dust and dirt.
4. Windows must be provided with colored curtains.

Biological factors

1. Avoid contact of book racks with walls (at least 15 cm away from the walls) to eliminate dampness.

2. Use paradichloro - benzene in the racks as it acts both as an insect repellent and insecticide.
3. The foundation of all new library buildings should be given anti-insect treatment.

Chemical factors

1. Filter the air intake into storage areas, by air conditioning system operating 24 hours.
2. Wrapping the books and manuscripts in cloth or placing them in book containers

Human Factors

1. Important books and manuscripts should be kept in specially prepaid containers.
2. For carrying a large number of books trolleys should be used.
3. Care should be taken while photocopying the books.
4. Corners of pages should not be folded to mark pages.

Disaster preparedness

1. Every library should have a written disaster preparedness and response plan containing description of emergency procedures, emergency supplies lest, disaster response outline, conservation expert's list of external contacts and names , addresses, home and work telephone number of personnel with emergency responsibilities.
2. Location of emergency gate must be clearly indicated.

CONCLUSION

The main aim of the library is not only the collection and dissemination of information but the storing and preservation of the information also. Due to the development of Information Technology there are various kinds of methods and techniques developed by the experts for preservation and conservation. In the electronic era the importance of the preservation and conservation has been increased and it is the responsibility of the library professionals to make acquainted with the latest technology available.

Index

American Library Association 238

American Society for Information Science and Technology 238

Assurance 154

Atkinson 144

ATSM Model 119

Ayurveda Information Users 253

Ayurvedic Information Sources 253

Bandyopathyay, AK 50

Bently 144

Bibliometric Analysis 23;79

Bibliometric study 20

Bibliometrics 3-4 Binding 300

Biological Factors, Deterioration of Books 307-08

Borse,TR 134

Bossard, James 17

British Council in India 202-203

British Council Libraries 195

British Council's Library Policy 195

CANARIE 268

Capezio, Peter 144

CAREO 269

Chartered Institute of Library and Information Professionals(CILIP) 238

Chemical Factors of Deterioratton, Books 308-309

Children's Book Trust 17

Children's Literature 16-19

Cito Analytical Study 49

Cochin University of Science and Technology 101

Collection Management 173

COLLOR 269

Commitment 159

Commonwealth of Learning 269

Computer-based Instruction 265

CONNEXIONS 270-71

Conservation Methods in Libraries 299

Continuous Improvement 159

Conventional Information System 187

Customer focus 158

Dabas,KC 131

Data 174

Davenport, TH 177
De-Acidification 300
Deterioration of Books, Preventive Measures 309-10
Deterioration of Library Materials 303
Devarajan,G,Biography Xvii-XXi
Devarajan, G, Bibliometrics of publications 4-12
Dhar 128
Digital warehouses 279
DLEARN 271
E-Book Aggregator 277-78
E-Book Aggregator, Advantages 278
E-Book Aggregators, Characteristics 283
E-Books, Bibliographical Issues 286
EDNA Online 272
Educational Software Components of Tomorrow(ESCOT) 267
Edusource Communications Layer (ECL) 268
E-GYANKOSH 272
E-Learning 265
E-Learning, Advantages 266
E-Learning Objects 267
E-Learning, Advantages 266
E-Learning, Programmes 268
Encapsulation 300
Environmental Factors of Deterioration, Books 305-07
Evans, GE 133
Explicit Knowledge 175-76
Flener, JC 131
Foskett, DJ 75
Fumigation 300
High Level Design 188
House-Keeping 302
Human Factors of Deterioration, Books 309
Human Resource Planning and Development 128
India, Country Plan 204
Indian Council of Social Science Research 75
Information 174
Information and Communication Technology 265
Intelligent Computer aided Instruction Systems 267
Internal use service 184
International Federation for Information and Documentation 238
Job Challenge 159
Job rotation 160
Kannur university 101
Karisiddappa, CR 234
Kedamani 3
Kerala Agricultural University 101
Kerala State Institutes of Children's Literature 17-18
Kerala University Act 100
Knowledge 175
Knowledge Acquisition 177
Knowledge and Learning Centres 225
Knowledge Management 172; 175
Knowledge Management Design 189-90
Knowledge Management in Libraries 176-77

Knowledge Management Organisation 186
Knowledge Objects 267
Kothari Commission 102
Kroto, HW 3
Lamination 300
Leadership 158
Learning Objects Repositories (LOR) 268
Learning Resources 267
Learning Technology Standards Committee 267
Library & Information Science education 2
Library Association (LA) 238
Library Associations 235
Library Associations, India 238-39
Library Associations and Development of Library Profession 236-37
Library Committee 141
Line MB 75
Little, Thoma M 75
Luthans,Fred 1989 Mahapatra,RK 50
Mahatma Gandhi University 101
Malayalam language 19-20
Mamoria 130
Manpower Development 127-129
Manpower Development, Factors 129-135
Manpower Model 118
Materials Digital Library (MATDL) 273
McGregor,Douglas 290
MERLOT 273
Merril, David 267
Motivation 129
MyiLibrary 283
Nadler 128
National Book Trust 17
National Centre for Children's Literature 18
NetLibrary 283
On-line Learning Materials 267
On-line Teaching 267
PakXchange 269
Pedagogical Documents 267
Performance Measurement 216
Pervaiz 234
Piaget, Jean 75
PLANET Digital Repository 273-74
Polanyi 175
Preservation Strategies 302
Preservation and Conservation 299
Preservation, Library Resources 301
Process Improvement 159
Process Improvement 159
Project Management 191
Quality Management in Libraries 143
Radhakrishnan Commission 102
Rajaleksmy 50
Ramachandran 3
Ranganathan, SR 2
Ranganathan, SR, Job Standard 105
Raza, M 50
Responsiveness 155
Sahoo, Jyotshna 50
Sangam 3
Savarnur, Kiran 3
Seligman 75

Simon, Herbert A 130
Social Science Information 73-74
Special Libraries Association 238
Spoken Word Project 274
Sree Sankaracharya University of Sanskrit 101
Sridhar, MS 134
Staff Management 158-59
Subramonium, CV 134
Survey 20
Survey of Literature 22
Tacit knowledge 175
Tangibles 155
Theory of X 290
Theory of Y 290
TILE 274
Total Quality Management 142-44
UGC Committee Formula 119
University Library Manpower 101 - 102
University of Calicut 101
University of Kerala 101
University of Travancore 100
User demand 184
Venketeswara Rao, T 128
Zarrin, Zeba 50